The Interior Landscape

BOOKS BY MARSHALL MCLUHAN
The Mechanical Bride: Folklore of Industrial Man
Understanding Media: The Extensions of Man
The Gutenberg Galaxy: The Making of Typographic Man
Verbi-Voco-Visual Explorations
The Medium Is the Massage (*with Quentin Fiore*)
War and Peace in the Global Village (*with Quentin Fiore and Jerome Agel*)
Through the Vanishing Point: Space in Poetry and Painting (*with Harley Parker*)
Explorations in Communication (*with Edmund S. Carpenter*)
Selected Poetry of Alfred Lord Tennyson (*Editor*)
Voices of Literature, Volumes One and Two (*Richard J. Schoeck, co-editor*)

BOOKS BY EUGENE MCNAMARA
For the Mean Time

THE INTERIOR LANDSCAPE

The Literary Criticism of Marshall McLuhan 1943-1962

Selected, compiled, and edited
by Eugene McNamara

McGraw-Hill Book Company
New York • Toronto
in association with the University of Windsor Press,
Windsor, Ontario

809
m

Designed by Christine Wilkinson

45443

FIRST EDITION

Library of Congress Catalog Number: 76-88886

Preface ❧ ❧ ❧

THE PURPOSE OF this book is simply to draw together from sources widely scattered in time and space representative literary essays written by Marshall McLuhan. Between 1934, when his first published essay, "G. K. Chesterton: A Practical Mystic," appeared in *Dalhousie Review,* and the present, he has published some thirty-seven critical articles on such writers as Joyce, Pound, Dos Passos, Poe, Tennyson, and Eliot in various learned journals. Many of these essays became classics: "The Analogical Mirrors," for example, which originally appeared in 1944 in *Kenyon Review,* was reprinted in the Kenyon Critics edition *Gerard Manley Hopkins.* His essays on Keats, Tennyson, Pound, and Coleridge, among others, have also found their way into the standard anthologies.

What is revealed in these essays is a widening concern for a larger context for literature than that afforded by conventional textual criticism. Professor McLuhan's early writings exhibit the kind of closeness that a concentration on a work of art to the exclusion of the world outside it can afford. But there is, as well, a faintly implied tone of moral disapproval for that world in these early essays. The 1934 Chesterton essay, for instance, takes occasion to praise Chesterton's "profound humility in the face of reality" as "the very condition of honest art and all philosophy" and sees the same humility as

> The reason for his energetic revival of tradition in so far as it dignifies and illuminates any present activity. In short, he is original in the only possible sense, because he considers everything in relation to its origins. It is because he is concerned to maintain our endangered institutions that he earnestly seeks to re-

v

establish *agriculture and small property, the only basis of any free culture.* (p. 456) (Italics supplied)

Later essays began to be more inclusive. By the mid-fifties, Professor McLuhan tended to see literature in a wider context, embracing finally, by 1962, the whole continuum of human experience that went into the art of printed creation and that went on in the aesthetic assumptions and psychological biases of the reading public. Since 1962, his interests have followed the same direction that he promised at the conclusion of *The Gutenberg Galaxy:*

> The new electric galaxy of events has already moved deeply into the Gutenberg galaxy. Even without collision, such co-existence of technologies and awareness brings trauma and tension to every living person. Our most ordinary and conventional attitudes seem suddenly twisted into gargoyles and grotesques and familiar institutions and associations seem at times menacing and malignant. (pp. 278–79)

Even if he never wrote on literature again, he has firmly established himself as a formidable literary critic, displaying awesome erudition and wide scope. He could, I submit, rest on his laurels and undeniable credentials. Obviously, literature has mattered to Professor McLuhan. No objective survey of his writings over the past thirty years could deny that. But his probes of the new media have unfortunately drawn to him the attention of the very forces he excoriated in *The Mechanical Bride.* In the pop mind, he has become the archetype of the post-Gutenberg critic, a "Pop Philosopher" or "Media Prophet." This present selection, one hopes, will be a step toward the rectification of a crude cartoon and a re-establishment of a truer picture of Marshall McLuhan, a distinguished and perceptive literary critic.

Despite the wider range of awareness implicit in his probes of the impact of new media on our modes of perception, the angle of vision, the interior landscape, remains the same. It is basically humanistic; one might even venture to say conservative, if by conservative I mean that he wishes to conserve what is worthwhile at all costs. For Professor McLuhan is man alive and aware of his

vii *Preface*

world. Whatever he wishes the world could be, he must first see that world as it is.

The last essay in this collection, "An Ancient Quarrel in Modern America," is one of the earliest, chronologically. Although there would appear to be no significant evolvement of a critical theory in Professor McLuhan's work, a simple chronological arrangement might appear, quite casually, to suggest an argument for such an evolution. We have therefore arranged the essays in clusters, following a clue buried in one of his metaphors: the galaxy.

Hence, instead of a temporal, linear progression of essays from 1943 to 1962, we have three galactic groups, polarized around three centers of interest. First, we see the "interior landscape," reflected analogically in the works which resulted from various modern artists' attempts to cope with their new, disturbing, and discontinuous universe. Second, a consideration of several Romantic and Victorian poets reveals the same "cubist" perspective, and suggests that the broken, refracted world of Joyce and Pound is not a limited twentieth-century phenomenon, but has its sources further back in time. The final piece in this cluster, on Pope's *Dunciad,* moves back into the eighteenth century and considers the impact of print technology on credulous masses.

Finally, three essays are brought together because they are more closely concentrated on the American landscape: the Southern tradition, Poe in the light of that tradition, and where it all began: the "ancient quarrel" between rhetoricians and dialecticians, between humanists and technologists, which persisted in various guises since the time of Socrates, and found new life in America, with the legalistic, forensic tradition finding hospitable soil in the South and the North opting for abstraction and technology.

Again, borrowing a metaphor: a work of art is often seen by Marshall McLuhan as a process of retrieval, of reconstruction after a moment of insight. There is, from the viewpoint afforded by this metaphor, an aptness in having "An Ancient Quarrel in Modern America" at the end.

Acknowledgments ❧ ❧ ❧

I WOULD LIKE to return special thanks to the Publications Committee of the University of Windsor and to those publishers, magazines, and reviews which have so generously granted their permission to reprint these essays:

THE SEWANEE REVIEW for "Edgar Poe's Tradition," copyright © 1944; for "The Southern Quality," © 1947; and for "Joyce, Mallarmé, and the Press,"© 1953; all of these essays copyright by The University of the South.

THE UNIVERSITY OF TORONTO QUARTERLY for "Aesthetic Patterns in Keats' Odes," © 1943.

NEW DIRECTIONS BOOKS, Norfolk, Connecticut, for "The Analogical Mirrors," which originally appeared in *Gerard Manley Hopkins: Kenyon Critics Edition,* © 1944 by *The Kenyon Review,* and for "Pound's Critical Prose," which originally appeared in *Examination of Ezra Pound: A Collection of Essays,* Peter Russell, Editor. All Rights Reserved.

THE CLASSICAL JOURNAL for "An Ancient Quarrel in Modern America (Sophists vs. Grammarians)," © 1946.

CHARLES SCRIBNER'S SONS, INC., New York, for "John Dos Passos: Technique vs. Sensibility," which originally appeared in *Fifty Years of the American Novel: A Christian Appraisal,* Charles Gardiner, Editor, © 1951.

ESSAYS IN CRITICISM for "Tennyson and Picturesque Poetry," © 1951.

COLUMBIA UNIVERSITY PRESS, New York, for "The Aesthetic Moment in Landscape Poetry," which originally appeared in *English Institute Essays: 1951,* Alan Downe, Editor, © 1952.

THOUGHT for "James Joyce: Trivial and Quadrivial," ©1953.

THE SOUTHERN ILLINOIS UNIVERSITY PRESS, INC., Carbondale, Illinois, for "Coleridge as Artist," which originally appeared in *The Major English Romantic Poets: A Symposium in Reappraisal,* edited by Clarence D. Thorpe, Carlos Baker, and Bennett Weaver, copyright ©1957 by Southern Illinois University Press. Reprinted by permission of Southern Illinois University Press.

THE UNIVERSITY OF TORONTO PRESS, INC. for "On Pope's *Dunciad,"* which originally appeared in The Gutenberg Galaxy, © 1962.

The collective support of the editors and publishers of the above publications was a crucial factor in bringing this book to life.

A debt of gratitude I can never adequately repay is due to my wife Margaret, to whose keen eye and boundless patience I owe whatever degree of accuracy this text affords, and my thanks also to Miss Mary Gerace, whose zeal in tracking down these materials is exceeded only by her enthusiasm for Professor McLuhan's work.

E.M.

Contents ✤ ✤ ✤

Foreword
by Marshall McLuhan

IN THE SUMMER OF 1932 I walked and biked through most of England carrying a copy of Palgrave's *Golden Treasury*. There had never been any doubt in my mind that art and poetry were an indictment of human insentience past and present:

> Aye, many flowering islands lie
> In the waters of wide Agony.

In the Lake Country I reveled in Wordsworth phrases:

> Most sweet it is with unuplifted eyes
> To pace the ground, if path be there or none,
> While a fair region round the traveller lies.

Every poem in that book seemed to have been written to enhance my pilgrimage:

> Yes, there is holy pleasure in thine eye!
> The lovely cottage in the guardian nook
> Hath stirr'd thee deeply; with its own dear brook,
> Its own small pasture, almost its own sky!

"Pied Beauty," the single poem of Hopkins in my copy, was quite startling. I assumed he was a Victorian eccentric who had been noted for one or two small poems such as this. Nobody could tell me about him.

After a conventional and devoted initiation to poetry as a romantic rebellion against mechanical industry and bureaucratic stupidity, Cambridge was a shock. Richards, Leavis, Eliot and Pound and Joyce in a few weeks opened the doors of perception on the poetic process, and its role in adjusting the reader to the contemporary world.

My study of media began and remains rooted in the work of these men. Thomas Nashe was a Cambridge pet in my terms there. I did my doctoral study on him, approaching him via the process of verbal training from the Sophists through Cicero and Augustine and Dante to the Renaissance. When Joyce quipped to a critic, "Some of my puns are trivial and some are quadrivial," he was being, as always, precise. When my critics imagine I am being vaguely metaphorical, I, too, am trying to be literal and precise.

That art is a means of giving us new awareness through an intensification of our sensory life is obvious. *TV Guide* for June 8–14, 1968, has a painting by Dali on the cover. Two thumbs exhibit two TV screens as thumbnails. That is pure poetry, acute new perception. Dali immediately presents the fact that TV is a tactile mode of perception. Touch is the space of the *interval,* not of visual connection. I have been trying to elucidate this fact for years. In vain. The somnambulist knows better. Can't he *see* TV with his eyes? How could it be *tactile?* Pasteur was thrown out of the medical profession because he insisted that doctors wash their hands before surgery. They knew better. They could *see* their hands were clean.

The *effects* of new media on our sensory lives are similar to the effects of new poetry. They change not our thoughts but the structure of our world.

All this is merely to say that my juvenile devotion to Romantic poetry is closely related to my present concerns with the effects of the media in our personal and political lives.

Must we continue to mow down the Kennedys in order to illustrate that the hot politics of the old machines won't work on the cool and involving TV medium?

The Interior
Landscape

Part One
The Nets of Analogy

McLuhan saw the popular press in the same manner as he was later to see electronic media, as a force subtly and radically shaping sensibility. Earlier technological innovations, such as the supplanting of gaslight by limelight in the theater, allowed a revolution in stagecraft to occur. The innovation of the tin tube of premixed oil paint freed artists from their studios, allowing them to paint on the scene. The direct apprehension of Nature, the Romantic urge of painters to be in the open air and immediately involved in nature thus owes more than is frequently acknowledged to metallurgical and industrial paint technology.

McLuhan suggests that picturesque art owed the same kind of debt to the spectroscope, and that the popular press, as a kind of static cinema, affords a simultaneous model of our common existence, which we are painfully aware is scattered and broken. In a concrete immediate way, any page of a modern newspaper reflects this random disorder. The serious is juxtaposed to the frivolous, the sublime is jammed next to the ridiculous, errors abound and are given grave and solemn existence simply because they exist in print. Joyce and Mallarmé were keenly aware of how the modern newspaper afforded a perspective, a model, for contemporary artists. Previously, artists were limited to the narrow scope of their

1

own personal conceptions of reality, shaped in a temporal sequence by both real and vicarious experiences. Now these experiences were widened, made spatial, simultaneous, and global through the casual medium of the newspaper page. Both Joyce and Mallarmé were very much aware of how that same newspaper page was an art form itself, or at least a model for art forms. *Ulysses,* as McLuhan points out, is a kind of newspaper, datelined June 6, 1904.

Joyce's fondness for puns is another key to the unlocking of modern sensibility. McLuhan sees the puns as indicators of meaning in the "communications network" of Joyce's work, as Techniques of handling a flow of messages. But McLuhan traces the device back to the traditional medieval disciplines of grammar, logic, and rhetoric (the *trivium*) and the *quadrivium* (arithmetic, geometry, music, and astronomy.) "Trivial" puns are therefore also "trivial" puns in another deeper sense. Joyce, as a symbolist, can be seen as a post-rhetorician. His renewed interest in these medieval structures then was not simply a love of archaism but sprang from a lively contemporary interest in linguistics, aesthetics, and anthropology. Take any one of these arts in the structure and trace it analogically through Joyce's work: music, for instance. Instantly, any serious student of the work will see the further unfolding of meaning.

"Landscape" is a key concept in McLuhan's critical practice. It is sometimes a metaphor for "model" in reference to works of art, and sometimes for "world view" or "perspective" in reference to individual artists. In "Joyce, Mallarmé, and the Press," he refers to the "new global landscape of the press," and the impact of this technological innovation on creative artists. In "James Joyce, Trivial and Quadrivial," he refers to *Finnegans Wake* unfolding as "an interior landscape." He comments on Dos Passos' "discontinuous city landscapes," and one could be tempted to look harder at his discussion of Hopkins' concept of the "inscape" as a clue to how rich and multidimensional the term "landscape" is for McLuhan, and how interlinked his ideas are. He derives two scenarios from Poe's work, for instance: the detective story written backward from its conclusion and being saved from a descent into the maelstrom by an uninvolved detached observation of the process of the maelstrom itself. These two metaphors are themselves "landscapes."

As he points out in "The Analogical Mirrors," the interior landscape of any work of art "masters the recalcitrance of matter." Mirrors, stereoscopes, cameras—all are modes of visual perception. Yet *words* remain as live artifacts, containing inherent in themselves the world so immediately and perfectly perceived through the visual modes.

He saw a modern sensibility reflected through Ezra Pound's early fascination with machines, technological discoveries as a coexisting force alongside an erudite sensitivity to language. So also Joyce's fascination with the modern newspaper can be seen, traced onward in Dos Passos' reduction and simplification of Joyce's techniques. Finally, Wyndham Lewis, as McLuhan sees him, viewed art as a means of gaining perspective, as a way of getting out of the mechanism of existence.

Now, at this juncture, any reader who wishes to do so may turn to the last essay in this collection to see one of the earliest statements made by McLuhan on the intellectual-historical dichotomy which he believes underlies our contemporary state of fragmentation. Or, you can read through the "galaxy" of essays back to it, discovering it through analogy here, seeing it restated there, failing to fetch it at once, keep encouraged, since it stops there waiting for you like the end of a detective story which was written at the outset.

Joyce, Mallarmé,
and the Press

♭ ♭ ♭ ♭ ♭

DECLINING TO WRITE for the *Revue Européenne* in 1831, Lamartine
said to its editor:

> Do not perceive in these words a superb disdain for what is
> termed journalism. Far from it; I have too intimate a knowledge
> of my epoch to repeat this absurd nonsense, this impertinent
> inanity against the Periodical Press. I know too well the work
> Providence has committed to it. Before this century shall run out
> journalism will be the whole press—the whole human thought.
> Since that prodigious multiplication which art has given to
> speech—multiplication to be multiplied a thousand-fold yet—
> mankind will write their books day by day, hour by hour, page by
> page. Thought will be spread abroad in the world with the rapid-
> ity of light; instantly conceived, instantly written, instantly un-
> derstood at the extremities of the earth—it will spread from
> pole to pole. Sudden, instant, burning with the fervor of soul
> which made it burst forth, it will be the reign of the human soul
> in all its plenitude. It will not have time to ripen—to accumu-
> late in a book; the book will arrive too late. The only book possi-
> ble from today is a newspaper.

It is strange that the popular press as an art form has often attracted the enthusiastic attention of poets and aesthetes while rous-
ing the gloomiest apprehensions in the academic mind. The same

5

division of opinion can be traced in the sixteenth century concerning the printed book. Two thousand years of manuscript culture were abruptly dissolved by the printing press. Failure to understand this arises from various overriding assumptions about the universal benefits of print. But today when technology has conferred ascendancy on pictorial and radio communication it is easy to detect the peculiar limitations and bias of the four-century span of book culture which is coming to a close.

In her recent study of George Herbert, Rosamund Tuve stressed the extent to which metaphysical conceits were direct translations into verbal terms of popular pictorial imagery of the late middle ages. She was able to show that the characteristic conceits of Herbert and others arose from the meeting of the old manuscript culture (with its marginal pictures) and the new printed medium. In the same way, many others have argued that the peculiar richness of effect of Elizabethan and Jacobean language was the result of a meeting of the oral tradition and the new printed culture. Mere literature didn't begin until the oral tradition was entirely subordinated to the silent and private studies of the bookman. It was the lifelong claim of W. B. Yeats that in Ireland this conquest over the spoken word was less complete than elsewhere in Anglo-Saxony.

So, if the metaphysicals owe much to their adaptation of medieval pictographs to the printed medium, it could be suggested that modern poetry with its elaborate mental landscapes owes much to the new pictorial technology which fascinated Poe and Baudelaire and on which Rimbaud and Mallarmé built much of their aesthetics. If the Jacobeans were receding from a pictographic culture toward the printed page, may we not meet them at the point where we are receding from the printed word under the impetus of pictorial technology? Manuscript technology fostered a constellation of mental attitudes and skills of which the modern world has no memory. Plato foresaw some of them with alarm in the *Phaedrus:*

> The specific which you have discovered is an aid not to memory, but to reminiscence, and you give your disciples not truth but only the semblance of truth; they will be hearers of many things

and will have learned nothing; they will appear omniscient and will generally know nothing; they will be tiresome company, having the show of wisdom without the reality.

Plato is speaking for the oral tradition before it was modified by literacy. He saw writing as a mainly destructive revolution. Since then we have been through enough revolutions to know that every medium of communication is a unique art form which gives salience to one set of human possibilities at the expense of another set. Each medium of expression profoundly modifies human sensibility in mainly unconscious and unpredictable ways. Alphabetic communication brings about an inevitable psychic withdrawal, as E. J. Chaytor showed in *From Script to Print,* with a train of personal and social maladjustments. But it secures a host of advantages. Psychic withdrawal is automatic because the process of literacy is the process of setting up the interior monologue. It is the problem of translation of the auditory into the visual and back again, which is the process of writing and reading, that brings the interior monologue into existence, as can be observed in the study of pre-literate cultures today. This introversion with its consequent weakening of sense perception also creates inattention to the speech of others and sets up mechanisms which interfere with verbal recall. Exact verbal recall is scarcely a problem for pre-literate cultures.

Throughout *Finnegans Wake* Joyce plays some of his major variations on this theme of "abcedmindedness" in "those pagan ironed times of the first city . . . when a frond was a friend." His "verbivocovisual" presentation of an "all nights newsery reel" is the first dramatization of the very media of communication as both form and vehicle of the flux of human cultures. Most of the problems of reading the *Wake* dissolve when it is seen that he is using the media themselves as art forms as in a "phantom city phaked of philm pholk." The lights go up in his "Feenichts Playhouse" as the sun dips at the end of the Anna Livia section, and he is ready to mime the war of light and dark, of Michael, the Devil, and the maggies in a zodiacal dance of the witches ("monthage") "with nightly redistribution of parts and players by the puppetry producer."

Throughout the *Wake* this interior "tubloid" or tale of a tub is linked both to the cabbalistic significance of the letters of the alphabet and to the psychological effect of literacy in creating a general "abcedmindedness" in human society.

But the arrest of the flux of thought and speech which is the written page permits that prolonged analysis of thought processes from which arise the structures of science. Pictographic Chinese culture, for example, would seem to stand midway between the extremes of our abstract written tradition and the plenary oral tradition with its stress on speech as gesture and gesture as "phatic communion." And it is perhaps this medial position between the noncommunicating extremes of print and pictorial technology which attracts us today to the Chinese ideogram.

A principal feature of manuscript culture was its relative unity. The rarity and inaccessibility of manuscript books fostered a habit of encyclopedism. And where scholars were not numerous there were additional reasons for each of them to be acquainted with the entire range of authors. Moreover, manuscripts were studied slowly and aloud. Silent reading was impossible until the presses created the macadamized highways of print. The handwritten book was a broken road which was traveled slowly and infrequently. It kept the reader close to the dimensions of oral discourse. The publication of a poem consisted in reading or reciting it to a small audience. The promulgation of ideas was by public disputation.

Print multiplied scholars, but it also diminished their social and political importance. And it did the same for books. Unexpectedly, print fostered nationalism and broke down international communication because publishers found that the vernacular audience was larger and more profitable. As H. A. Innis has shown in *The Bias of Communication,* the printed word has been a major cause of international disturbance and misunderstanding since the sixteenth century. But pictorial communication is relatively international and hard to manipulate for purposes of national rivalry. H. A. Innis has been the great pioneer in opening up the study of the economic and social consequences of the various media of communication; so that today any student of letters is necessarily indebted to him for insight into changing attitudes to time and space which result from shifting media. In particular his studies of the newspaper as a major branch of the technology of print are relevant to the study of modern literature. Beginning as an economic historian, Innis was gradually impelled to consider not just the external trade routes of the world but also the great trade routes of the mind. He became aware that the modern world, having solved the problem of commodities, had turned its technology to the packaging of information and ideas.

If the manuscript tradition encouraged encyclopedism, book culture naturally tended to specialism. There were enough books to make reading a full-time occupation and to ensure an entirely withdrawn and private existence for the whole class of bookmen. Eventually there were enough books to splinter the reading public into dozens of noncommunicating groups. This has meant a large degree of unawareness in our culture of the meaning and drift of its most obvious developments. The bookman as such is not easily interested even in the technology and art of the book form of communication. And as this form has been modified by the popular press, and later developments, the exponents of book culture have registered various emotions but little curiosity. It is not, therefore, incongruous that real understanding of the changes in modern communication should have come mainly from the resourceful technicians among modern poets and painters.

Much of the novelty of the *Portrait, Ulysses,* and the *Wake* is an illusion resulting from inattention to technical developments in the arts since Newton. That manipulation of a continuous parallel between modern Dublin and ancient Ithaca which Mr. Eliot has noted as the major resource of *Ulysses* was a transfer to the time dimension of a "double-plot," a technique which had been the staple of all picturesque art for two hundred years. De Gourmont observed that one achievement of Flaubert had been the transfer of Chateaubriand's panoramic art from nature and history to the industrial metropolis. And Baudelaire had matched Flaubert in this witty reversal of the role of picturesque landscape. But English landscape art in painting, poetry, and the novel was decades in advance of France and Europe, a fact which was inseparable from English industrial experiment and scientific speculation. In her fascinating book *Newton Demands the Muse,* Marjorie Nicolson records the impact of Newtonian optics on the themes of the poets. But the techniques of rendering experience were equally modified in the direction of an inclusive image of society and consciousness. The new vision of space and light as outer phenomena which were precisely correlative to our inner faculties gave a new meaning and impetus to the juxtaposition of images and experiences. The taste for the discontinuities of Gothic art was one with the new interest in the juxtaposition of various social classes in the novels of the road (Fielding, Smollett, Mackenzie) and in the juxtaposition of historical epochs as well as primitive and sophisticated experience in Scott and Byron. More subtle was the juxtaposition of various states of the same mind in *Tristram Shandy* and the sleuthlike quest for the origins of such states on the part of Sterne and later of Wordsworth.

But the parallel development of the arts of spatial manipulation of mental states which was occurring in the popular press has been given no attention. Innis has shown how the new global landscapes of the press were not only geared to industry but were themselves the means of paying for new roads, for railway and telegraph and cable. The physical landscape of the earth was changed very quickly by the landscapes of the newspaper, even though the political scene has not yet caught up. The networks of news, trade, and transport were one. And newspapermen like Dickens who had no stake in established literary decorum were quick to adapt the technology of print to art and entertainment. Well before the French impressionists and symbolists had discovered the bearings for art of modern technology, Dickens had switched the picturesque perspectives of the eighteenth-century novel to the representation of the new industrial slums. Neurotic eccentricity in the sub-world of the metropolis he proved to be a much richer source for the rendering of mania and manic states of

mind than the crofters of Scott or the yokels of Wordsworth. And
Dostoevsky mined from Dickens freely, as G. B. Shaw did later still.
But just how valid were the impressionist techniques of the pic-
turesque kind familiar to the news reporter appears in the notable
essay of Eisenstein in *Film Form* where he shows the impact of
Dickens on the art of D. W. Griffiths.

How deeply English artists had understood the principles of picturesque art by 1780 appears from the invention of cinema at that
time. In 1781 De Loutherbourg, the theatrical scene-painter, contrived in London a panorama which he called the "Eidophusikon"
so as "to realize pictures in all four dimensions." His "Various Imitations of Natural Phenomena, Represented by Moving Pictures"
were advertised in these words and caused a sensation. Gainsborough, we are told by a contemporary, "was so delighted that for
a time he thought of nothing else, talked of nothing else, and passed
his evenings at the exhibition in long succession." He even made
one of these machines for himself capable of showing sunrise and
moonrise as well as storms and ships at sea. Gainsborough through
this cinema was experiencing the novelty of cubism with *"lo spetta-
tore nel centro del quadro."*

Another familiar instance of the abrupt newspaper juxtaposition
of events in "picturesque perspective" is *The Ring and the Book,* an
explicitly newspaperish crime report given as a series of "inside
stories," each one contained within another like Chinese boxes. But
it was Mallarmé who formulated the lessons of the press as a guide
for the new impersonal poetry of suggestion and implication. He
saw that the scale of modern reportage and of the mechanical mul-
tiplication of messages made personal rhetoric impossible. Now
was the time for the artist to intervene in a new way and to manipulate the new media of communication by a precise and delicate adjustment of the relations of words, things, and events. His task had
become not self-expression but the release of the life in things. *Un
Coup de Dés* illustrates the road he took in the exploitation of all
things as gestures of the mind, magically adjusted to the secret
powers of being. As a vacuum tube is used to shape and control vast

reservoirs of electric power, the artist can manipulate the low current of casual words, rhythms, and resonances to evoke the primal harmonies of existence or to recall the dead. But the price he must pay is total self-abnegation.

The existentialist metaphysic latent in Mallarmé's aesthetics was stated in 1924 in *In Praise of Newspapers* by Karel Čapek:

> The newspaper world like that of the wild beasts exists solely in the present; Press consciousness (if one can speak of consciousness) is circumscribed by simple present time extending from the morning on to the evening edition, or the other way round. If you read a paper a week old you feel as if you were turning the pages of Dalimil's chronicle: no longer is it a newspaper but a memorial. The ontological system of newspapers is actualized realism: what is just now exists . . . literature is the expression of old things in eternally new forms, while newspapers are eternally expressing new realities in a stabilized and unchangeable form.

By extending the technique of reporting the coexistence of events in China and Peru from global space to the dimension of time, Joyce achieved the actualized realism of a continuous present for events past, present, and future. In reverse, it is only necessary to remove the dateline from any newspaper to obtain a similar if less satisfactory model of the universe. That is what R. L. Stevenson meant when he said he could make an epic of a newspaper if he knew what to leave out. Joyce knew what to leave out.

For that school of thought for which the external world is an opaque prison, art can never be regarded as a source of knowledge but only as a moral discipline and a study of endurance. The artist is not a reader of radiant signatures on *materia signata* but the signer of a forged check on our hopes and sympathies. This school has supported the idea of the function of art as catharsis which, as G. R. Levy shows in *The Gate of Horn,* was a preparation for the lesser Greek mysteries. But if the world is not opaque and if the mind is not of the earth earthy, then this moral view of art should yield to the cognitive view. However that may be, the cathartic, ethical view of art has led to a doctrinaire hostility to the use of discontinuity in art (the theme of Arnold's preface to *Poems,* 1853) and indifference to all popular art. And in the past century with every technological device advancing the discontinuous character of communication the stand taken by the cathartic and ethical school has enveloped the entire world of popular culture in a haze of esoteric nescience, disguised, however, as a profound moral concern with the wider hope and the higher things. Joyce had a phrase for this anti-cognitive attitude, "the cultic twalette."

Moral and aesthetic horror at the ignobility of the popular scene gave way to an opposite attitude in the symbolists, and Mallarmé is, before Joyce, the best spokesman of the new approach. In his *Shop-Windows* (*Étalages*), while analyzing the aesthetics of commercial layout, he considers the relations between poetry and the press.

A shop window full of new books prompts his reflection that the function of the ordinary run of books is merely to express the average degree of human boredom and incompetence, to reduce to a written form the horizon of the human scene in all its abounding banality. Instead of deploring this fact as literary men tend to do, the artist should exploit it: "The vague, the commonplace, the smudged and defaced, not banishment of these, occupation rather! Apply them as to a patrimony."

Only by a conquest and occupation of these vast territories of stupefaction can the artist fulfill his culturally heroic function of purifying the dialect of the tribe, the Herculean labor of cleaning the Augean stables of speech, of thought and feeling. Turning directly to the press, Mallarmé designates it as "a traffic, an epitomization of enormous and elementary interests . . . employing print for the propagation of opinions, the recital of divers facts, made plausible, in the Press, which is devoted to publicity, by the omission, it would seem, of any art." He delights in the dramatic significance of the fact that in the French press, at least, the literary and critical features form a section at the base of the first page. And even more delightful:

> Fiction properly so called, or the imaginative tale, frolics across the average daily paper, enjoying the most prominent spots even

to the top of the page, dislodging the financial feature and pushing actuality into second place. Here, too, is the suggestion and even the lesson of a certain beauty: that today is not only the supplanter of yesterday or the presager of tomorrow but issues from time, in general, with an integrity bathed and fresh. The vulgar placard, bawled . . . at the street corner thus sustains this reflection . . . on the political text. Such experience leaves some people cold because they imagine that while there may be a little more or less of the sublime in these pleasures tasted by the people, the situation as regards that which alone is precious and immeasurably lofty, and which is known by the name of Poetry, that this situation remains unchanged. Poetry (they suppose) will always be exclusive and the best of its pinions will never approach those pages of the newspaper where it is parodied, nor are they pleased by the spread of wings in our hands of those vast improvised sheets of the daily paper.

Mallarmé is laughing at these finicky and unperceptive people for whom the press appears as a threat to "real culture"; and continues:

> To gauge by the extraordinary, actual superproduction, through which the Press intelligently yields its average, the notion prevails, nonetheless, of something very decisive which is elaborating itself: a prelude to an era, a competition for the foundation of the popular modern Poem, at the very least of innumerable Thousand and One Nights: by which the majority of readers will be astonished at the sudden invention. You are assisting at a celebration, all of you, right now, amidst the contingencies of this lightning achievement!

The author of *Ulysses* was the only person to grasp the full artistic implications of this radically democratic aesthetic elaborated by the fabulous artificer, the modern Daedalus, Stéphane Mallarmé. But Joyce was certainly assisted by Flaubert's *Sentimental Education* and *Bouvard and Pécuchet* in adapting Malarmé's insights to his own artistic purposes. A very little reflection on the scrupulously banal character of Flaubert's epics about industrial man illuminates much of the procedure in *Ulysses* and the *Wake*.

Crise de Vers, Étalages, and *Le Livre, Instrument Spirituel* all belong to the last few years of Mallarmé's life, representing his ultimate insights (1892–1896). And in each of these essays he is probing the aesthetic consequences and possibilities of the popular arts of industrial man. In *Le Livre* he turns to scrutinize the press once more, opening with the proposition, self-evident to him, that the whole world exists in order to result in a book. This is a matter of metaphysical fact, that all existence cries out to be raised to the level of scientific or poetic intelligibility. In this sense "the book" confers on things and persons another mode of existence which helps to perfect them. And it is plain that Mallarmé regarded the press as this ultimate encyclopedic book in its most rudimentary form. The almost superhuman range of awareness of the press now awaits only the full analogical sense of exact orchestration to perfect its present juxtaposition of items and themes. And this implies the complete self-effacement of the writer, for "this book does not admit of any signature." The job of the artist is not to sign but to read signatures. Existence must speak for itself. It is already richly and radiantly signed. The artist has merely to reveal, not to forge the signatures of existence. But he can only put these in order by discovering the orchestral analogies in things themselves. The result will be "the hymn, harmony and joy, as a pure ensemble ordered in the sharpest and most vivid circumstance of their interrelations. Man charged with divine vision has no other mode of expression save the parallelism of pages as a means of expressing the links, the whims, the limpidity on which he gazes."

All those pseudo-rationalisms, the forged links and fraudulent intelligibility which official literature has imposed on existence must be abandoned. And this initial step the press has already taken in its style of impersonal juxtaposition which conveys such riches to the writer. This work of "popular enchantment" which is the daily paper is not lacking in moral edification, for the hubbub of appetites and protests to be found among the advertisements and announcements proclaims each day the "original servitude" of man and the confusion of tongues of the tower of Babel. But the very format of the press resembles "a retracted wing which is ready to spread itself," awaiting only the "intervention of folding or of rhythm" in order to rid us of all that passes for "literature."

Mallarmé sees this impersonal art of juxtaposition as revolutionary and democratic also in the sense that it enables each reader to be an artist: "Reading becomes a solitary, tacit concert given to itself by the mind which recaptures significance from the least sonorities." It is the rhyming and orchestrating of things themselves which releases the maximum intelligibility and attunes the ears of men once more to the music of the spheres. We are finished, he says, with that custom of an official literary decorum by which poets sang in chorus, obliterating with their personal forgeries the actual signatures of things. In fact, the new poet will take as much care to avoid a style that is not in things themselves as literary men have in the past sought to achieve and impose one.

In approaching the structure of *Ulysses* as a newspaper landscape it is well to call to mind a favorite book of Joyce's, *The Purple Island* of Phineas Fletcher, the author's name suggesting Finn the arrow-maker. Fletcher presents the anatomy and labyrinths of the human body in terms of an enchanted Spenserian landscape. Many have pointed out the importance of the human form of the sleeping giant, the collective consciousness, as the structure of the *Wake*. And Joyce was careful to instruct his readers in the relation between the episodes of *Ulysses* and our bodily organs. (In 1844 the American press greeted the telegraph as "the first definite pulsation of the real nervous system of the world.") In *Ulysses* in episode seven we find ourselves in a newspaper office in "the heart of the Hibernian metropolis." For Joyce the press was indeed a "microchasm" of the world of man, its columns unchanging monuments to the age-old passions and interests of all men, and its production and distribution a drama involving the hands and organs of the entire "body politic." With its dateline June 16, 1904, *Ulysses* is, newspaperwise, an abridgement of all space in a brief segment of time, as the *Wake* is a condensation of all time in the brief space of "Howth castle and environs."

The dateline of *Ulysses,* the day of the end of the drought in the land of "The Dead," the day of the meeting of Joyce and Nora Barnacle, was the day that Joyce was to preserve in exile as Aeneas carried to New Troy the ashes and hut-urn of his ancestors (Fustel de Coulanges' *The Ancient City* is a useful introduction to this aspect of Joyce's filial piety). But whereas the techniques of the *Wake* are "telekinetic" and are explicitly specified as those of radio, television, newsreel, and the stuttering verbal gestures of H. C. E., it is the newspaper as seen by Mallarmé that provides most of the symbolist landscapes of *Ulysses*. As a daily cross-section of the activities and impulses of the race the press is an inclusive image affording possibilities of varied orchestration. A passage in *Stephen Hero* suggests the direction in which Joyce has modified the superficial cross-section of the popular press:

> The modern spirit is vivisective. Vivisection itself is the most modern process one can conceive. . . . All modern political and religious criticism dispenses with presumptive states. . . . It examines the entire community in action and reconstructs the spectacle of redemption. If you were an esthetic philosopher you would take note of all my vagaries because here you have the spectacle of the esthetic instinct in action. The philosophic college should spare a detective for me. (p. 186)

The key terms here, vivisection, community in action, reconstruction, detection, are related to every phase of Joyce's aesthetic. In *Modern Painters* Ruskin discusses the discontinuous picturesque techniques in medieval and modern art under the term "grotesque," noting it as the avenue by which popular and democratic expression enters the serious levels of art:

> A fine grotesque is the expression, in a moment, by a series of symbols thrown together in bold and fearless connection of truths which it would have taken a long time to express in any verbal way, and of which the connection is left for the beholder to work out for himself, the gaps, left or overleaped by the haste of the imagination, forming the grotesque character. . . . Hence it is an infinite good to mankind when there is a full acceptance of the grotesque . . . an enormous amount of intellectual power is turned to use, which in this present century of ours,

evaporates in street gibing. . . . It is with a view to the reopening of this great field of human intelligence, long entirely closed, that I am striving to introduce Gothic architecture . . . and to revive the art of illumination . . . the distinctive difference between illumination and painting proper, being, that illumination admits no shadows, but only gradations of pure colour.

Ruskin in describing the grotesque gives the very formula for "vivisection" or the community in action, though he hadn't the faintest idea of how to adapt this ideal to contemporary art. It was not misleading on Joyce's part, therefore, when he spoke of his work as a Gothic cathedral or of the *Wake* as an activated page of the Book of Kells. In presenting "history as her is harped," Joyce concludes: "And so the triptych vision passes out of a hillside into a hillside. Fairshee fading. Again am I deliciated by the picaresqueness of your irmages." (*Wake,* 486). It is the Mallarméan method of orchestration of the qualities of ordinary speech and experience that recurs, again, and again in the *Wake:*

> and inform to the old sniggering publicking press and its nation of sheepcopers about the whole plighty troth between them, malady of milady made melody of malodi, she, the lalage of lyonesses, and him, her knave errant . . . for all within crystal range.

The last "crystal" image gives the typical translation of the auditory into the visual, music into color, the harp of Aeolus into the harp of Memnon, time into space, which is the kind of metamorphosis which is going on everywhere in the *Wake.*

But the world of *Ulysses,* being primarily a modulation of space, is relatively static and newspaperish in its landscapes. It stands as inferno to the purgatorio of the *Wake.* However, in the Aeolus section of *Ulysses,* which is governed specifically by the organ "lungs" and the art of rhetoric, "everything," as Bloom says, "speaks for itself." The sheets of the newspaper become the tree harp for the wind of rhetoric. And the tree harp of the newspaper office is appropriately located beside the rock pillar of the hero:

Before Nelson's Pillar, trams glowed, shunted, changed trolley, started for Blackrock.

The trams with their rows of cast steel provide a parallel network to the linotype machines and the rows of printed matter. But if the tree and pillar provide the true image of a hero cult, the rhetoric that blows through the leaves of this tree is that of an alien speech. Much is made of this contretemps throughout the episode, and the climax brings this dramatic conflict to an issue. J. J. O'Malloy recites John F. Taylor's defense of the Gaelic revival, the theme of which is the Mosaic refusal to accept the gods and cult of the dominant Egyptians, a refusal which made possible his descent from Sinai "bearing in his arms the tables of the law graven in the image of the outlaw." This passage, the only one Joyce seems to have recorded from *Ulysses,* has an obvious bearing on the relation of his own art to English culture.

In his *Dialogue de l'Arbre* Valéry expounds the Aeolian cosmology of trees, roots, trunks, branches, leaves:

> *Chacun dit son nom. . . . O langage confus, langage qui t'agites, je veux foudre toutes tes voix. Cent mille feuilles mues font ce que le rêveur murmure aux puissances du songe.*

And he proceeds to contemplate the tree as a labyrinth merging with river and sea yet remaining a giant. In the same way the Aeolean tree music of the press "reamalgemerges" with the Mosaic eloquence of Sinai and the mountain, just as Anna Livia is also ALP (and Aeolus was a volcano spirit, that is, a cyclopian or mountain figure. He was the reputed father of Ulysses and hence of Bloom). The cyclopean aspect of Aeolus and the press provides an important motif, that of crime detection and the private eye. The press man as a "Shaun the cop" or cyclops type ("though he might have been more humble there's no police like Holmes") is presented in this episode as a parody or ape of the artist. Editor Myles Crawford, soliciting the services of Stephen, boasts of the sleuthing feats of "we'll paralyze Europe" Ignatius Gallaher. Gallaher's idea of scare journalism is paralysis as opposed to the artist's idea of awakening.

Gallaher reconstructed the pattern of the Phoenix Park murders to paralyze Europe; the artist reconstructs the crime of history as a means of awakening the dead. As "bullock-befriending bard," Stephen is the threader of that Labyrinth described by Vergil in the fourth Georgic, the fable of the ox and of the bees of poetic inspiration.

Nevertheless Joyce is not questioning the parallel between journalism and art in respect to the retracing process. The very conditions of journalism fostered insight into artistic production, because daily or periodic publication led to a great deal of serial composition. This in turn compelled authors to write their stories backwards. Edgar Poe, a journalist, in "The Philosophy of Composition," begins:

> Charles Dickens, in a note now lying before me, alluding to an examination I once made of the mechanism of *Barnaby Rudge,* says—"By the way, are you aware that Godwin wrote his *Caleb Williams* backwards?"

Poe then develops the familiar symbolist doctrine of poem as an art situation which is the formula for a particular effect. The same method of composition in reverse enabled Poe to pioneer the detective story. There is nothing accidental, therefore, about the Aeolus episode being crammed with instances of reversal and reconstruction. Applying the same principle to language yields, in the *Wake,* a reconstruction of all the layers of culture and existence embedded in the present forms of words and speech gesture.

It was natural that eighteenth-century writers should have been attracted to the retracing and reconstruction principle of art, which made Horace Walpole say of *Tristram Shandy* that it was the first book which consists "in the whole narrative going backwards." A little later Dr. Thomas Brown of Edinburgh argued that the poet's imagination differed from the ordinary man's by the power of reversing the direction of association. Once picturesque art, following the spectroscope, had broken up the continuum of linear art and narrative the possibility of cinematic montage emerged at once. And montage has to be arranged forwards or backwards. Forwards it yields narrative. Backwards it is reconstruction of events. Arrested it consists of the static landscape of the press, the co-existence of all aspects of community life. This is the image of the city presented in *Ulysses.*

James Joyce:
Trivial and Quadrivial

🙚 🙚 🙚 🙚 🙚

"We've had our day at triv and quad and writ our bit as inter-midgets."

(I)

MANY PEOPLE WOULD PROBABLY welcome an elucidation of Joyce's celebrated retort to a critic of his puns: "Yes, some of them are trivial and some of them are quadrivial." For, as usual, Joyce was being quite precise and helpful. He means literally that his puns are crossroads of meaning in his communication network, and that his techniques for managing the flow of messages in his network were taken from the traditional disciplines of grammar, logic, rhetoric, on one hand, and of arithmetic, geometry, music, and astronomy, on the other.

At the time when Joyce was studying the trivium with the Jesuits there had occurred in the European world a rebirth of interest in the traditional arts of communication. Indirectly, this had come about through the reconstruction of past cultures as carried on by nineteenth-century archeology and anthropology. For these new studies had directed attention to the role of language and writing in the formation of societies and the transmission of culture. And the total or gestalt approach natural in the study of primitive cultures

23

had favored the study of language as part of the entire cultural network. Language was seen as inseparable from the tool-making and economic life of these peoples. It was not studied in abstraction from the practical concerns of society.

It was at this time that Vico came into his own. At the beginning of the eighteenth century Vico's *Scienza Nuova* had proposed language as the basis for anthropology and a new science of history. Extant languages, he argued, could be regarded as working models of all past culture, because language affords an unbroken line of communication with the totality of the human past. The modalities of grammar, etymology, and word-formation could be made to yield a complete account of the economic, social, and spiritual adventures of mankind. If geology could reconstruct the story of the earth from the inert strata of rock and clay, the *scienza nuova* could do much better with the living languages of men. Previously, historians had attempted to create working models of some segment of the human past in their narratives. These were necessarily hypothetical structures eked out by scraps of recorded data. The new historian need never attempt again to revivify the past by imaginative art, because it is all present in language. And it is present, Joyce would add, as a newsreel re-presents actual events. We can sit back and watch the "all night news reel" of *Finnegans Wake* reveal as interfused the whole human drama past and present. This can be done by directing an analytical camera-eye upon the movements within and between words.

Joyce came to this kind of awareness through the symbolists. It is typical of them that vers libre, for example, should be a return to the formal rhythms of early litanies, hymns, and to the psalter. But going with this liturgical bias in art was a new sense of the neglected resources of classical rhetoric. Until the eighteenth century, rhetoric had been taught much as Cicero and Quintilian had presented it. But the ancient linguistic theory which had supported the rhetorical structure had receded. Newtonian science knocked ancient rhetoric off its much reduced pedestal by making the spatial and pictorial aspects of the external world supreme. So that from Thomson to Tennyson poets are concerned to establish and communicate states of mind in terms of external landscape. Psychology is managed in terms of external landscape. Psychology is managed in terms of space. The dimensions of time, tradition, and language are given minimal scope. But it was precisely to these neglected aspects of art and language that the later nineteenth century was turning. And the symbolists habitually work in terms of an interior landscape in which by the juxtaposition of more than one time (e.g., the opening of *Prufrock* or *The Waste Land* of Mr. Eliot) the poet reacquires his proprietorship of the human past.

It is necessary to see the century of neglect of the ancient trivium in order to explain how the revival of the trivium could have been what it was. The new context provided by anthropology and modern psychology really put grammar, logic, and rhetoric in an ancient rather than in a medieval or Renaissance context. Modern linguistic theory is quite sympathetic to the semimagical views of the ancients. Our idea of language as gesture, as efficacious, and as representing a total human response is a much better base for a study of the figures and arts of speech than any merely rationalistic approach can provide. But for Mallarmé, Valéry, Joyce, and Eliot the figures of rhetoric are discriminated as notable postures of the human mind. The linguistic studies of Edward Sapir and B. L. Whorf have lately shown that language is not only the storehouse of scientific thought. All actual and potential scientific theories are implicit in the verbal structure of the culture associated with them. By 1885 Mallarmé had formulated and utilized in his poetry these concepts about the nature of language uniting science and philology, which nowadays are known as "metalinguistics." However, these views of languages were commonplaces to Cratylus, Varro, and Philo Judaeus. They were familiar to the Church Fathers, and underlay the major schools of scriptural exegesis. If "four-level exegesis" is back in favor again as the staple of the "new criticism," it is because the poetic objects which have been made since 1880 frequently require such techniques for their elucidation. *Finnegans Wake* offers page by page much of the labyrinthine intricacy of a page of the

Book of Kells. And the central feature of the *Wake* is the exegesis of a letter dug up by the musical fowl Belinda. Pope wrote "A Key to the Lock" by way of an elaborate exegesis of the symbolic senses of his poem. Joyce made his poem in the shape of the key which unlocks it. But for Joyce as much as for St. Augustine the trivial and quadrivial arts form a harmony of philology and science which is indispensable to the exegetist of scripture and of language, too.

One way of seeing how ancient philology was linked to the quadrivial arts is found in St. Augustine's treatise *De Musica,* which is a discussion of metrics, astronomy, and prosody. In the milieu of St. Augustine it was natural to consider metrics in relation to numbers and arithmetic, for the entire order of the cosmos was supposed to be based on number just as all earthly music was but an approximation to the music of the spheres. Music was, esthetically speaking, the meeting place of poetics and mathematics, of grammatica and astronomy. Each letter of the alphabet had its numerical power attached to it quite as definitely as Rimbaud joined vowel and color. So that to speak of medieval illumination, as Ruskin did, as the art of color chords would have seemed as trite and obvious to St. Augustine as it is basic for the work of Joyce. For example, one of the most persistent and deeply embedded motifs in *Ulysses* is that of the "series of empty fifths" which Stephen plays on Bella Cohen's piano, expounding their ritual perfection "because the fundamental and the dominant are separated by the greatest possible interval which . . . is the greatest possible ellipse. Consistent with the ultimate return. The Octave. . . . What went forth to the ends of the world to traverse not itself. God, the sun, Shakespeare, a commercial traveller. . . . The longest way round is the shortest way home." The musical chord is a means of linking with the stages of human apprehension, the growth of the soul, the movement of the sun through the zodiacal signs, the Incarnation and Ascension, the mental labyrinth of art and the cloacal labyrinth of commerce. Nor are these diverse themes merely introduced casually in the Circe episode. They pervade this epic which unites the trivial and quadrivial arts by means of the same solar ritual which underlies

Homeric and other epic structures. Every incident becomes a point crossed and recrossed by the seven arts. For example, the above theme of the return and the commercial traveler recurs in the Ithaca episode in connection with Bloom as the Wandering Jew. The "technic" of the episode is "catechism (impersonal)."

> Would the departed never nowhere nohow reappear? Ever he would wander, selfcompelled, to the extreme limit of his cometary orbit, beyond the fixed stars and variable suns and telescopic planets, astronomical waifs and strays, to the extreme boundary of space passing from land to land, among peoples, amid events. Somewhere imperceptibly he would hear and somehow reluctantly, suncompelled, obey the summons of recall.

Astronomy is operative in two modes in *Ulysses,* an Eastern and a Western mode, as befits a work which follows the course of the rising and setting sun. Moreover, the opening episode of the book, organized in accord with the art of theology, is liturgical. One of the little epics contained analogously within the larger action of *Ulysses* concerns the wanderings of a cake of lemon soap purchased by Bloom early in the day. At one level the soap is a comic and cloacal variant on the ritual labyrinth traversed by Bloom that day (Pope's *Rape of the Lock* is a similar comic epic ending in a similar apotheosis). The soap says from the heavens:

> We're a capital couple are Bloom and I;
> He brightens the earth, I polish the sky.

At another level the soap is a sign of grace uniting earthly and stellar, hermetic and astrologic, East and West labyrinths. These two levels of reality, which are in conflict all during Bloomsday, are thus reconciled among the stars. In the same context Dante is invoked obliquely as another sign of the reconciliation of Bloom and Stephen. For Dante, like Joyce and Eliot, employs grace to reconcile East and West. Reconciliation is not merging, however. This is made explicit in the Ithaca episode where Bloom's "Eastern" creed of perfectibility, "vital growth through convulsions of metamorphosis" is counterpointed with Stephen's "Western" way: "He affirmed his significance as a conscious rational animal proceeding syllogistically from the known to the unknown and a conscious rational reagent between a micro- and macrocosm ineluctably constructed upon the incertitude of the void." These two labyrinths are counterpointed throughout *Ulysses*. The one is "Eastern," Hermetic, earthly and cloacal, proceeding by peristaltic convulsions to metamorphosis (e.g., the Marxian materialistic dialectic of history). The other is "Western," a cognitive labyrinth cognizant and constitutive of the word and of analogy. As a true analogist Joyce attempts no reduction of these realities, but orders their ineluctable modalities to the reconciliation of vision rather than of fusion. But, roughly, the two modes correspond to quadrivium and trivium.

Ulysses as concerned primarily with Bloom carries him over the sea of matter. His quest is social, ethical, political, in contrast to the spiritual quest of Stephen. Joyce pursues a rigorous classical decorum in his delineation of these themes which can best be enjoyed by a reader possessing some acquaintance with the traditional scope of the trivium and the quadrivium. As St. Thomas says (*De Trinitate* V, 3), "These subjects are known as the trivium and quadrivium because by them, as if by certain roads, the eager mind enters into the secrets of philosophy." They are propaedeutic to other studies.

If St. Augustine's *De Musica* affords a view of the traditional way of seeing the relation between metrics and astronomy, his *De Doctrina Christiana* links the trivium and quadrivium to the business of scriptural exegesis and sacred oratory. It amounts to an adaptation of the Ciceronian ideal of the *doctus orator* to the new tasks of the Christian theologian and teacher.

In this regard Cicero's *De Oratore* is itself a charter of classical humanism, an attempt to unify the Graeco-Roman culture in a vision of the ideal orator. As such it underlies not only St. Augustine and St. Jerome but most medieval and Renaissance books of advice to princes and courtiers. However, it is far from being a mere résumé of ancient cultural ideals, for Cicero is consciously pre-Socratic in his bias. His synthesis is directed to the end of forming the perfect man of action rather than the man of speculation and science. He is Isocratean and Sophist, therefore, rather than Socratic or Platonic and Aristotelian. This preference, as well as the conflict it involves, has dominated the culture of Western Europe until today. Joyce gives these themes full play in his work. His Bloom is Homer's prudent "man of many devices" and he is also Cicero's orator.

Since the principal sphere of rhetoric and social guidance is advertising in these latter days of the Gutenberg era, Bloom is presented as a copywriter and canvasser for ads. He is peripatetic, encyclopedic, and able, like Cicero's orator, to speak eloquently on all subjects. As the Citizen says in the Cyclops episode:

> I declare to my antimacassar if you took up a straw from the bloody floor and if you said to Bloom: *Look at, Bloom, Do you see that straw? That's a straw.* Declare to my aunt he'd talk about it for an hour so he would and talk steady.

At this particular moment Bloom is elsewhere examining *The Awful Disclosures of Maria Monk* and Aristotle's *Metaphysics.* As type of the encyclopedic and prudent citizen Bloom's network of communication stretches from heaven to earth and includes especially all aspects of corporate social life. With respect to the conditions of modern life Joyce characterizes Bloom with exact classical decorum as the perfect rhetorician and type of Homer's "man of many devices."

> What were habitually his final meditations? Of some one sole unique advertisement to cause passers to stop in wonder, a poster novelty, with all extraneous accretions excluded, reduced to its simplest and most efficient terms not exceeding the span of casual vision and congruous with the velocity of modern life.

The ideal orator will be a man of encyclopedic knowledge because learning precedes eloquence. And because he will be the type of the perfect citizen he will be eloquent about everything which concerns corporate life. But eloquence implies great tact, a sense of the propriety of word and thing as befits each contingency. Bloomsday is a prolonged demonstration of Bloom's learned sense of decorum. But decorum in language or action is of all things, observed Aristotle, in common with antiquity, the hardest thing to hit, calling, as it does, for an agile perception and adjustment to the fluctuating circumstances of times, places, and persons.

Joyce underlines the skill of Bloom's social decorum in a peculiarly witty way. Homer's Odysseus learns from Circe that after passing the Sirens there were two courses open to him. One is by way of the Wandering Rocks, which Jason alone had passed in the *Argo*. The other is the way of Scylla and Charybdis, rock and whirlpool. Odysseus avoids the labyrinth of the Wandering Rocks. But Bloom navigates both labyrinths safely, thus excelling Odysseus. The Rocks are citizens and society seen in abstraction as mindless, Martian mechanisms. The "stone" men are children of the sun, denizens of space, exempt from time, and linked with the Druidic culture. Opposed to them are "The Dead" (see last story in *Dubliners*) children of the moon, the Celtic twilight ("cultic twalette"), moving in the aquacities of time, memory, and sentiment. On these dual labyrinths of stone and water Joyce has built almost every line he has written. And all the antithetic pairs of the *Wake* embrace these polarities, as H. C. E. bricklayer and A.L.P. river, male and female; Shem and Shaun, poet and policeman. Since, moreover, the letters of the alphabet are easily polarized in the same way, it is a matter of main consequence to recognize their hermetic signatures in order to get around in the *Wake*.

In the same episode of the Wandering Rocks there is another aspect of decorum seen in the contrasting monologues of Stephen and Bloom. The leaping movement of Stephen's wide-ranging thoughts counterpoint the slow-footed earthbound progress of Bloom as each threads his way through a world of contrived illusions and fake identities.

If Bloom represents the actualized modern embodiment of classical decorum in *Ulysses*, Stephen illustrates the sense in which the poet is dispensed from the bonds of social decorum. The Aeolus or newspaper episode in which the art is rhetoric shows Stephen declining the editorial invitation to a journalistic career. The episode opens with an evocation of the stone-steel labyrinth of the Dublin trainway system and then shifts to the analogous network of movable type and the world of spatial communication controlled by the press. (Mr. Eliot's *Coriolan* poems traverse the same labyrinths of spatial organization represented by government in a technological age.) By counterpoint, this episode concerned with the spatial power and emptiness of the press proceeds by reminiscences of great orations (communication in time) and moves backwards out of the one-day press world to the stone labyrinth of Sinai and the Mosaic fables of the law. Professor MacHugh recalls "a speech made by John F. Taylor at the college historical society" in a debate about the revival of the Irish tongue. Taylor's argument is that "had the youthful Moses listened to and accepted that view of life (i.e., the Egyptian-English view of Hebrew-Irish culture and language). . . . He would never have spoken with the Eternal amid lightnings on Sinai's mountaintop nor ever have come down with the light of inspiration shining in his countenance, and bearing in his arms the tables of the law graven in the language of the outlaw."

That this speech has the same central role in *Ulysses* as the Anna Livia passage in the *Wake* may be concluded from the fact that they are the only two passages that Joyce ever consented to record for gramophone. Stephen's comment on this speech is his "parable of the plums," after which the group noisily recedes from the stone-steel labyrinth of the press world to the aquatic labyrinth of the pub. In the *Wake* Shem the penman is, like Moses, an "outlex." The seer cannot be a rhetor. He does not speak for effect, but that we may know. He is also an outlet, a shaman, a scapegoat. And the artist, in order that he may perform his katharsis-purgative function, must mime all things. (The katharsis-purgative role of the Herculean culture hero dominates the nightworld of the *Wake* where the hero sets Alpheus, the river of speech and collective consciousness, to the task of cleansing the Augean stables of thought and feeling.) As mime, the artist cannot be the prudent and decorous Ulysses, but appears as a sham. As sham and mime he undertakes not the ethical quest but the quest of the great fool. He must become all things in order to reveal all. And to be all he must empty himself. Strictly within the bounds of classical decorum Joyce saw that, unlike the orator, the artist cannot properly speak with his own voice. The ultimate artist can have no style of his own but must be an "outlex" through which the multiple aspects of reality can utter themselves. That the artist should intrude his personal idiom between thing and reader is literally impertinence. Decorum permits the artist as a young man (*The Portrait*) to speak with his master's voice—the voice of Pater, his father in art. (Joyce like Chesterton delighted in the multivalent wit of nature and reality so that, no matter how far-fetched his analogues and paradoxes, they are never concocted nor forced. They not only bear but require intent scrutiny.)

Whereas the ethical world of *Ulysses* is presented in terms of well-defined human types, the more metaphysical world of the *Wake* speaks and moves before us with the gestures of being itself. It is a nightworld and, literally, as Joyce reiterates, is "abcedminded." Letters ("every letter is a godsend"), the frozen, formalized gestures of remote ages of collective experience, move before us in solemn morrice. They are the representatives of the age-old adequation of mind and things, enacting the drama of the endless adjustment of the interior acts and dispositions of the mind to the outer world. The drama of cognition itself. For it is in the drama of cognition, the stages of apprehension, that Joyce found the archetype of poetic imitation. He seems to have been the first to see that the dance of being, the nature imitated by the arts, has its primary analogue in the activity of the exterior and interior senses. Joyce was aware that this doctrine (that sensation is imitation because the exterior forms are already in a new matter) is implicit in Aquinas. He made it explicit in *Stephen Hero* and the *Portrait,* and founded his entire poetic activity on *these* analogical proportions of the senses.

The doctrine of decorum, the foundation of classical rhetoric, is a profoundly analogical doctrine, so that to discuss it as it operates in Joyce is to be at the center of his communication network. In

Ulysses each character is discriminated by his speech and gestures, and the whole work stands midway between narrative and drama. But the *Wake* is primarily dramatic and the techniques proper to this form are taken from the fourth part of rhetoric, *"pronuntiatio"* or action and delivery. This division of rhetoric was a crux of communication theory in former times, being the crossroads of rhetoric, psychology, and other disciplines. St. Thomas discusses the issue, for example (*S.T.* I, 57, 4, ad 3), apropos of the modes of communication between men and angels:

> Since, therefore, the angels know corporeal things and their dispositions, they can thereby know what is passing in the appetite or in the imaginative apprehension of brute animals, and even of man, in so far as man's sensitive appetite sometimes acts under the influence of some bodily impression. . . .

The analogical relation between exterior posture and gesture and the interior movements and dispositions of the mind is the irreducible basis of drama. In the *Wake* this appears everywhere. So that any attempt to reduce its action, at any point, to terms of univocal statement results in radical distortion. Joyce's insistence on the "abcedminded" nature of his drama can be illustrated from his attitude to the alphabet throughout. He was familiar with the entire range of modern archeological and anthropological study of pre-alphabetic syllabaries and hieroglyphics, including the traditional kabbalistic lore. To this knowledge he added the Thomistic insights into the relation of these things with mental operations. So that the polarity between H.C.E. and A.L.P. involves, for one thing, the relation between the agent and possible intellect. H.C.E. is mountain, male and active. A.L.P. is river, female and passive. But ALP equals mountain and historically "H" is interfused with "A," and "A" is both ox-face and plough first of arts and letters; so that, dramatically, the roles of HCE and ALP are often interchangeable. Punning on "Dublin," he constantly invites us to regard his drama as the story of "doublends joined." Irremediably analogical, Joyce's work moves as naturally on the metaphysical as on the naturalistic plane.

But there is always the liturgical level as well. Nothing Joyce ever wrote lacks that dimension. One significance of Stephen's surname Dedalus (the French form of Daedalus) is that Daedalus, the inventor of the labyrinth, was accredited with having been the first to reduce the ancient initiation rituals to the form of art. That is to say, Daedalus was the first to grasp the relation between the pagan rebirth rituals and the labyrinthine retracings of the artistic process. The pagan rituals were imitations of nature *in sua operatione,* because the soul imprisoned in existence could only be released by retracing the stages of its fall and descent through the various degrees of material being. Necessarily, therefore, all artistic imitation first arose from the pagan liturgies or mysteries. If Daedalus was the first to note this relation, Joyce was the first to see in these ancient rituals of descent and return the perfect externalization, in drama and gesture, of the stages of human apprehension. The retracing of any moment of cognition will thus provide the unique artistic form of that moment. And its art form coincides with its quiddity, except that the artist arrests what is otherwise fleeting. (M. D. Chénu, O.P., has explained the larger pattern of the *Summa* of St. Thomas to be based on the Neo-Platonic theme of emanation and return which pagan rituals have derived and expressed in the pattern of solar movement: "This brief scheme . . . is utilized by St. Thomas not as a commodious frame in which he can dispose at his pleasure the immense material of his sacred doctrine, but as an order of knowledge, which produces intelligibility at the heart of revealed truth" [*Cross Currents* II 2, p. 72].)

It is the liturgical sense of Joyce that enables him to manipulate such encyclopedic lore, guided by his analogical awareness of liturgy as both an order of knowledge and an order of grace.

In this respect it could be suggested that Austin Farrer's *A Rebirth of Images* (Dacre Press, 1949), which is a commentary on the Book of Revelation, is probably the ideal introduction to the work of Joyce. His conclusions are relevant to the Joycean procedure: "If John is keeping so many concerns in mind, following the symbolical week and the sacred year, the scheme of traditional eschatology, of

Christ's prophecy, and of multiple Old Testament typology, how can he move at all, and how can he keep his pattern firm? The diagram supplies the answer [a diagram of the Hebrew plus the Christian liturgical year laid out on the zodiacal plan]. He makes each movement of the poem by working round the diagram: each such movement, or group of such movements, is a day in the week, a quarter of the year, and so on—he will never get lost. The diagram, as St. John comes back over it, retains the enrichments of meaning with which the previous movements have overlaid it. These afford materials for the fresh movement and give rise to that continually varied embellishment of a standing cyclic pattern which is the literary miracle of the Apocalypse. . . . St. John started with the diagram ready drawn . . . it was not enough to contemplate the diagram; the diagram must, as it were, be persuaded to speak, and, in its own order, to reveal its mysteries. As the mind passed over and over it, the several stages of ascent were built up . . . until the World to Come burst on the seer's vision, charged with the weight of all he had seen by the way.

"What it is so hard for us to recover is the thought-world in which the diagram, and the diagram simply, could be viewed as a sacred and illuminating thing." But such a thought-world is entirely congenial to the twentieth century, as its art and criticism testify. Representative as he is of that return to the plenary scope of patristic exegesis, Dr. Farrer unintentionally provides a splendid introduction to Joyce (as Joyce does to these other fields). This can perhaps be taken as a mark of the profound coherence of modern culture when viewed at its best levels.

As Hugh Kenner indicated in his essay on the *Portrait,* the first page provides the standing cyclic pattern which is the track which Joyce traverses over and over again with deepening awareness and ever richer epiphanies of being. That track is the order of the expanding sensuous, moral and intellectual development of a human being. It is an order of knowledge. Because it is a standing cycle, Joyce can record the growth of an artist's mind as a portrait rather than a narrative. In *Ulysses* Bloom's day is a solar cycle including the social and political dimensions. *Finnegans Wake* is a full-scale liturgical cycle involving the total experience of the race. The *Wake* follows the track of the Christian liturgical year, but at any moment the four quarters of this track may shift to H.C.E.'s four-poster bed or to the four evangelists. It is at some moments a hippodrome, at another a conducted tour of a museum, or a radio-television network. The use of these analogous patterns as projective techniques is parallel to what Dr. Farrar notes in St. John: "For the already written part of his work becomes formative of the rest. . . . In writing the Candlestick-vision, he underwent the control of Zecariah and Daniel, in writing the Seven Messages he underwent the control of the Candlestick-vision. . . . The vision thrust upon him the symbol of the lamps and stars, and of their mysterious equivalence . . . . Passing back over the text of the vision, he heard in it the messages of Christ to the Seven Churches. . . . The meaning of the Name works itself out in the short pattern of the Greeting, Doxology, Advent, Promise and Amen . . . the short pattern has set forth the Name, but a longer pattern must set forth the short pattern. . . . The fulfilment must begin in further oracle or vision."

(I I)

Dr. Farrar provides not only insight into Joyce but saves space here as a contemporary instance of that encyclopedic scriptural exegesis which has been undertaken whenever the trivial and quadrivial studies have flourished. At the outset it was suggested that renewed interest in the trivium and quadrivium was not love of archaism but of a piece with recent developments in linguistics, esthetics, and anthropology. Now that some of the general bearings of this situation have been given with respect to Joyce it is possible to move a little closer to the particular facets of these disciplines as he employed them. It needs to be understood that only short discontinuous shots of such a work as Joyce's are possible. Linear or continuous perspectives of analogical structures are only the result of radical distortion, and the craving for "simple explanations" is the yearning for univocity.

To glance in brief succession at the trivium and quadrivium in Joyce is to begin with grammatica or philology. This involves speech itself, which has been properly named as the main protagonist of every work of Joyce. "Our speech is, as it were," says Julius Caesar Scaliger in his *Poetics,* "the postman of the mind, through the services of whom civil gatherings are announced, the arts are cultivated and the claims of wisdom intercede with men for man." Joyce employs this image of speech as letter in the Belinda episode of the *Wake,* as well as in the section on Shaun the Poet cycling back through the night of history and collective consciousness. Words as a network of tentacular roots linking all human culture, and "reaching down into the deepest terrors and desires," as Mr. Eliot says, were the study of ancient grammatica. So that it is easy to see how a Quintilian could say that in a certain sense grammar embraces all other studies, and why Varro's *De Lingua Latina* is an encyclopedic work. There was a "nominalist" school in antiquity but the main tradition was via the Stoics or analogists for whom speech was a specific level of communication in the divine Logos which distinguished men from brutes. From this point of view it followed naturally that the cultivation of eloquence and verbal precision was the principal means of achieving human excellence. "Every letter is a godsend," wrote Joyce. And, much more, every word is an avatar, a revelation, an epiphany. For every word is the product of a complex mental act with a complete learning process involved in it. In this respect words can be regarded not as signs but as existent things, alive with a physical and mental life which is both individual and collective. The conventional meanings of words can thus be used or disregarded by Joyce, who is concentrating on the submerged metaphysical drama which these meanings often tend to overlay. His puns in the *Wake* are a technique for revealing this submerged drama of language, and Joyce relied on the quirks, "slips," and freaks of ordinary discourse to evoke the fullness of existence in speech. All his life he played the sleuth with words, shadowing them and waiting confidently for some unexpected situation to reveal their hidden signatures and powers. For his view of the poet was that he should read, not forge, the signatures of things. As he explains in *Stephen Hero,* this involves the poet in a perpetual activity of retracing and reconstructing the ways of human apprehension. A poem is a vivisection of the mind and senses in action, an anagenesis or retracing, begetting anagnorosis or recognition. This is the key to the theme of memory and history embodied in Anna Livia of the *Wake.* She runs forward but "ana" is Greek for backwards, and spells the same both ways. Anna Livia is also the Liffey nourishing the Guinnesses (anagenesis) of all things. It is the business of grammarian and poet to see this cyclic process of emanation and return as the origin and term of all words and creatures.

Paul Valéry (*Variety V*) expresses our contemporary sense of these matters: "It is the domain of the 'figures' with which the ancient rhetoric was concerned and which today has been almost abandoned by pedagogy. This neglect is regrettable. The formation of figures is inseparable from that of language itself, in which all 'abstract' words are obtained by some abuse or transfer of signification, followed by oblivion of the primitive meaning. . . . Moreover, in considering these things from the highest point of view, one cannot but see Language itself as the supreme literary masterpiece, since every creation in this order reduces itself to a combination of forces in a given vocabulary, according to forms instituted once and for all." In a word, there is no such thing as a primitive language. As Joyce once said to Frank Budgen (*The Making of Ulysses*), he had embedded all of Quintilian's figures of rhetoric in The Oxen of the Sun episode as part of the technic of "embryonic development" of the ovum, man and society. These figures dramatize all the possible stages and dispositions of body and mind in womb and society.

It is, however, in the third or Proteus episode of *Ulysses* that Joyce explicitly deploys the resources of traditional grammatica. The binding of Proteus or primal matter is achieved by Stephen the poet by philology:

Ineluctable modality of the visible. At least that if no more, thought through my eyes. Signatures of all things I am here to read, seaspawn and seawrack, the nearing tide, that rusty boot.

The scene is the strand, border between two worlds, type of the condition of man "that great amphibian." The first work of Adam in the Garden, says Bacon, was the viewing of creatures and the imposition of names. Such is the work of Stephen, poet and philologian, on the strand—the binding of Proteus, the reading of signatures and evocation of quiddity by the imposition of names. Some power more than human, says Socrates in the *Cratylus* (a dialogue named for the grammarian who was Plato's teacher) gave things their first names.

In the *Wake* the origins of speech as gesture are associated with "Bygmeister Finnegan of the stuttering hand." This seems to tie up with Vico's view that the earliest language was that of the gods of which Homer speaks: "The gods call this giant Briareus" of the hundred hands. The idea of speech as stuttering, as arrested gesture, as discontinuities or aspects of the single Word, is basic to the *Wake* and serves to illustrate the profundity of the traditional philological doctrine in Joyce. On the other hand, as Vico suggests, popular speech and script are the people's domain, the world of Bloom and the newspaper. In the Proteus episode there are brief speech gestures from many languages, but the external world utters itself most richly of all: "Listen: a four-worded wave speech: seesoo, hrss, rsseeiss, ooos. Vehement breath of waters amid seasnakes, rearing horses, rocks. In cups of rocks it slops: flop, slop, flop."

There is a speech of the giant Sir Lout whose toys are the big boulders of the shore, and his words are neolithic-heroic in a manner which reveals much of the technique of the *Wake,* where we learn to note "what age is at" by such gestures: "I'm the bloody well gigant rolls all them bloody well boulders, bones for my stepping-stones. Feefaw-fum. Izmellz de bloodz oldz an Iridzman." The Druidic sacrificial stone altar is evoked.

Heraldry provides Joyce with a ready-made shorthand language of creatures: "on a field tenney a buck, trippant, proper, unattired" fades to "the bloated carcass of a dog lolled on bladderwrack and a boat sunk in sand. *Un coche ensablé,* Louis Veuillot called Gautier's prose. These heavy sands are language tide and wind have silted here."

Joyce employs here specially the lore associated with the ancient conception of the auditory side of the external world as an Aeolian harp. His color symbolism employs the complementary conception of the visual aspect of creation as the harp of Memnon. With the development of the spectroscope in the eighteenth century both these ancient images became popular again. The color chord of the spectrum suggested that there exists a rapport between the outer world and the inner world of our faculties which developed into the symbolist doctrine of "correspondences." In 1856 Georges Kastner produced an encyclopedic work entitled *La Harpe D'Eole et la Musique Cosmique.* Its subtitle runs: *Etudes des phénomènes sonores de la Nature avec la science et l'art suivies de Stephen ou la Harpe D'Eole, Grand Monologue Lyrique avec choers.* Joyce students will find much that is useful in this work which includes a full-scale catalogue of the musical resonances of animals, plants, trees, groves, metals, rocks, waters, caves, grottos, storms, and of artifacts as well. The relations with ancient doctrine and modern art are discussed. Berlioz he regards as a composer who has tried to reduce this natural symphony to the limits of art. Dante had counterpointed the music of heaven with the sounds of hell. Since, "under the name of cosmic music we intend the multiple harmonies of nature speaking to man," it is necessary to include arithmetic, Pythagorean number theory and to see their harmonic relation with physics, astronomy, psychology, and morals.

Kastner is apropos as a nineteenth-century artist-philosopher concerned with the language of Nature, since he indicates very explicitly not only the scope of ancient grammatica but also the interests of the symbolist writers. Moreover, he enables us to see how grammatica or philology embraces the other liberal arts. Joyce would have regarded him in general as crude and trite, but not as mistaken. The experiments of Lipps at the end of the last century illustrated how all possible musical structures were contained in a single clang of a bell. A technique for electrically spatializing such complex sounds made such demonstrations possible. Mallarmé approached words and states of mind likewise, tracing their subtlest derivatives in a way which eventually returned the poetry of Joyce and Eliot to the contemplation of "the Beatrician moment" from which Dante had derived his complex structure of physical, mental, and spiritual states. The theme of Tennyson's "flower in the crannied wall" was really put to poetic uses which might well have astonished him. Properly, then, philology includes all the arts and sciences, but their individual, specialized characters and uses are also indispensable. The one which in *Ulysses* Joyce singled out next is rhetoric, in the Aeolus episode. Something has already been said of this large subject in connection with decorum and Cicero's ideal orator, as the type of encyclopedic eloquence, social propriety, and political prudence. For it is this Ciceronian character of Bloom which enables him to act as the center of so complex a network as *Ulysses*. As Stuart Gilbert writes:

> James Joyce is, in fact, in the great tradition which begins with Homer; like his precursors he subjects his work, for all its wild vitality and seeming disorder, to a rule of discipline as severe as that of the Greek dramatists; indeed, the unities of *Ulysses* go far beyond the classic triad, they are as manifold and yet symmetrical as the daedal network of nerves and bloodstreams which pervade the living organism.

In an important book, *Communication, the Social Matrix of Psychology*, a psychologist and an anthropologist, Jurgen Ruesch and Gregory Bateson, have recently followed the method of *Ulysses* in attempting to convey the working image of cultural communication. Their work serves as a useful approach to Joyce, if only because it demonstrates how in some ways modern science falters along in the distance behind the art of *Ulysses*. For Joyce has solved numerous problems which science has not yet formulated as problems. And Joyce's superiority to Freud and Jung is not so much one of a talent as his ability to avail himself of the entire wisdom of the collective human past. The propriety, for instance, of using a solar day as the ground plan of a presentation of the body politic would require a treatise to explain. It can only be suggested that the movement of the sun, controlling and paralleling the movements of individual and social organs, is an archetypal situation which is infinitely responsive to poetic manipulation. It is also all-inclusive and, literally, encyclopedic. Such an archetype permits Joyce to utilize Cicero's entire doctrine of the orator and the body politic with ease. It also enables him to include the corpus of Eastern wisdom in the structure of the emanation and return theme which is traditionally associated with solar myth. As A. P. Sinnett writes in *Esoteric Buddhism:* "Man has a manvantara and pralaya every four-and-twenty hours . . . vegetation follows the same rule from year to year as it subsides and revives with the seasons."

Ponchielli's "Dance of the Hours" enters into *Ulysses* at many levels, the feet of the hours weaving and unweaving Penelope's veil, as well as evoking the Egyptian ritual dance of the sungod.

The scene of the Aeolus episode is the newspaper offices of the *Freeman's Journal and National Press* which Bloom visits in order to place an ad for a client. Stephen has come about a letter on the foot-and-mouth disease. And the tentacles attached to the ad and the letter are involved in everything else. For instance, the ad concerns Alexander Keyes; the house of keys and cross keys are the sign of the isle of Man, as well as St. Peter. The letter which gets for Stephen the title of bullockbefriending bard is linked to Virgil's fourth Georgic and to the theme of ox and bees as type of the labyrinths of the poetic process.

But the principal relevance of the newspaper with reference to rhetoric and decorum concerns the one-day world of press and advertisement alike, a fact linking the press to the solar ritual. The press exists primarily as a means of spatial communication and control. Its time-binding powers are quite puny. This fact is handled in several facetious modes in the episode. As Stuart Gilbert notes, for example: "The style of the captions is gradually modified in the course of the episode; the first are comparatively dignified, or classically allusive, in the Victorian tradition; the time dimension still clinging to the spatial. Later captions reproduce in all its vulgarity, the slickness of the modern press. This historico-literary technique, here inaugurated, is a preparation for the employment of the same method, but on the grand scale, a stylistic tour de force in . . . The Oxen of the Sun." The effect in both episodes is serio-comic, the comic effect resulting from the revelation of the mechanical aspect of embryonic development. The main theme of the Aeolus episode is Roman and cloacal, the countertheme Mosaic and spiritual. As journalism is the ape of literature so there is a detective story embedded in the episode as ape of the poetic process. "Aeolus" refers not only to the press as the cave of the winds and rhetoric but to such esoteric data as the illicit unions of the children of Aeolus being reflected in the journalistic union of aspiration and compromise, idealism and opportunism, art and "what the public wants."

Dialectic, the third member of the trivium, appears as "technic" in the ninth episode whose "art" is literature. Typical of the "trivial" punning of Joyce is the fact that "Scylla" is derived from a Semitic word "skoula," a rock which also permits Joyce to link dialectic both to scholasticism and the Chair of Peter. As correspondences for the Rock, Joyce himself offers Aristotle and dogma. Antithetic to Scylla, the rock, is Charybdis, the whirlpool, corresponding to which are Plato and mysticism. The presiding "art" of literature, which barely survives the passage between the antithetic dialectics of Aristotle and Plato. Dialectics, the traditional enemy of letters and poetry, gives literature a very thin time as Stephen steers the theme of literary paternity and Shakespeare past the twin enemies which are yet necessary to the existence of literature. Every literary and theological crux concerning the relation of poet and product, Father and Son is broached in this episode, reminding us that St. Thomas explains the procession in the Trinity by the analogue of the artistic process. For example, John Eglinton tackles

Stephen over his "theory" of Shakespeare and Hamlet: "You are a delusion. You have brought us all this way to show us a French triangle. Do you believe your own theory?"

"No," said Stephen promptly.

This is the dialectical crux of "poetry and beliefs" which has wrecked so many critical craft in recent decades. Dialectics seeks a syllogistic certitude which is alien to the mode of vision of art. Art must employ dialectics as matter, not as the way or conclusion of its quest. As Stuart Gilbert sums up:

> The mystery of paternity, in its application to the First and ' Second Persons of the Trinity, to King Hamlet and the Prince, and, by implication to the curious symbiosis of Stephen and Mr. Bloom, is ever in the background of Stephen's Shakespearian exegesis. All through the chapter he is capturing in a net of analogies, is *symbolizing* (in the exact meaning of this word: *throwing together*), the protean manifestations of the creative force (one of whose dynamics in the animate world is the rite of creation, paternity). . . . And the artist himself, creator of the saga of Dublin, the Viking City, is by a subtle cross-allusion drawn into the net.

Dialectics shuns the way of these nets of analogies, seeking to reduce them to univocal discourse and linear statements. So there is special propriety in the analogical juxtaposition of the antithetic modes of dialectics, Scylla and Charybdis, Aristotle and Plato, as providing the true course of the poet.

The net of analogies or symbolic juxtapositions of *Ulysses* can also be seen with reference to the dateline June 16, 1904. The frankly newspaperish aspect of this epic derives from the speculations and practice of Mallarmé who regarded the press as a new kind of popular poetry, collective in origin and appeal. If the trivium and quadrivium represent seven crossroads for the meeting of the various degrees and levels of reality, a page of the press is an even more complex set of crossroads, juxtaposing events representative of many times and multiple spaces under a single dateline. In the press an Eskimo item will repose beside a Parisian event, the neolithic and the atomic man meet in the same flat paper landscape of the press. In the same way *Ulysses* is 1904 A.D. but also 800 B.C. And the continuous parallel between ancient and modern provides a "cubist" rather than a linear perspective. It is a world of a "timeless present" such as we meet in the order of objections in a Thomistic article, but also typical of the nonperspective discontinuities of medieval art in general. History is abolished not by being disowned but by becoming present. "History is now," as Eliot sees it in *Four Quartets*. This "cubist" sense of the past as a dimension of the present is natural in four-level scriptural exegesis and ancient grammatica. It is necessary to enjoyment of *Ulysses* or the *Wake* with its theme that "pastimes are past times," that the popular press, popular games, and ordinary speech are charged with the full historic weight of the collective human past.

(I I I)

In the same way that instantaneous communication of news from many cultures, times, and places, which is characteristic of modern technology, tends to create the art of a "timeless present," so Joyce in the *Wake* deals with the conventional meanings which words have picked up in their long history. For the conventional meanings like the dateline of a newspaper often disguise the fact that "pastimes are past times." The timeless or simultaneous aspect of words leaps out at us (the literal sense of "object") when they are used not as conventional signs but as metaphysical existents. It is, therefore, only necessary to free words from their immediate contemporary contexts in order to reveal their substantial character. One of the many techniques for freeing words from their conventional contexts is the pun and the "slip" of the tongue or pen. In Book II, chapter 2 of the *Wake,* the study period is presented as a universal drama of "triv and quad." Dialectics is presented in terms of strife. Pictures of boxers adorn the twins' nursery. The twins have been studying the battles of history and intercultural strife.

And so, these things being so or ere those things having done, way back home in Pacata Auburnia (untillably holy gammel

Eire) one world burrowing on another . . . have discust their
things of the past, crime and Fable with shame, home and profit,
why lui lied to lei and tried to kill ham. . . . Spell me the
chimes. They are tales all tolled. Today is well thine but where's
May tomorrow be . . . dirging a past of bloody altars. . . .
Yet sung of love and the monster man. What's hiccuper to hem or
her to Hagaba? Ough, ough brieve kindli.

This, as Joyce says elsewhere, is "History as her is harped," the
quadrivial art of music carrying the theme of a cultural concor-
dance of discordant motifs. The marginal gloss for the above passage is in the style of Hegel's dialectic of the historic process: "From
cenogenetic dichotomy through diagnostic conciliance to dynastic
continuity."

"One world burrowing on another" is a typical pun which in-
vokes the two-way process of borrowing and burrowing plus the
image of burial mounds and the tree-pillar cults which themselves
were modes of communication between the living and the dead.
Every word in the *Wake* is dramatically active in this kind of way,
following not a road of meaning but carrying us on an every-way
roundabout with intrusions from above and below:

> Begin to forget it. It will remember itself from every sides,
> with all gestures in each our word. . . . Our wholemole mill-
> wheeling vicociclometer . . . receives through a portal vein the
> dialytically separated elements of precedent decomposition for
> the very pet purpose of subsequent recombination so that the
> eroticisms, catastrophes and eccentricities transmitted by the
> ancient legacy of the past, type by tope, letter from letter, word at
> ward. . . . Well, we have frankly enjoyed more than anything
> these secret workings of natures (thanks ever for it, we humbly
> pray) and, well, was really so denighted of this lights time.

Such is Joyce's conception of his puns as now trivial, now quadrivial. If Shakespeare, as Johnson said, loses the world for a quibble,
Joyce re-creates it by the same means. But like Shakespeare and
Chesterton, Joyce uses the pun as a way of seeing the paradoxical
exuberance of being through language. And it was years after he
had begun the *Wake* before he saw that the babble of Anna Livia

through the nightworld of the collective consciousness united the towers of Babel and of sleep. In sleep "the people is one and they have all one language" but day overcomes and scatters them. Of this nightworld Joyce says, "it is dormition," linking it in a single gesture to Domitian, damnation, and all the senses of "subliminal," or doormission, with its links with dormitory, dormeuse, doormouse (Lewis Carroll), door-muse and the daughters of memory.

> Triv and quad are the "keys to dreamland,"
> As you sing it it's a study . . . This nonday diary,
> this allnight's newseryreel

But the *Wake,* as is fitting, although compact of every mood and state of mind, is mainly a world of uproarious fun. No more joyous or funny book was ever conceived or executed:

> ₋ You is feeling like you was lost in the bush, boy? . . . Lead kindly fowl! They always did; ask the ages. What bird has done yesterday man may do next year, be it fly, be it moult, be it hatch, be it agreement in the nest. For her socio-scientific is sound as a bell, sir, her volucrine automutativeness right on normalcy: She knows, she just, feels she was kind of born to lay and love eggs. . . . Yes, before all this has time to end the golden age must return with its vengeance.

The *Wake* unfolds as an interior landscape, "a phantom city, phaked of philim pholk," and has a flexibility and range as much greater than *Ulysses* as the latter enjoyed over the *Portrait.* The tradition that links Zoroaster with the origin of the Seven liberal arts and sees the arts as the long road back from the Fall, can be caught and dramatized in a few clauses: "Since primal made alter in garden of Idem. The tasks above are as the flasks below, saith the emerald canticle of Hermes . . . solar systemised, seriocosmically, in a more and more almightily expanding universe under one, there is rhymeless reason to believe, original sun. Securely judges orb terrestrial. *Haud certo ergo.* But O felicitous culpability, sweet bad cess to you for an archetypt!"

John Dos Passos:
Technique vs. Sensibility

☙ ☙ ☙ ☙ ☙

MOST ELABORATE of the many spoofs made by James Joyce was his obeisance to Dujardins as his "master" of the interior monologue. Only less elaborate have been the jokes played by Mr. Eliot, as in presenting to Harvard his copy of Jessie Weston with many pages uncut. To darken the counsel of those who choose to live in darkness has always been a form of light-bringing among the wits. But easily the most esoteric literary high-jinx of our time is the very formal debate, conducted far above the heads of Bloomsbury, between Wyndham Lewis and James Joyce. Lewis' "attack" on Joyce as a romantic time-snob, and Joyce's "counterattack" in *Finnegans Wake* are not just obscurantist trifling but a means of offering important insights to those readers who have acquired certain preliminary disciplines.

The reader of Dos Passos, however, is not required to have much more reading agility than the reader of the daily press. Nor does Dos Passos make many more serious demands than a good movie. And this is said not to belittle an excellent writer who has much to offer, but to draw attention to the extreme simplification to which Dos Passos has submitted the early work of James Joyce. *Three Soldiers* (1921), *Manhattan Transfer* (1925), and *U. S. A.* (1930–1936) would not exist in their present form but for the *Portrait of the Artist as a Young Man, Dubliners,* and *Ulysses.* It is as a slightly super-realist that Dos Passos has viewed and adapted the work of Joyce in his own work. And since his technical debt to Joyce is so considerable, one useful way of placing the achievement of Dos Passos is to notice what he took over and, especially, what he did not take.

As a young man in Chicago and at Harvard Dos Passos was much alive to the imagists, Sandburg, Fletcher, Pound, Amy Lowell, and the French poet Cendrars. From them he learned much that has continuously affected his practice. Their romantic tapestries and static contemplation of the ornate panorama of existence have always held him in spite of his desire to be a romantic of action. The same conflict, between the man who needs to participate in the life of his time and the artist who wishes to render that life more luminous by self-effacement in his art, appears also in Whitman and in Hemingway. Hemingway's solution may prove to have been in some ways the most satisfactory insofar as he has succeeded occasionally in holding up the critical mirror to the impulse of romantic action, and not just to the action itself.

Dos Passos has been less sure than Hemingway of his artistic direction, though more confident in his politics. But everywhere from *One Man's Initiation* (1917) to the trilogy *U.S.A.* he has been conscious of the need for some sort of detachment and some sort of commitment. *Three Soldiers* is a portrait of the "artist" as G.I. in which, as in E. E. Cummings' *The Enormous Room,* the demand of the individual for some kind of intelligibility in a merely bureaucratic order is met by savage group reprisal. That has remained the vision of Dos Passos.

For in recent decades the artist has come to be the only critical spectator of society. He demands and confers the heightened significance in ordinary existence which is hostile to any self-extinction in the collective consciousness. So that when the balance is lost between individual responsibility and mass solidarity, the artist automatically moves to the side of the individual. With equal inevitability, the less resourceful man, faced with the perplexities of planned social disorder, walks deeper into the collective sleep that makes that chaos bearable to him. The work of Dos Passos is almost wholly concerned with presenting this situation. His people are, typically, victims of a collective trance from which they do not struggle to escape. And if his work fails, it is to the extent that he clings to an alternative dream which has little power to retract the dreamers from their sleep, and even less power to alert the reader to a sense of tragic waste.

Born in 1896, John Dos Passos grew up in a milieu that had brought to a focus a number of discordant themes and motivations. The popularity of Darwin and Spencer had by then led to the profession of a doctrinaire individualism which got melodramatic treatment at the hands of a Frank Norris. Louis Sullivan and Frank Lloyd Wright were considerably affected by the spirit associated with the flamboyant extroversion and aggression of "frontier" Darwinism. Carl Sandburg's "Chicago" illustrates the curious blend of democratic lyricism and megalomaniac brutality that existed at that time. Robinson Jeffers has the gloomy distinction of representing today the then fashionable code of doctrinaire sadism which found a center in Chicago at the turn of the century.

Superficially it may appear odd that the cosmic humanitarianism of Whitman should have fostered such diverse expressions as the work of Sandburg and Jeffers. But as Sidney Lanier pointed out long ago, Whitman himself was a Byronic dandy turned inside out. Reared on the picturesque art of Scott with its preoccupation with the folk and their crafts, nurtured equally on the heroic panoramas of Byron with his vistas of world history, Whitman found no difficulty in transferring this aristocratic art to the democratic scene. Had not the aristocratic Chateaubriand earlier acquired in America the palette and the scenes which were to attract to him the discipleship first of Lord Byron and later of Stendhal and Flaubert? And the Jeffersonian dream of democracy was of a leveling-up rather than a leveling-down process. An aristocratic dream after all.

Co-existing with the fashionable Darwinism of Midwest tycoons was the grass-roots populism which found an academic spokesman in the formidable Thorsten Veblen. Veblen is ably presented in *The Big Money,* the last of the *U.S.A.* trilogy, as are Henry Ford and Sam Insull. Taken together, Veblen, Ford, and Insull are strikingly representative of the unresolved attitudes and conflicts of the milieu in which Dos Passos grew up. Nor does Dos Passos attempt any reconciliation of these conflicts. While his sympathies are entirely with the agrarian Veblen and the grass-roots, his art is committed to rendering the entire scene. And it is attention to the art of Dos Passos that the critic finds most rewarding. For Dos Passos is not a thinker who has imposed a conceptual system on his material. Rather, he accepted the most familiar traditions and attitudes as part of the material which his art brings into the range of the reader's vision. It is by the range of his vision and the intensity of his focus that he must receive criticism.

As a boy in Chicago, Dos Passos was devoted to Gibbon's *Decline and Fall of the Roman Empire.* Artistically, Gibbon's late use of baroque perspectivism, the linear handling of history as a dwindling avenue, concurred with the eighteenth-century discovery of the picturesque, or the principle of discontinuity as a means of enriching artistic effect. So that the later discovery of contemporary imagism and impressionism by Dos Passos, and his enthusiasm for the cinematic velocity of images in the French poet Cendrars, corresponded pretty much with the original revolution in eighteenth-century taste and preception which carried letters from the style of Gibbon to Sterne.

Looking first at the technical means which he employs as a writer, there is the basic imagistic skill in sharpening perception and defining a state of mind with which *Manhattan Transfer* opens:

> Three gulls wheel above the broken boxes, orangerinds, spoiled cabbage heads that heave between the splintered plank walls, the green waves spume under the round bow as the ferry, skidding on the tide, crashes, gulps the broken water, slides, settles slowly into the slip.

Many passages of this wry lyricism counterpoint the episodes of the book. The episodes and characters are also features of a landscape to which these lyric chapter overtures give point and tone. The point is readily seized and the tone extends over a very narrow range of emotions: pathos, anger, disgust. But Dos Passos employs the impressionist landscape monotonously because he has never chosen to refract or analyze its components to zone a wide range of emotions. Open any page of Pound's *Cantos* and the same impressionist landscapes will be found to be presenting a variety of carefully discriminated mental states. Pound does not accept the landscape as a homogeneous lump of matter. Even satire is managed by Dos Passos in a direct, lyric mode though the technique seems to be impersonal:

> He's darn clever and has a lot of personality and all that sort of thing, but all he does is drink and raise Cain . . . I guess all he needs is to go to work and get a sense of values.

or:

> The terrible thing about having New York go stale on you is that there's nowhere else. It's the top of the world. All we can do is go round and round in a squirrel cage.

Manhattan Transfer is full of such planned incongruities which achieve a weak pathos when they could more successfully have effected a robust guffaw. The author is sensitive to the ugliness and misery as things he can see. But he is never prepared to explore the interior landscape which is the wasteland of the human heart:

> Ellen stayed a long time looking in the mirror, dabbing a little superfluous powder off her face, trying to make up her mind. She kept winding up a hypothetical dollself and setting it in various positions. Tiny gestures ensued, acted out on various model stages. Suddenly she turned away . . . "Oh, George I'm starved, simply starved . . . we've got to be sensible. God knows we've messed things up in the past both of us. . . . Let's drink to the crime wave."

The effect is comparable to that of *The Great Gatsby,* which sustains this Hansel-and-Gretel sort of wistful despair to create a child-pastoral world. Out of the same situations Hemingway at his best

—as in the first page of *A Farewell to Arms*—can obtain moments of tragic intensity—landscapes of muted terror which give dignity to human suffering.

But Dos Passos too often seems to imply that the suffering is sordid and unnecessary or that some modification of the environment might free his characters from the doll-mechanism that is their private and collective trap. Seeing nothing inevitable or meaningful in human suffering, he confronts it neither in its comic, intelligible mode, nor in a tragic way. It angers and annoys him as something extraneous.

The difference from Joyce is instructive. For in *Ulysses* the same discontinuous city landscape is also presented by imagistic devices. The episodes are musically arranged to sound concordantly. But Joyce manipulates a continuous parallel at each moment between naturalism and symbolism to render a total spectrum of outer and inner worlds. The past is present not in order to debunk Dublin but to make Dublin representative of the human condition. The sharply focused moment of natural perception in Joyce floods the situation with analogical awareness of the actual dimensions of human hope and despair. In *Ulysses* a brief glimpse of a lapidary at work serves to open up ageless mysteries in the relations of men and in the mysterious qualities of voiceless objects. The most ordinary gesture linked to some immemorial dramatic mask or situation sets reverberating the whole world of the book and flashes intelligibility into long opaque areas of our own experience.

To match Joyce's epiphanies Dos Passos brings only American know-how. And, indeed, there seems to be no corner of the continent with whose speech and cooking he is not familiar. There is no trade or profession which he does not seem to know from the inside. Joyce contemplates things for the being that is theirs. Dos Passos shows how they work or behave.

Earlier, Joyce had opened the *Portrait* with an overture representative of the stages of human apprehension, which with Aristotle he held to be a shadow of the artistic process itself, so that the development of the artist concurs with the retracing of the process of poetic experience. By a technique of cubist or overlayering perspectives both of these processes are rendered present to the reader in an instant of inclusive consciousness. Hence the "portrait" claim of the title. The very setting side-by-side of these two operations is typical, therefore, of the level and extent of symbolic implication in Joyce. (The Oxen of the Sun section of *Ulysses* fused both these processes with both the human biological and civilized processes, as well as with the parts and totality of the book itself, and yet has been read as a series of parodies of English prose styles.)

The difference between this kind of art and that of Dos Passos is that between one of univocal, psychological and one of properly analogical effect. Joyce constantly has his attention on the analogy of being while Dos Passos is registering a personal reaction to society.

It is not a serious criticism of Dos Passos to say that he is not James Joyce. But Joyce is his art master and the critic is obliged to note that Dos Passos has read Joyce not as a greater Flaubert, Rimbaud, or Mallarmé, but as it were through the eyes of Whitman and Sandburg, as a greater Zola or Romains. This is negative definition which does not bring into question the competence of Dos Passos or belittle the quality of positive delight he affords. His *U.S.A.* is quite justly established as a classic which brought into a focus for the first time a range of facts and interests that no American had ever been able to master. But it is in the main an ethical and political synthesis that he provides, with the interest intentionally at one level—the only level that interests Dos Passos.

Manhattan Transfer, which corresponds roughly to Joyce's *Dubliners,* cuts a cross-section through a set of adult lives in New York. But the city is not envisaged as providing anything more than a phantasmagoric backdrop for their frustrations and defeats. The city is felt as alien, meaningless. Joyce, on the other hand, accepts the city as an extension of human functions, as having a human shape and eliciting the full range of human response which man cannot achieve in any other situation. Within this analogy Joyce's individuals explore their experience in the modes of action and passion, male and female. The stories are grouped according to the expanding awareness of childhood, adolescence, maturity, and middle age. Man, the wanderer within the labyrinthine ways at once of his psyche and of the world, provides an inexhaustible matter for contemplation. Dos Passos seems to have missed this aspect of *Dubliners.* But in *U.S.A.,* while extending his backdrop from the city to the nation, he did make the attempt to relate the expanding scene to the development of one mind from childhood to maturity. That is the function of "Camera Eye." "Newsreel" projects the changing environment which acts upon the various characters and corresponds to riffling the back issues of *Life* magazine.

But *Ulysses,* with which *U.S.A.* invites comparison, shows a very different conception of history in providing a continuous parallel between ancient and modern. The tensions set up in this way permit Joyce to control the huge accretions of historic power and suggestion in the human past by means of the low current of immediate incident. The technological analog of this process occurs in the present use of the electronic valve in heavy-power circuits. So that Joyce does not have to step up the intensity of the episode or scene so long as he maintains its function in the total circuit. Deprived of this symbolic "feedback" process implicit in the historic sense, and which is manipulated alike by Joyce, Pound, and Eliot, Dos Passos is left with little more current or intensity than that generated by his immediate episodes.

Since criticism, if it is to be anything more than a review of the "content" of works of art, must take cognizance of the technical means by which an artist achieves his effects, it is relevant to consider some of the stages by which the kind of art found in *U.S.A.* came into existence. If there is anything to be explained about such a work it can best be done by noting the extraordinary preoccupation with landscape in eighteenth-century art. For it was the discovery of the artistic possibilities of discontinuity that gave their form to the novels of Scott as well as to the poems of Byron and Whitman.

Whitman, a great reader of Scott in his youth, later took pains to bring into his poetry as much of the contemporary technology as he could manage. Whitman's poems are also camera-eye landscapes in which human tasks are prominent. In his numerous portraits which he strove to bring into line with the techniques of the impressionists' painting, he wove the man's work into his posture and gestures. His aim was to present the actual, and he took pride that in his *Leaves of Grass* "everything is literally photographed." As for the larger lines of his work, it is plain that he uses everywhere a cinematic montage of "still" shots.

It is not only in the details but in the spirit of much of his work that Whitman resembles Dos Passos. And it is hard to see how anyone who set himself to rendering the diverse existence of multitudes of people could dispense with the technique of discontinuous landscapes. In fact, until the technique of discontinuous juxtaposition was brought into play it was not even possible to entertain such an ambition. "Remember," he said of the *Leaves* to Dr. Bucke, "the book arose out of my life in Brooklyn and New York from 1838 to 1853, absorbing a million people, for fifteen years, with an intimacy, an eagerness, an abandon, probably never equalled." Taken in connection with his technical inventiveness, this enables us to see why the French were from the start so much more interested in Whitman than either his countrymen or the English. Hopkins, struggling with similar technical problems at a more serious level, remarked, however, that he had more in common with Whitman than with anybody else of his time.

From this point of view it is plain, also, why Tolstoy and Hugo could take Scott and Byron with the same artistic seriousness with which Dostoevsky regarded Dickens. Dickens was probably the first to apply the picturesque to discoveries in technique, to the entire life of an industrial metropolis. And the brilliance of his technical development of this matter provided W. D. Griffiths with his cinematic principles seventy years later.

However, it was in Flaubert's *Sentimental Education* that the acceptance of the city as the central myth or creation of man first leads to the mastery of that huge material by means of the technique of discontinuous landscape. Moreover, Flaubert makes a continuous parallel between the fatuity of Frederic Moreau's "education" and the deepening disorder and banality of nineteenth-century Paris.

It is slightly otherwise in *U.S.A.,* where the development of political consciousness of the "Camera Eye" persona is not so much parallel with as in contrast to the unfolding landscape of the nation. And this again is close to the way in which the development of Stephen Dedalus in the *Portrait* as a self-dedicated human being runs counter to the mechanisms of the Dublin scene. The author's political and social sense unfolds without comment in the "Camera Eye" sections, with "Newsreel" providing the immediate environmental pressures which are felt in different ways by everybody in the book. Both of these devices are successfully controlled to provide those limited effects which he intends. But the insights which lead to these effects are of a familiar and widely accepted kind.

That, again, in no way invalidates the insights but it does explain the monotony and obviousness which creeps into so many pages. The reader of Dos Passos meets with excellent observation but none of the unending suggestiveness and discovery of the *Sentimental Education* or *Ulysses*. For there is neither historical nor analogical perception in the *U.S.A.,* and so it fails to effect any connections with the rest of human society, past or present. There is a continuous stream of American consciousness and an awareness that there are un-American elements in the world. But as much as in any political orator there is the assumption that iniquity inside or outside the U.S.A. is always a failure to be true to the Jeffersonian dream. The point here is that this kind of single-level awareness is not possible to anybody seriously manipulating the multiple keyboards of Joyce's art.

Dickens as a newspaper reporter had hit upon many of his characteristic effects in the course of his daily work. Later, when he turned to the serial publication of his stories, he was compelled to do some of that "writing backwards" which, as Edgar Poe saw, is the principle underlying the detective story and the symbolist poem alike. For in both instances the effect to be attained is the point at which the writer begins. The work finally constructed is a formula for the effect which is both the beginning and the end of the work.

It is interesting to note how Browning moved toward a fusion of these interests in the *Ring and the Book,* turning a police romance into a cross-section of an inclusive human consciousness by the technique of the reconstruction of a crime. Artistically he is more complex than Dos Passos in the use he makes of the dramatic process of retracing or reconstruction. For that retracing reveals many of the labyrinthine recesses of the human heart which the merely panoramic impressionism of Dos Passos cannot even attempt to do. And it is also this profound drama of retracing the stages of an experience which enables the popular detective story to sound varied depths of the greatest human themes in the hands of Graham Greene. In the art of Eliot (as in *The Cocktail Party*) it permits the sleuth and the guardian of souls to meet in the figure of Harcourt-Riley, as in Browning's Pope.

The failure of Dos Passos' insights to keep pace with the complex techniques at his disposal is what leaves the reader with the sense of looseness and excessive bulk in *U.S.A.* In the equally bulky *Finnegans Wake,* on the other hand, which exploits all the existing techniques of vision and presentation in a consummate orchestration of the arts and sciences, there is not one slack phrase or scene. *U.S.A.,* by comparison, is like a Stephen Foster medley played with one finger on a five keyboard instrument. There is that sort of discrepancy between the equipment and the ensuing concert; but it is not likely to disturb those readers who have only a slight acquaintance with Joyce.

Manhattan Transfer and the *U.S.A.* trilogy are not novels in the usual sense of a selection of characters who influence and define one another by interaction. The novel in that sense was a by-product of biological science and as such persists today only among book-club practitioners. The novel as it has been concerned with the problems of "character" and environment seems to have emerged as a pastime of the new middle classes who were eager to see themselves and their problems in action. Remove from these novels the problems of money and the arts of social distinction and climbing and little remains. From that point of view Flaubert's *Madame Bovary* was the deliberate reduction of the middle-class novel to absurdity. And Sinclair Lewis' *Babbitt* is, as Ford Madox Ford pointed out, the America *Madame Bovary*. But the *Sentimental Education* is a great step beyond this, and taken with *Bouvard and Pecuchet,* provided the framework for the symbolic epic of the commonplace which is *Ulysses*. The middle classes found romance and glamour in the commonplace, but they were not prepared for the profound existentialist metaphysic of the commonplace which Joyce revealed.

In such a perspective as this the collective landscapes of *U.S.A.* represent only a modest effort at managing the huge panorama of triviality and frustration which is the urban milieu of industrial man.

But the fact that a technological environment not only induces most people into various stages of automatism but also makes the family unit socially noneffective, has certainly got something to do with the collective landscapes of *U.S.A.* Its structure is poetic in having its unity not in an idea but a vision; and it is cubist in presenting multiple simultaneous perspectives like a cycle of medieval mystery plays. It could readily be maintained that this method not only permits comprehensiveness of a kind indispensable to the modern artist, but makes for the intelligible rather than the concupiscible in art. The kind of pleasure that Dos Passos provides in comparison with Hemingway is that of detached intellectual intuition rather than that of sympathetic merging with the narrative and characters.

The current conception of art as vicarious experience, on the other hand, seems mainly to support the attitude of behavioristic merging with the lives of the characters portrayed. And since this tendency is geared commercially with the demands of an untrained reader mass, it is irresistible. It helps to explain why a Dos Passos is considered highbrow although he offers no more strain on the attention than a detective story. It is because of the kind rather than the degree of effort he invites that he is deprecated as highbrow by readers who accept the cubist landscapes of the newspaper, and the musical equivalent in jazz, without perturbation.

Although Dos Passos may be held to have failed to provide any adequate intellectual insight or emotion for the vast landscape of his trilogy, his themes and attitudes are always interesting, especially in the numerous biographies of such folk heroes as Edison and the Wright brothers, Debs and La Follette, Steinmetz and Isadora Duncan, Ford and Burbank. These sections are often masterly in their economy and point. The frustration of hopes and intentions in these public figures provides the main clue to the social criticism which underlies the presentation of dozens of nonentities. For it is usually pointed up that the great are as helplessly ensnared in merely behavioristic patterns irrelevant to their own welfare as the crowd of nobodies who admire them.

The frustration and distortion of life common to the celebrated and the obscure is, in Dos Passos, to be attributed to "the system." No diagnosis as crude as this emerges directly. But over and over again in the contrast between humble humanity and the gormandizing power-gluttony of the stupidly arrogant few, there is implied the preference for a world of simple, unpretentious folk united in their common tasks and experience. It has often been noted that there is never love between the characters of Dos Passos. But there is the pathos of those made incapable of love by their too successful adjustment to a loveless system. Genuine pathos is the predominant and persistent note in Dos Passos, and must be considered as his personal response to the total landscape. Yet it is a pathos free from self-pity because he has objectified it in his analysis of the political and economic situation.

The homelessness of his people is, along with their individual and collective incapacity for self-criticism or detachment, the most obvious feature about them. And home is the positive though unstated and undefined dream of Dos Passos. In wandering from the Jeffersonian ideal of a farmer-craftsman economy in the direction of Hamiltonian centralism, power, and bigness, Dos Passos sees the main plight of his world. Hamilton set up the false beacon that brought shipwreck. But out of that shipwreck, which he depicts, for example, as the success of Henry Ford's enterprise, we can recover the dream and create a reality worthy of it. That is an unfailing note. For those who are critically aware he prescribes the duty of selfless dedication to the improvement of the common civilization. And in three uninteresting, short novels since *U.S.A.* he has explored the problem of discovering a self worth giving to such a cause. The current need would seem to be for a historic sense which can resolve the Hamilton-Jefferson dichotomy.

There is, perhaps, little point in dwelling on these aspects of Dos Passos, in which without new insight he reflects the ordinary attitude of the great majority. Yet, there is great social hope in the fact that this common intellectual ground is so large and so admirably chosen. But it is outside the province of criticism, which is concerned with the means employed and effects obtained by an artist. By the time the critic comes to the point of confronting Dos Passos the Jeffersonian radical, he has moved into a territory shared by Frank Capra.

And Dos Passos may have lost his stride as an artist through the very success of those social causes which were the militant theme of *U.S.A.* To have a cause to defend against a blind or indifferent world seemed to give tone and snap to the artist in him who has since been overlaid by the reporter. But if this is the case, nobody would be happier than Dos Passos to have lost his artistry on such excellent terms.

The Analogical Mirrors

Hopkins is full of pitfalls for the unwary. There is a double difficulty: his Catholic beliefs and experience on one hand; his individual use of the resources of English on the other, to say nothing of his irrelevant theory of prosody. The non-Catholic reader—especially the non-Christian reader—is timid or hostile in the presence of Hopkins' faith and doctrine. He is beset with "mnemonic irrelevance" and stirred to a thousand acts of undemanded vigilance and depreciation which inevitably distort the pattern and texture of the poems.

For the Catholic reader Hopkins has, understandably, a great deal of prestige value. Long accustomed to a defensive position behind a minority culture, English and American Catholics have developed multiple mental squints. Involuntarily their sensibilities have been nourished and ordered by a century or more of an alien literary and artistic activity which, *faute de mieux,* they still approach askance. However, their intellectual distrust in the presence of, say, the emotional chaos of Shelley or Browning has not in the least prevented the assimilation of the vision of those poets. (One might add that it has not in the least prevented them from hailing as "Catholic poetry" the febrile immaturities of Francis Thompson and Joyce Kilmer.)

63

Thus there was no Catholic magazine which would accept any poem of Hopkins in his lifetime. With Bloomsbury's sudden acclaim of Hopkins as a major poet, however, Catholics were caught off-guard. They hastened to enshrine but not to understand him. Somewhat inconsequentially they have begun to feel at home in the present world of art because "their" poet is a big gun on the literary front. That is the catch. The Catholic reader comes to Hopkins with a mechanism of sensibility which came off the line in 1850. His sensibility has been unmodified by the impact of Baudelaire, Laforgue, Pound, or Eliot. Bloomsbury was at least readied for Hopkins by these and *The Seafarer*. But the Catholic assumes his proprietary manner on the strength of doctrinal affinity alone. With equal justification the professors of Anglo-Saxon might have staked out an exclusive claim in Hopkins. Insentience or modesty has prevented them so far; or is it simply that they are incapable of seeing that the work of Hopkins is almost the sole civilized fruit of their brain-starved plodding?

Before there can be any basis for Catholic complacency in the presence of Hopkins we must explain our tardy recognition of him. Again, if Catholic doctrine made Hopkins a major poet, why aren't there more like him? All, I think, that need be said of this peculiarly Catholic pitfall is that some knowledge (the more the better) of Catholic doctrines and Scotist philosophy is needed for the full elucidation, though not for the immediate enjoyment, of Hopkins. Such knowledge, however, will never reveal his poetic excellence. The Catholic reader has the advantage only in that he is disposed to give Hopkins a chance. And, of course, he is not inclined to urp, with Bridges, when Hopkins speaks of the Virgin or the Trinity. The problem, in short, is much the same as that of reading, say, Dante or John Donne. The ancillary scholarly effort should, but seldom does, keep ever sharply focused the stereoscopic gaze at the work itself.

Before looking at "The Windhover," as our chosen text, let us consider the crux of Hopkins' sensibility—"inscape." It is the "fineness, proportion of feature" mastering the recalcitrance of matter which he saw everywhere in the world. It is the ontological secret:

> It is the forgèd feature finds me; it is the rehearsal
> Of own, of abrupt self there so thrusts on, so throngs the ear.

Hopkins finds this Euclid peeping from the chaos of matter alike in the veins of a violet, the "roped" sides of a mountain, or the bright shoe on the anvil. (Note the precise yet witty implications of "forged feature" in this connection.) That Hopkins should take the further step of greeting Christ at such moments of natural perception should cause even the non-Catholic reader very little inconvenience, for the poet is making no pantheistic claims whatever:

> Since, tho' he is under the world's splendour and wonder,
> His mystery must be instressed, stressed.

Hopkins is not a nature mystic at all, nor a religious mystic, either, but an analogist. By stress and instress, by intensity and precision of perception, by analogical analysis and meditation he achieves all his effects. His is literally a sacramental view of the world since what of God is there he does not perceive nor experience but takes on faith. It may sound at first strange to hear that Hopkins is not a mystic but an analogist. That he does not lay claim to a perception of natural facts hidden from ordinary men is evident in every line of description he ever wrote. As for religious experience, it is the same. Nowhere in his work does he draw on an experience which is beyond the range of any thoughtful and sensitive Catholic who meditates on his Faith. Let the authoritative statement of Jacques Maritain clarify this matter at once. He begins a chapter on "Expérience Mystique et Philosphie" this way:

> Nous entendrons ici le mot "expérience mystique," que cela soit convenu une fois pour toutes, non pas en un sens plus ou moins vague (extensible à toutes sortes de faits plus ou moins mystérieux ou préternaturels, ou même à la simple religiosité), mais au sens de *connaissance expérimentale* des profondeurs de Dieu, ou de *passion des choses divines,* menant l'âme, par une suite d'états et de transformations, jusqu'à éprouver au fond

d'elle-même le toucher de la déité, et à "sentir la vie de Dieu."
Les Degrés Du Savoir (Paris, 1935), pp. 489–490.

But there is nothing of this in Hopkins. He deals sensitively with
the commonplaces of Catholic dogma in the order of Faith, and he
records a vigorous sensuous life in the order of nature. Since for the
agnostic no precision is possible in these matters, and all distinc-
tions are nugatory, he will continue to call both Blake and Hopkins
"mystical."

Hopkins looks at external nature as a Scripture exactly as Philo
Judaeus, St. Paul, and the Church Fathers had done. Their views,
which have never ceased to be current, though their prevalence has
fluctuated, are summarily expressed by the conventional patristic
divine, Jeremy Taylor:

> Thus when [God] made the beauteous frame of heaven and
> earth, he rejoyced in it, and glorified himself, because it was the
> glasse in which he beheld his wisdom, and Almighty power.
> . . . For if God is glorified in the Sunne and Moon, in the rare
> fabric of the honeycombs, in the discipline of Bees, in the œcon-
> omy of Pismires, in the little houses of birds, in the curiosity of
> an eye, God being pleased to delight in those little images and
> reflexes of himself from those pretty mirrours, which like a
> crevice in a wall thorow a narrow perspective transmit the spe-
> cies of a vast excellency: much rather shall God be pleased to
> behold himself in the glasses of our obedience. . . .

Hopkins habitually shifts his gaze from the order and perspectives of nature to the analogous but grander scenery of the moral
and intellectual order. And he does this methodically:

> . . . O the mind, mind has mountains; cliffs of fall
> Frightful, sheer, no-man-fathomed.

Or the book of nature provides parallel passages with the supernatural revelations of Scripture:

> . . . For Christ plays in ten thousand places,
> Lovely in limbs and lovely in eyes not his
> To the Father through the features of men's faces.

As the microcosm of man is a nobler, a more perfect mirror of God's beauty and grandeur, so Christ, as Taylor goes on to say in the same place, "was the image of the Divinity . . . designed from eternal ages to represent as in a double mirrour, not onely the glories of God to himself, but also to all the world; and he glorified God by the instrument of obedience, in which God beheld his own dominion. . . ." Hopkins freely employs these three traditional mirrors (physical, moral, divine) of God's beauty and grandeur, using them sometimes simply ("Pied Beauty"), doubly ("The Caged Skylark"), or triply ("The Wreck of the Deutschland"). Naturally, these combinations admit of infinite variations since the particulars reflected in each "mirror" can be chosen from a great store.

"The Windhover" exploits all three mirrors of God's grandeur.

I caught this morning morning's minion, king-
    dom of daylight's dauphin, dapple-dawn-drawn Falcon, in his
        riding
Of the rolling level underneath him steady air, and striding
High there, how he rung upon the rein of a wimpling wing
In his ecstasy! then off, off forth on swing,
    As a skate's heel sweeps smooth on a bow-bend: the hurl and
        gliding
Rebuffed the big wind. My heart in hiding
Stirred for a bird, —the achieve of, the mastery of the thing!

Brute beauty and valour and act, oh, air, pride, plume, here
    Buckle! AND the fire that breaks from thee then, a billion
Times told lovelier, more dangerous, O my chevalier!

    No wonder of it: shéer plód makes plough down sillion
Shine, and blue-bleak embers, ah my dear,
    Fall, gall themselves, and gash gold-vermilion.

The bird "literally" mirrors the physical order of subrational "valour and act." But, analogously, as "kingdom of daylight's dauphin," it mirrors Christ. As Hopkins transfers his gaze from the first mirror to the second, we see that his own heart is also a hidden mirror (moral obedience) which flashes to God the image not of "brute beauty and valour and act" but a "fire" which is "a billion times told lovelier"—the chevalier image of Christ. We can thus simply, and, I believe for the first time, fully explain the function of "here Buckle!" Rhetorically, fire bursts from Hopkins as he looks at the fiery falcon whose action mirrors the mastery of Christ over the world. Now, he says, let us take this mirror (St. Paul's "armour") and buckle it here in my hidden heart, raising the image of Christ in the bird to the image of Christ in the obedience and humility of the heart. Christ's fire will burst on and from the second mirror "a billion times told lovelier" than from the falcon. This is the basic structure of this image. The superstructure of its ambiguity will be shown later on. Hopkins would even seem to have this mirror mechanism in the forefront of his mind as he compares his obedient day-by-day plodding to the homely ploughshare whose polished surface is hidden in the earth ("my heart in hiding") but which imparts a sheen even to the mud and dirt which it turns up. (Compare with this "sheer plod" image "the jading and jar of the cart"—"Deutschland," stanza 27.)

To have seen the dialectic or mechanism of the poem is not, however, to have seen anything of what constitutes its dramatic action. In other words, we have yet to see that it is a poem at all. There is a logical movement which has been indicated. There is also dramatic surprise achieved by a striking peripateia. This happens when the ecstatic hyperboles of the octet are yet rendered trite by the merely homely images of the sestet. Moreover, while the sestet is in a lower key, befitting the change to the theme of humble obedience, it is more intense, fuller of compressed implication. Hopkins has Spiritual humility act out its easy victory over "brute beauty and valour and act." Yet this victory is not won by crushing "brute beauty" but by catching it to the hidden heart which reflects it back to God.

The assonance and alliteration in the first three lines perform just the opposite of their usual functions in Hopkins' verse—the opposite of "gall" and "gash" in the last line, for example. Here, in conjunction with the even phrasing, they convey the delicate poise, the hovering emphasis of the falcon's movements. The falcon is seen as a chevalier, a horseman glorying in the great power under him and the quick response to the rein as he sweeps "forth on swing." (The skate on ice image shifts the point of view only to stress the precision and sharply etched movements of the bird. Compare: "It is the forgèd feature finds me" in "Henry Purcell." "Dapple-dawn-drawn Falcon" also insists upon the etched quality of the scene. The bird is drawn to the light but it is also drawn, etched, against the dawn.)

To a member of a militant order whose founder was a Spanish soldier or chevalier, the feudal character of the opening imagery is quite natural. "Minion," "dauphin," "valour," "plume," and "buckle" alike evoke the world of dedicated knighthood and shining panoply of armor. Thus the mounted chevalier flashing off exploit as he "rung upon the rein" enables Hopkins later to reverse the situation with great dramatic effect in "sheer plod makes plow down sillion Shine." The paradox consists in the fact that Hopkins as lowly plowman following a horse flashes off infinitely more exploit than Hopkins the imagined chevalier.

More central still to the dramatic movement of the poem is the way in which the cavalier images of the octet are concentrated in "here Buckle!" Buckling is the traditional gesture of the knight preparing his armor for action. A buckler is the bright shield of defense bearing insignia, flashing defiance. (The relevance of the sense of "buckle" as "collapse" or "crumple" has often been debated in this context. It has been suggested that Hopkins, in shifting his point of view, here means that the sensuous beauty of the world is a feeble prop, that he is making a conventional renunciation of "mortal beauty" as dangerous to the spiritual life. But this is to ignore the dramatic development, to blur it with cliché. It ignores the excited emphasis of "here" at the end of the line and "Buckle!" at the beginning of the next. It is, of course, almost impossible not to accept these suggestions so long as the basic mirror images of his analogist vision are not grasped.) Whichever way one looks at this image the implication of shining brilliance, of enthusiastic gesture, is present. I have already said that "here" means "in the obedient and humble heart," and that "Buckle" means that the "brute beauty" of the bird as mirror of God's grandeur is to be transferred or flashed to the "heart in hiding," just as the burnished surface of the plow in action is hidden in the earth. The high-spirited but obedient heart of a man is a "billion Times" better a mirror of Christ the chevalier than is the mirror of the external world. "AND the fire that breaks from thee then" (note how the eager stress on "AND" serves to flash attention intensely on what follows as being an inevitable result) is ambivalent in suggesting both the fire and ecstasy which the poet has felt as he watched the bird as well as the much greater fire which Christ will flash on him and from him, and which will flame out at the world. The mirror of man's moral life can "give beauty back to God," the beauty of God's world, and in so doing it becomes the mirror in which (by the imitation of Christ) God can flash out more brilliantly. ("Give beauty back," as in a mirror, is also the theme of "The Leaden Echo and the Golden Echo," as the title suggests.)

Once it is seen that the shining armor of the falcon's imitation of Christ's mastery is to be buckled in the hidden heart of the poet it is easy to find other passages in Hopkins which show that this image obsessed him. In the sonnet to St. Alphonsus Rodriguez there is the same running image of military brilliance and valor:

> But be the war within, the brand we wield
> Unseen, the heroic breast not outward-steeled,
> Earth hears no hurtle then from fiercest fray.

The whole sonnet is helpful to an understanding of "Windhover." But there is especial relevance in the second line:

> And those strokes that once gashed flesh or galled shield.

There is here a direct clue to the last lines of our poem:

> No wonder of it: shéer plód makes plough down sillion
> Shine, and blue-bleak embers, ah my dear,
> Fall, gall themselves, and gash gold-vermilion.

"Gall" and "gash" are in both places associated with shield and mirror and flesh—mortified or obedient flesh, of course. The underlying image in these last three lines is that of mortal *clay* transformed. It is made to shine and to fructify by the humble service of the plough (the obedient will). The "blue-bleak" earth provides the transition to the embers covered with claylike ash. Just as "the fire that breaks from thee then" (after the mirror of mortal beauty has been buckled to the hidden heart) is not a fire produced by any direct action or valor, so the fire that breaks from the "blue-bleak embers" is not the effect of *ethos* but *pathos,* not of action but of suffering or patience. The true "achieve of, the mastery of the thing" from which flashes the most dangerous and daring exploit

> dates from day
> Of his going in Galilee
> Warm-laid grave of a womb-life grey;

Here again is the image of the fire in the hidden heart which evokes the "blue-bleak embers," and, which, as some have suggested, leads on to the image of the vermillion side of Christ on the Cross.

One might even suggest that as the ash-covered coals gash gold-vermilion when touched by the poker (spear), so when Hopkins "kissed the rod, Hand rather" ("Carrion Comfort"), he becomes a mirror of Christ, flashing gold-vermilion:

> I kissed the rod,
> Hand rather, my heart lo! lapped strength,
> Stole joy, would laugh, chéer.
> Cheer whom though? the hero whose heaven-handling
> flung me, fóot tród
> Me? or me that fought him?

The *crucial* ambivalence which Hopkins stresses is owing to the double mirror image which he keeps always in mind. As a mirror of Christ he must imitate both the valor and also the obscure sufferings of Christ. He must overcome and be overcome at the same instant—at every instant. But this complexity does not exist in the mirror of mortal beauty, the "brute beauty and valour and act" which is a simple reflection of Christ's mastery but not of His suffering and love.

Familiarity with Hopkins soon reveals that each of his poems includes all the rest, such is the close-knit character of his sensibility. A relatively small number of themes and images—such is the intensity of his perception—permits him an infinitely varied orchestration. Thus it is really impossible to feel the full impact of "The Windhover" without awareness of the tentacles which its images stretch out into the other poems. To take once more the analogy of "sheer plod makes plough down sillion Shine," its paradox is brightly illuminated in the poem "That Nature Is a Heraclitean Fire." Contemplating his "joyless days, dejection," "flesh fade, and mortal trash," he reflects that:

> This Jack, joke, poor potsherd, patch, matchwood, immortal
> diamond,
> Is immortal diamond.

This "Jack, joke" plodding behind the plough makes the trash and mud of earth shine like diamond, "wafting him out of it." And diamond flashing from the silicates of the soil is also, once again, the mirror of Christ in the hidden and humble heart of mortal clay.

Another aspect of this analogy of the plough grinding through the gritty soil is seen in the last line of "Spelt from Sybil's Leaves":

> Where, selfwrung, selfstrung, sheathe- and shelterless, thóughts
> agáinst thoughts in groans grínd.

This aspect of the plough and the soil is the more obviously dramatic one—immortal beauty won from the harshest dullest toil, suffering, and discipline.

An inevitable dispersal of attention has accompanied the above elucidation of this poem. But then only an oral reading with all the freedom and flexibility of spoken discussion can really point to the delicate interaction, at each moment of the poem, of all its cumulative vitality of logic, fancy, musical gesture.

"The Windhover" could never have become the richly complex poem it is if Hopkins had not tested and explored all its themes beforehand, in other poems. There is no other poem of comparable length in English, or perhaps in any language, which surpasses its richness and intensity or realized artistic organization. There are two or three sonnets of Shakespeare (for example, "They that have power to hurt" and "The expense of spirit") which might be put with Donne's "At the round earth's" for comparison and contrast with this sonnet. But they are not comparable with the range of the experience and multiplicity of integrated perception which is found in "The Windhover."

Pound's Critical Prose

☙ ☙ ☙ ☙ ☙

THE SENECAL OR Jonsonian vigor and precision of Mr. Pound's critical writing has been too much the foil for the urbane sinuosities of Mr. Eliot's prose—a fact which reflects on the twentieth-century reader and not on these writers. Mr. Pound is the only writer of our time whose prose achieves the effect of actual conversation as it occurs among those who exist in an intense focus of complex interests. It shocks again and again with the dramatic stress of the spoken word, and yet amid all that has been said of "salty Yankee speech" it has not been recognized for what it is. Mr. Pound has incorporated in his prose the radical individualism of generations of seaboard Yankees—not the mannerisms only but the entire movement of mind—the intensity, the shrewdness, and the passion for technical precision. And these are just the qualities which he brought to bear on the reshaping of poetry in London in 1908–1922.

By contrast with Pound's sharp and alert sentences the gentle rhythms of Eliot's paragraphs are a balm for minds which find only distress in the violence of intellectual penetration. Mr. Eliot has said the same things, for example, about Dante and the French Symbolists as Mr. Pound. They share an immense interest in verbal technique and poetic structures. But whereas Mr. Pound has been vehement and explicit about these things, Mr. Eliot has been unobtrusive and casual. Mr. Eliot has adjusted the "frequency modula-

75

tion" of his prose so that it causes little perturbation in foolish ears, but Mr. Pound insists on his readers' attention even where no likelihood of understanding is present. And for this he has not been forgiven by the literate. With entire Yankee optimism he has insisted on the universal import of his interests, while Mr. Eliot's sceptical wisdom has led him to soothe the literate and to seek understanding only from a few. Mr. Pound brought to letters the evangelical public spirit of the American town meeting. It thus never occurred to him to apologize for having serious intellectual and literary interests at a time when such things were of even less general account than they now are. And he has likewise omitted the various rituals of self-flagellation which our world still exacts from the literary man who ventures to present his views directly:

> It appears to me quite tenable that the function of literature as a generated prize-worthy force is precisely that it does incite humanity to continue living; that it eases the mind of strain, and feeds it, I mean definitely as *nutrition of impulse*. . . . It has to do with the clarity and vigour of "any and every" thought and opinion . . . the individual cannot think and communicate his thought, the governor and legislator cannot act effectively or frame his laws, without words, and the solidity and validity of these words is in the care of the damned and despised *literati*. When their work goes rotten—by that I do not mean when they express indecorous thoughts—but when their very medium, the very essence of their work, the application of word to thing goes rotten, i.e., becomes "slushy" and inexact, or excessive or bloated, the whole machinery of social and of individual thought and order goes to pot. This is a lesson of history, and a lesson not yet half learned.

It is also the lesson of *The Cantos*. Human association, it is implied, depends on the utmost fidelity of sensuous and intellectual discrimination. Let there be complete humility in the presence of the actual diversity of things and absolute intolerance of the obfuscators of language. This is an existential philosophy which makes Mr. Pound impatient with the average degree of human apathy and confusion. So that in the drama of human history he finds as little to admire as did Gibbon. His roots are in the America of Adams and Jefferson, who also sought to make things new and whose limitation was also to see past and present as no more than philosophy, teaching by examples.

However, the America which Mr. Pound left about 1908 gave him a great deal which he translated into literary perception and activity. It was the technological America which Siegfried Giedion has been the first to explore in *Space, Time and Architecture* and in *Mechanization Takes Command*. It is also the America which appears obliquely in Henry James' prefaces and in his notes on the technique of the novel. Commenting on James' notes to *The Ivory Tower* Mr. Pound says,

> I give this outline with such fullness because it is a landmark in the history of the novel as written in English. It is inconceivable that Fielding or Richardson should have left, or that Thomas Hardy should leave, such testimony to a comprehension of the novel as a "form." . . . The Notes are simply the accumulation of his craftsman's knowledge, they are, in all their length, the summary of the things he would have, as a matter of habit, in his mind before embarking on composition.

In the America of 1908 the most authentic aesthetic experience was widely sought and found in the contemplation of mechanical tools and devices, when intellectual energies were bent to discover by precise analysis of vital motion the means of bringing organic processes within the compass of technical means. Mr. Pound records in his *Gaudier-Brzeska* the delight of his young contemporaries in examining and commenting on machinery catalogues, "machines that certainly they would never own and that could never by any flight of fancy be of the least use to them. This enjoyment of machinery is just as natural and just as significant a phase of this age as was the Renaissance 'enjoyment of nature for its own sake,' and not merely as an illustration of dogmatic ideas." The impersonal concerns and impatience of Mr. Pound's critical outlook are everywhere associated with this passion for technical excellence: "The experimental demonstrations of one man may save the time of many—hence my furore over Arnaut Daniel—if a man's experiments try out one new rhyme, or dispense conclusively with one iota of currently accepted nonsense, he is merely playing fair with his colleagues when he chalks up his result."

This fascination with technological discovery co-existing with erudition and sensitivity in language and the arts was what gave Mr. Pound his peculiar relevance in London, 1908. It was a combination of interests indispensable to anybody who wished to undertake the task of importing into English letters the achievement of the French from Stendhal to Mallarmé. (It may not be irrelevant to consider that this same combination of interests which also appears in Edgar Poe's *Philosophy of Composition* had helped to guide those very French developments which in turn Mr. Pound did so much to introduce into English.) As Mr. Pound saw it, the job was to acclimatize seventy years of French discovery within a single decade. And with the assistance of Wyndham Lewis, T. E. Hulme, T. S. Eliot, and Joyce, that job was mainly done by 1922. But it could not have been done without Mr. Pound's intense concern for technique:

> Later it struck me that the best history of painting in London was the National Gallery, and the best history of literature, more particularly of poetry, would be a twelve-volume anthology in which each poem was chosen, not merely because it was a nice poem or a poem Aunt Hepsy liked, but because it contained an invention, a definite contribution to the art of verbal expression.

The *ABC of Reading* was a later issue of this project. The exactitude of the dissociations of style and technique which appear in the selections and comments of that small book give it the distinction of being at once the shortest and the most heavily freighted account of English poetry. The short section on Chaucer is the only appreciation he has received since Dryden that relates him to the mind of Europe or that indicates, in contrast, the defects of Elizabethan culture.

Mr. Pound's technical interests exist in so sharp a focus that they have had a decisive impact only on those who shared them in equal measure. So that while Joyce, Yeats, and Mr. Eliot have never stinted their tributes to him for his direct effect on their work, no critical comment has so far risen to that level of perception where this influence could be evaluated. Perhaps such criticism cannot be conducted without literary and rhythmic analysis as severe as they themselves directed, especially to Dante and the French Symbolists. At any rate this advent of rigor after a long period of slackness in English letters was mainly owing to Mr. Pound. Now this rigor which is everywhere apparent in his prose criticism has long passed current as the irresponsible and scornful expression of a hasty mind. If there is any critical prose more exact, more pointed, more weighted with perception it may be found in the last essays of Mallarmé, but nowhere else in English. For English letters depth of perception has tended to be associated with opacity and suggestiveness. So that the values of plastic hardness and precision in Chaucer and Ben Jonson are readily overlooked in favor of the rich associations of Shakespeare. Not unrelated to this preference for psychological atmosphere to the exclusion of other qualities in poetry is our related expectation that prose is obliged to carry the reader forward by the appearance at least of casually connected conceptions. But in both poetry and prose Mr. Pound has not only disappointed such ordinary expectation, he has resolutely avoided any such means of effect. They are not the means pursued by anybody whose tool is the engraver's or whose presentation is analogical.

Thus when he says that *Sweeney Agonistes* contains more essential criticism of Seneca than Mr. Eliot's essays on English Senecanism we have a typical observation whose form is that of exact juxtaposition. It is not a casual statement but an ideogram, a presentation of an analogical proportion depending on a precise analysis of Seneca, on one hand, and of *Sweeney Agonistes,* on the other. Syntactically elaborated it would fill many pages. But Mr. Pound seldom translates himself into ordinary prose. And anecdotes and reported conversations which enrich his essays are, in the same way, never casually illustrative but ideogrammatic. In the language of the schoolmen, for whose precision of dissociation Mr. Pound has so frequently expressed his admiration, the ideogram represents the "copula of agglutination." That is to say, the copula of existential reality and not the copula which connects enunciations and conceptions in rationalistic discourse. And it is the consequent solidity and sharpness of particularized actuality (in which the Chinese excel) that baffles the reader who looks for continuous argumentation in Mr. Pound's prose and verse alike.

So that if there is one theme which emerges everywhere in Mr. Pound's critical prose it is the seeking out of those qualities and techniques in a writer which lead to the economical rendering of complex actualities. Writing of Henry James he says

> 1907. *The American Scene,* triumph of the author's long practice. A creation of America. . . . I know of no such grave record, of no such attempt at faithful portrayal as *The American Scene.* Thus America is to the careful observer.

Implied, of course, is the absolutely bracing effect of such an artistic realization. Greater in scope than *The American Scene* and much more exacting in execution, Mr. Pound's *Mauberley* is "The London scene" for the same period, and *The Cantos* are the human scene for a long period. This may be said, at least, by way of illustrating the mode in which any poet's prose criticism directs the keenest possible ray on his own poetic practice. And it is the neglect of close study of Mr. Pound's prose which has deprived *The Cantos* of due understanding. His *Guide to Kulchur* is the inevitable prose companion of *The Cantos,* constructed like them without any overlayering or underlying concepts but existing by the affirmation of the proportions which are present in the juxtapositions of persons, places, things. Yet *Kulchur* offers only a preliminary training in perception which is presumed to be fully developed in the contemplator of *The Cantos.*

Mr. Eliot has held the interest of a whole generation of readers by making basic concessions in his prose to their demand for dialectic and persuasive charm. What he has to say, however, is neither dialectical nor charming, but profoundly analogical and even unpleasant. Mr. Pound's prose on occasion follows the procedure of

Mr. Eliot's poetry when it is for most readers extremely obscure, just as the organization of the sections of *The Waste Land* employs the analogical "music" of *Mauberley*. It is "to live in the wink," in the concentration of those timeless moments when the eye of mankind has been most open to intelligible form. And this method of proportionality is "symbolic" in the strict sense of the Greek. It dispenses entirely with syntax and rhetoric and leaves the reader naked to the diversity of existence. Mr. Pound's poetry has finally swallowed his prose. But it remains essentially a critical prose, always carrying the method of direct comparison and contrast of specific qualities to a point of decisive discrimination.

Permettre à ceux qui en valent la peine d'écrire franchement ce qu'ils pensent—seul plaisir d'un écrivain.

Wyndham Lewis:
His Theory of Art
and Communication

𝄞 𝄞 𝄞 𝄞 𝄞

FOR THIRTY YEARS and more Wyndham Lewis has been a one-man army corps opposed to these forces which seek to use art, science, and philosophy in order to reduce our world to the nocturnal womb from which they suppose it to have been born. As he put it in *Time and Western Man:*

> For me art is the civilized substitute for magic; as philosophy is what, on a higher or more complex plane, takes the place of religion. By means of art, I believe Professor Whitehead and M. Brémond wish to lead us down and back to the plane of magic, or mystical, specifically religious, experience.

The recent *Gate of Horn* by G. R. Levy presents the Greek effort to devise a civilized substitute for magic. The later dialogues of Plato "are in general of an Orphic or Pythagorean colour."

> There are the cosmic cycles, the harmony of the spheres, necessity with her whirling spindle at the centre of existence, the Judgment of the Dead, the Waters of Remembrance and Forget-fulness, and the soul's imprisonment in the Cave. In general they describe the fall from and the return to divine life.
> Plato's theory of Ideas institutes a gigantic effort to establish

the mystic doctrine upon an intellectual basis. The relation of created things to "the pattern laid up in heaven" is, as we saw, that *methexis,* or participation, which Aristotle equated with *mimesis,* the "imitation" by which the living world was built upon the Pythagorean numbers. Thus the relationship created by the earliest man, and the means of his growth as already described; the vehicle of the first-known religion, is now made articulate. The wheel has come full-circle.

From this point of view, Greek Philosophy and science were a means of arresting the wheel of existence or of delivering us from the time mechanism of existence. In the opinion of Wyndham Lewis, that is the function of art as well. There is no need to immerse ourselves again in the destructive element of the Time flux or to return to that "Primitive Past saturated with blood and incest so generally favoured." We have, as *Finnegans Wake* also proclaims, the means to awaken permanently from the repetitive nightmare of history. This is also the basis of the Lewis attack on Spengler:

> We are perhaps in the last phases of Greek "progress"—phases that are extremely unGreek, however. Progress may even itself bring Progress to an end. Indeed, already the bottom seems to be entirely knocked out of Spengler's "historical" periodic picture by such things as wireless, air-travel and so forth—actually by progress itself. How *can,* in fact, the old competitive "rising" and "declining" clashing of crowds of rival states, continue at all, unless science is abolished, or else unless that state of historical rivalry is artificially maintained?

We have, then, to consider that modern technology is itself mainly a product of art. It is explicitly the rival of the primitive artist. For it has been the prime characteristic of science and philosophy since Newton and Kant, that they seek to control the world rather than to understand it. We can, they say, control by magical formula what necessarily eludes our understanding or comprehension. The artist was always a magician in this sense. But the civilized artist has differed from the primitive artist in seeking to arrest the flux of existence in order that the mind may be united with that which is permanent in existence. Whereas the modern artist has used his factive or creative intelligence to manipulate matter and experience into a pattern which could arrest the mind in the presence of a particular aspect of existence, the modern scientist has sought to merge the functions of the primitive and civilized magicians. He has developed formulas for the control of the material world and then applied these to the control of the human mind. He invades the human mind and society with his patterned information. That is the key to the nature of the new "mass media."

In recent years Lewis returned to this theme in *America and Cosmic Man,* in which he took America as the laboratory in which was being produced the new ahistoric man. His attacks on the romancers of Progress and the romancers of the Past have this single aim, to deliver us from the bondage of primitive religion with its obsession with recurrence, and the way of destruction as the way of rebirth. And it has been his sense of equal menace presented to any living present by the cultist of East and West that has procured his exclusion from the public attention which they control.

Shelley, says Whitehead, "thinks of nature as changing, dissolving, transforming as it were at a fairy's touch . . . this is one aspect of Nature, the elusive change . . . a change of inward character. That is where Shelley places his emphasis."

And that, Lewis points out, is where Whitehead, Bergson, Spengler, and their school place their emphasis. But, continues Whitehead, there is another aspect of nature, namely its opposite. And Lewis comments: "Wordsworth, we are told, because he was born upon a hill, saw the other aspect of nature. He is the poet of endurance. And Spengler tells us that all Greeks, whether born on a hill or elsewhere, always had the misfortune to see that side of the medal—the enduring and concrete as opposed to the changing."

Such is also the misfortune of Wyndham Lewis. But it is important for an understanding of his vortex view of art and civilization to notice his insistence that the world of Space as opposed to the world of memory and history is the world of a "pure Present." "The world of the 'pure Present' of the Classical Ages is obviously the world that is born and dies every moment." By comparison with the intensity that is revealed in the contemplation of this spatial reality, the vision of the Time mind, argues Lewis, is that of the sentimental tourist:

> The pretentious omniscience of the "historical" intelligence makes of it an eternal dilettante, or tourist. It does not live in, it is *en touriste,* that is tastes its time-district, or time-climate. . . . This mental world becomes for it an interminable time-preserve, laid out for critical, disembodied journeyings.

A striking illustration of his point occurs in *The Lion and the Fox.* In Renaissance Italy:

> The prince or commander of an army of a state had often started as a free captain . . . we can agree that it must have been "singular to see these men—generally of low origin and devoid of culture—surrounded in their camps by ambassadors, poets and learned men, who read to them Livy and Cicero, and original verses in which they were compared to Scipio and Hannibal, to Caesar and Alexander." But they were all acting on a tiny scale the past that was being unearthed. . . . With the more intelligent of them like Caesar Borgia, this archaeological and analogic habit of mind assumed the proportion of a mania. His *Aut Caesar aut nihil* is the same type of literature as is concentrated in the small maniacal figure of Julien Sorel, Stendhal's little domestic Napoleon. . . . For every type of relatively small adventurer there was an antique model. . . . They attempted to bring to life the heroes of antiquity, and recall in their own lives the events recorded in the codices, and it was this immediate application of everything to life in Italian renaissance society (like the substitution of a cinema for a history-book in a school) that made the Italian influence so vivid in the rest of Europe. Renaissance Italy was very exactly a kind of Los Angeles where historical scenes were tried out, antique buildings imitated and roughly run up, and dramatic crimes reconstructed.

In a word, Lewis' attitude to the Time-and-psychology-enchanted Bergsonian and Proustian twentieth century extends to the Renaissance. Along with T. E. Hulme he would substitute for the naturalistic values of that era those of the ahistoric cultures of Egypt and Byzantium. He is not enchanted by gimcrack approximations to past grandeur:

When, as in the present age, life loses its exterior beauty, and all the ritual of grandeur has become extinct, the intellect and character everywhere deteriorates. "It is always the form that imposes the fact. But in its turn the form originates in some fancy or desire that seeks a ceremonious expression, just as an ardent mind seeks for itself a personal expression in some suitable medium."

It is the magical form of Shakespeare's verse which evokes the leonine splendors of his heroes:

. . . the poetry overwhelms the prose: the chivalry substitutes itself for the self-interest, a mystical religion for a "scientific truth," the Lion for the Fox.

Lewis' theory of art and communication is a traditional one. The hero, the genius, is a god-intoxicated man. He communes with the noumenal world. And the contrast of this knowledge with the misery of his human condition constitutes his dementia or madness:

It is as outcasts, as men already in a sense out of life, and divested of the functional machinery of their roles . . . Lear, Hamlet, Timon, Thersites, and so forth are in the position of disincarnate spirits, but still involved with and buffeted by life. Their "truth" is an angry one usually, but they have the advantage of having no "axe to grind."

Thersites is always in that unfortunate position! Lear and Hamlet only become so when they grow demented . . . we assume that if undisturbed by calamity they would be respectable members of society, and not have, much less express, all these horrible thoughts. It is this assumption of conditions that do not exist at all in the plays . . . that is usually the basis of English Shakespearian criticism.

The sense in which Lewis envisages his artist as genius and as the Enemy also appears in another passage from *The Lion and the Fox:*

The child is made to feel that the individual in himself or in herself is the enemy. The death or subjection of that enemy is the task of the child. He must deaden himself before engaging as a qualified human being in the world-wide occupation of making life mechanical and uniform, and fit for even the vastest herd to live in.

Honour is not your own "good" for there is no you. Honour is a faculty of the gentleman: Its exercise consists in doing as much for somebody else (for the Not-You) as is consistent with the natural reluctance to do anything of the sort, and where the circumstances ensure complete safety: in order to get the maximum for yourself, while pretending all the while that the self does not exist, and that the Not-You (or you might say the NOT) does.

The artist, gifted with mania from above, is always confronted with the great collective mania from below:

But without the scientific organization of revolution . . . men have always had this much wider instinct for the divine — that is of course, the instinct to destroy it, isolate it, or corrupt it to their uses. In a time when there is no accredited divinity, or "divine right," left, it is in a sense easier to observe the universal operation of this instinct. . . . So that dark competitive self, in the smallest organism, that makes it murderous, becomes organized into the type of herd-war against the head, where almost anything high, unusual and unassimilable is sighted. . . . It is the person wrenched out of the organic context by the impulses of some divine ferment, and this being suddenly appearing free, that is the signal for those dispensations and adjustments, culminating in his pathos. . . .

It must be remembered that human beings are congeries of parasites subsisting on the Individual, subsisting on a very insufficient supply of Individuals. . . . And anything representing the principle of individuality they attack. . . . On the back of every great human intelligence there are millions of contingent forms, which it propels and feeds. The relations subsisting between this lonely host and the organisms which it propels and feeds. The relations subsisting between this lonely host and the organisms to whom he is appropriated is not very marked by a warm mutual sympathy.

In considering the meaning for art and communication of this war of the collective puppetry against the individual person there is another passage in G. R. Levy's *The Gate of Horn* which indicates the traditional bearings of the position:

Plato's theory of Ideas constitutes a gigantic effort to establish the mystic doctrine upon an intellectual basis. . . . But it must be noted that Plato's Ideas are of two kinds, and both of the nature of the Soul. Like daemons, some of whom are conceived as descending as watchers from the higher spheres of being, and others as rising from the body or group, but infected by it, and so always drawn back into incarnation. . . .

This would seem to be the basis of Lewis' distinction between the space-mind and the Time-ridden mentality. As he writes in *Wyndham Lewis the Artist:*

> If you conclude from this that I am treading the road to the platonic heaven, my particular road is deliberately chosen for the immanent satisfaction that may be found by the way. You may know Schopenhauer's eloquent and resounding words, where, in his forcible fashion, he is speaking of what art accomplishes: "It therefore pauses at this particular thing: the course of time stops: the relations vanish for it: only the essential, the idea is its object." . . . A sort of immortality descends upon these objects. It is an immortality, which, in the case of painting, they have to pay for with death, or at least with its coldness and immobility.

That is, the moment of art is not a moment of time's covenant. And art emotion is specifically that experience of arrest in which we pause before a particular thing or experience. It is also, at such moments, the sense of disproportion between our mental and our physical dimensions from which Lewis derives his view both of the tragic and the comic:

> It is to feel that our consciousness is bound up with this non-mechanical phenomenon of life; that, although helpless in the face of the material world, we are in some way superior to and independent of it; and that our mechanical imperfection is the symbol of that. In art we are in a sense playing at being what we designate as matter. We are entering the forms of the mighty phenomena around us, and seeing how near we can get to being a river or a star, without actually becoming that. . . . The game consists in seeing how near you can get, without the sudden extinction and neutralization that awaits you as matter, or as the machine. In our bodies we have got already so near to extinction.

This provides the perfect view of the great Lewis line in painting and his watchful game with his characters in fiction. It is a perpetual poise on a razor's edge. It explains at once his lack of enthusiasm not only for Bergson's passionate merging with the Time flux, but his scepticism about Eliot's doctrine of impersonality in art. The above views also help to explain that affinity which Lewis has with Dostoevsky despite the superficial lack of resemblance between the great Romantic and the Lewis stylization. As he himself suggests in *The Lion and the Fox,* apropos of Falstaff and Don Quixote:

> Hamlet, Lear, Othello, Timon are all demented or halluci-
> nated, as so many of the celebrated figures in nineteenth century
> Russian fiction were. It is the supreme liberty it is possible to
> take with your material. That it should be so often taken in the
> case of the great characters of dramatic fiction is the most evi-
> dent testimony to the dependence on untruth, in every sense, in
> which our human nature and environment put us. In the case of
> Muishkin, Dostoevsky had to call in express and abnormal
> physiological conditions to help him incarnate his saint. And the
> heightening everywhere in Shakespeare is by way of madness.
> Since it is made to behave in the way the hero does, he has to be
> maddened by some means or other more often than not in order
> to make him at all probable.

The hero, in short, is, as such, a type of mania from above and a type of the misery as well as of the grandeur of the human condition. Along these lines it would be easy to establish the affinities not only between Lewis and Dostoevsky but between Lewis and Swift.

His theory of the comic as stated in *The Wild Body* is the exact reverse of the Bergsonian theory of laughter:

> The root of the comic is to be sought in the sensations result-
> ing from the observations of a thing behaving like a person. But
> from that point of view all men are necessarily comic: for they
> are all things, or physical bodies, behaving as persons. It is only
> when you come to deny that they are "persons" or that there is
> any "mind" or "person" there at all, that the world of appearance
> is accepted as quite natural, and not at all ridiculous. Then, with
> the denial of "the person," life becomes immediately both "real"
> and very serious.

In a word, life is always serious for Bergson because our personal reality depends not on moments of detachment from the flux but on moments when we are merged in it. Lewis, on the contrary, adopts the Schopenhauer intellectualism in seeing the movements of vision as an arrest and detachment of the great mechanism of the world as will and idea: "moments of vision are blurred rapidly, and the poet sinks into the rhetoric of the will." And "no man has ever continued to live who has observed himself in that manner for longer than a flash. Such consciousness must be of the nature of a thunderbolt. Laughter is only summer-lightning. But it occasionally takes on the dangerous form of absolute revelation."

Between this view and the earlier quotation concerning art as a game played on the edge of the abyss of extinction, it is possible to get a very adequate image of Lewis' activity as painter and novelist. He is a mystic or visionary of the comic, moving toward the pole of intelligibility instead of that of feeling. Joyce establishes a similar distinction in his notebooks as quoted by Gorman:

> When tragic art makes my body to shrink terror is not my feeling because I am urged from rest, and moreover this art does not show me what is grave, I mean what is constant and irremediable in human fortunes, nor does it unite me with the secret cause. . . . Terror and pity, finally are aspects of sorrow comprehended in sorrow—the feeling which the privation of some good excites in us.

In short, Joyce tends like Lewis to reject the way of connatural gnosis and emotion favored by Bergson, Eliot, and theosophy, in which the emotions are used as the principal windows of the soul. And Joyce continues ". . . but a comedy (a work of comic art) which does not urge us to seek anything beyond itself excites in us the feeling of joy. . . . For beauty is a quality of something seen but terror and pity and joy are states of mind." Joyce, that is, argues that beauty is entirely of intellectual apprehension whereas the passions or states of mind are gnostic windows of the soul which cause us to be merged with that particular quality. The intellectual, comic perception is for Lewis what beauty is for Joyce. But so far as the term "beauty" goes Lewis identifies it with "ideal conditions for an organism," much as Burke does in *The Sublime and the Beautiful.*

Compared with Joyce, however, there is in Lewis a Manichean abjurgation of delectation.

But Joyce, Lewis, Eliot, and Pound are perhaps nearer in agreement on the subject of the vortices of existence. If "the world of the 'pure present' of the Classical Ages is obviously the world that is born and dies every moment," it is clear that it is such a world that Lewis seeks to arrest in his paintings (and novels), especially in that "creation myth" which appears in this issue of *Shenandoah*.* If we can elucidate the vortex concepts in Lewis we shall be finally in a position to see his grounds for rejecting the thought and work of the Time and Flux school of this century. At first glance it might seem that Lewis was a candidate for the same school in being the observer of a "world that is born and dies every moment." But there is even at that level the habit of the observer substituted for the sympathetic merger. In place of the gnostic and nostalgic contemplation of flowers that give thoughts too deep for tears, Lewis would as soon "say it with locomotives." In *Wyndham Lewis the Artist* he writes:

> In the case of a dynamic shape like an aeroplane there is neither any reason nor any need for the collaboration of engineer and artist. All such machines, except for their colouring, or some surface design, to modify their shape, develop in accordance with a law of efficient evolution as absolute as that determining the shape of the tiger, the wasp, or the swallow. They are definitely, for the artist, in the category of animals. When we come to the static cell-structures (houses) in which we pass our lives there is far more latitude and opportunity for his inventiveness.

That is to say, Lewis is not without affinities with Samuel Butler, who viewed the evolutionary impulses as existing in an accelerated form in machinery. But Lewis is not much interested in the time vistas of evolution if only because:

> The artist goes back to the fish. The few centuries that separate him from the savage are a mere flea-bite to the distance his memory must stretch if it is to strike the fundamental slime of creation. And those are the conditions—the very first gust of

* *Editor's Note:* Refers to Mr. Lewis' artwork Creation Myth No. 17, first of a collection of reproductions of Lewis' paintings which appeared in this issue of *Shenandoah* (pp. 88–94).

creation in this scale of life in which we are set that he must reach, before he, in his turn, can create!

The creation of a work is an act of the same description as the evolution of wings on the sides of a fish, the feathering of its fins; or the invention of a weapon within the body of a hymenopter to meet the terrible needs of its life. The ghostly and burning growths—the walking twigs and flying stones—the two anguished notes that are the voice of a being—the vapid twitter; the bellows of age-long insurrection and discontent—the complacent screech—all these may be considered as types of art, all equally perfect, but not all equally desirable.

Corresponding to this notion of creativity is Lewis' theory of communication:

> For what the artist's public has to be brought to do is to see its world, and the people in it, as a stranger would. There have been so far principally two methods of achieving this. One is to display a strange world to the spectator, and yet one that has so many analogies to his that, as he looks, startled, into attention by an impressive novelty, he sees his own reality through this veil, as it were, momentarily in truer colours. The other method is the less objective one of luring the spectator to the point from which, inevitably, the world will appear as the artist sees it, and the spectator from that point of vantage paints the picture for himself, but with the artist's colours and his more expert eyes. The first of these methods can be described very roughly as the impersonal and objective method, and the second as the personal and subjective one. The latter method (contrary to what is sometimes supposed) seems to be more assured of a positive result: for a lesser effort of intelligence is required on the part of the public. . . . The artist, unless of a very lucky or privileged description, can only exist even, by pretending to be one of the audience. Nothing less democratic than that will be tolerated. . . . Bergson's view that the permanence of the work of art, or its continued interest for us, depends on its uniqueness, on the fact that such and such a thing will never happen again, would make of everything in life a work of art.

Lewis has made plain enough what he considers to be the relation between the artist and nature. He holds the traditional view of imitation as working in the way that nature works, so that art is another nature: "As much of the material poetry of Nature as the plastic vessel will stand should be taken up into the picture. Nowadays though when Nature finds itself expressed so universally in specialized mechanical counterpart, and cities have modified our emotions, the plastic vessel, paradoxically, is more fragile. The less human it becomes, the more delicate from this point of view." That suggests that as more and more of the actual material world has been brought under the manipulation of the global art of applied science, and as our emotions are attenuated by the impact of these artifacts, the balance of the individual artist becomes more precarious. It is, naturally, in relation to the artist's operating in the way that nature works that brings Lewis to a direct statement of his notion of the vortex:

> Da Vinci recommends you to watch and be observant of the grains and markings of wood, the patterns found in Nature everywhere. The patterned grains of stones, marble, etc., the fibres of wood, have a rightness and inevitability that is similar to the rightness with which objects arrange themselves in life—the objects upon your work-table, for instance . . . the finest artists—and this is what Art means—are those men who are so trained and sensitized that they have a perpetually renewed power of doing what Nature does, only doing it with all the beauty of accident, without the certain futility that accident implies.

It is in this sense that art for Lewis appears as a natural vortex of patterned energy, presenting us with creative cores or vortices of causality. In the heart of these cores or vortices there is an absolute calm, but at the periphery there is violence and the unmistakable character of great energy. These "untumultuous vortices of power" are at the center of every vital work of art as they are in any vital civilization. And it is presumably the view of Lewis that the role of the artist in society is to energize it by establishing such intellectually purified images of the entelechy of nature. The alternative mode is the swoon upon death, the connatural merging in the indiscriminate flux of life, the reflexive feeling and expressing of one's time. It is Lewis' constant theme that the art of our time has chosen the second mode and that its Mona Lisa appeal is to the death swoon.

Part Two
The Beatrician Moment

Many of us in the twentieth century assume that we live in the post-Romantic era. In a time when our conceptions of ourselves and of our world seem dominated by the theories of Freud and Marx, the Romantic assumptions about man, about the fecund powers of his creative imagination seem, if not hopelessly dated and naïve, at least irrelevant to our present condition.

McLuhan does not begin with these assumptions. In the following essays, through a variety of approaches to such writers as Keats, Coleridge, Tennyson, and Pope, he provides abundant argument for our seeing our world as co-existent with theirs, our awareness of our condition as co-extensive with their awareness. In brief, we are contemporaneous with Pope and Keats.

First of all, McLuhan traces a movement, through a very useful analogy to musical structure, in the major odes of Keats. Each ode, McLuhan argues, has its own separate principle of organization, which we will become sensitive to if we first free ourselves from the semantic bind of seeing (or *hearing*) language as the "handmaid of exposition and persuasion." Our ears have become dulled to the frequency ranges on either end of the scale and we therefore resist listening itself as an activity. McLuhan pierces through this habit of filtering out the subtle and non-expository uses of language and provides a pattern of apprehension which makes the great odes available once again to us, if we are willing to listen to them.

The next useful analogy is to landscape painting and how Tennyson could best be understood when seen as a landscape poet:

> . . . thoroughly trained in the picturesque school, Tennyson never fails to compose his larger pictures with the utmost care for the texture and placing of objects (and words as objects), light and shade.

However, Tennyson, like the Romantics before him, was limited by the science of his time to external landscapes. We had to wait for a post-Newtonian science to free us to create the interior landscapes of the Symbolists. The "aesthetic moment" of arrested cognition, a moment in and at once out of time, of simultaneity, could only exist when cinema was technologically possible.

McLuhan posits Coleridge's development as an artist of "rhetorical statement" to "a master of symbolic ritual" as a prophetic enactment of the history of art and poetry in our century. Our casual acceptance of cubist discontinuity, of ironic juxtaposition in art today owes a profound debt to Coleridge's technical innovations. What had been outer, external, and spatial in the poetic tradition before him became progressively more internal.

> Since Rimbaud, Mallarmé, Eliot, and Joyce the enormous advantages in scope, learning, and precision of the interior landscape over external landscape have become evident, and the poems of Coleridge have accordingly gained in interest.

Finally, McLuhan examines Pope's *Dunciad* from the perspective of how the revolution of print and the resulting availability on a mass level of powerfully persuasive words created a new factor in the aesthetic process: the anarchic tribal force of "mesmerized" readers. For Pope, the "dunces" were not specific contemporaries, but the power unleashed by the technology of print itself, which could now create what Ortega y Gasset was later to call the "learned ignoramus," a very dangerous monster indeed.

McLuhan, in this cluster of essays, thus sees the artistic process itself as a deliberate movement backward from a moment of insight, forming and creating through analogy a word structure which we can most fruitfully apprehend through analogy itself: to music, to painting, to an understanding of the science and technology of the artist's own time. The original aesthetic moment will then become possible for us in our own prison of space and time.

Aesthetic Pattern
in Keats' Odes

ᴄ⊧   ᴄ⊧   ᴄ⊧   ᴄ⊧   ᴄ⊧

LESS THAN JUSTICE has been done to the great odes of Keats since
they lend themselves so easily to the uses of his biographers. They
have been so much quoted for casual illumination of his moods that
few people are able to think of them as anything but self-
expression. The highly successful labors of the editors and biographers, which no careful reader will ignore, have impressively established the fact that there is scarcely a mood or impression or image
in the great odes which cannot be paralleled again and again in the
least interesting of Keats' poems. There has, however, been only a
small effort to point the obvious corollary from this fact; namely,
that the high place which the odes have held in the regard of those
who care for poetry is owing to qualities which they do not share
with the bulk of Keats' poems—qualities of intense organization
arising from the strict discipline of a critical intelligence. It is not
the themes themselves, nor their private significance for Keats, but
their immediate and successful realization in these odes, which is of
decisive interest. The object of this paper is to show that the odes
rise far above the level of self-expression, that they are fully realized works of art, and that each of them is organized upon its own
independent principle. The *Ode to a Nightingale,* which is the most
intensely organized of the group, is also the most difficult and

99

varied, and so necessarily draws the main amount of attention here.

Before commencing a detailed consideration of this very subtle and varied poem, the reader may find it convenient to anticipate one conclusion concerning its basic movements. It is to be shown that there are two negative and two positive, or two "down" and two "up" movements of sense and rhythm, in the first four stanzas. (The first movement is "down"; the next "up," and so on.) The fifth stanza, which contributes something unheard till that point, achieves a basis of stability after the violent oscillations of the preceding stanzas. In relation to the fifth stanza, the sixth and seventh stanzas give to the themes of the first four a wholly new mode of expression, leading with ease and inevitability to the resolution in "rational" wakefulness in the eighth. It is well, perhaps, to keep this, which is the "action" of the poem, in mind while considering the rich details, whose varied interaction is the means by which this dramatic movement is realized.

Since the seventeenth century, language has been increasingly the handmaid of exposition and persuasion, until the general reader is merely baffled and annoyed by the quite different uses and arrangements of words which interest and concern the poet. So far, indeed, has the awareness of the non-expository and non-persuasive functions of language been lost that some analogy from the minor and neutral art of music is often helpful. In the case of these odes it is necessary to grasp that the relations between their parts rather resemble the internal structure of a fugue or a sonata than a paragraph of statements. An insight into this fact is quite as relevant to the understanding of works so diverse as *King Lear* or *At the round earth's imagin'd corners*. It would, of course, be futile to try to imagine the *Ode to a Nightingale* as a piece to be set to music, because the theme is so vividly and variously realized that there is nothing left for music to do. In the very nature of things, words in a poem are capable of a much richer texture than non-significant musical phrases. This is the reason that not even a Debussy could attempt the interpretation of any poetry more complex than that of Verlaine or Louÿs. Similarly, Monteverdi is fully adequate to setting a Petrarch sonnet, but the dramatic lyrics of a Donne are too complexly articulated for any music but their own.

The central image or symbol of the *Ode to a Nightingale* is intimately, though not always explicitly, functional to the whole poem. The basic paradox of its beautiful song born of a harsh and brutal persecution is integral to the tensions which constitute the dramatic power of the poem; but this major paradox or conflict naturally gives rise to others, as at the very outset where the heavy, depressive, and negative movement of the lines is the effect of "being too happy in thine happiness." This theme is in its turn intimately associated with the paradox that ideal or disembodied beauty is richer in ontological content than actual life with its defeats and deprivations and "leaden-eyed despairs." It is in terms of these paradoxes that "I have been half in love with easeful Death" gets its force and justification. The stark negation of death is viewed as a positive good ("rich to die"), not so much as an evasion of difficulties as a seemingly easy means of transmuting the leaden stuff of life into glorious beauty. The basic reference is to the nightingale's song, which had its origin in this manner.

The paradoxes stated at the beginning of the last stanza occur on a different level and may conveniently be reserved for comment since they concern the dénouement of the poem. Perhaps it is unnecessary to say that the interest of all these paradoxes does not lie in their statement but in their rich dramatic realization, their "local habitation" within the poem. However, they are magnificently stated in *The Fall of Hyperion:*

> "None can usurp this height," returned that shade,
> "But those to whom the miseries of the world
> Are misery, and will not let them rest."

The same paradox, when it is stated in the *Ode on Melancholy,* sounds, in comparison, hollow and affected:

> Ay, in the very temple of delight
> Veil'd Melancholy has her sovran shrine.

"Heard melodies are sweet, but those unheard are sweeter," is like-wise less impressive. But this serves to indicate that there is some-thing basically characteristic of Keats' artistic mode arising from his preoccupation with these paradoxes or conflicts in the very heart of experience. How very far he was from refusing to undertake their resolution with the full intellectual energy of a great artist has been quite insufficiently recognized. His merely personal efforts to re-solve these teeming antinomies have, on the other hand, absorbed the main attention.

The Greek legend concerning the nightingale gets no explicit statement in the ode. But just how important the Greek atmosphere of this legend is for the poem is indicated by the recurrence of images rich in Greek associations: "hemlock," "Lethe-wards," "Dryad," "Flora," "Hippocrene," "Bacchus." Here, of course, is no conflict with the evidence produced by Mr. Finney that Keats is aware of the medieval tradition of the nightingale as a "happy" bird, the sponsor of sensuous pleasure. This facet of the nightingale symbol sustains rather than annuls the paradox which is the basic dramatic tension of the poem and gets its statement in "Singest of summer in full-throated ease."

(I)

My heart aches, and a drowsy numbness pains
    My sense, as though of hemlock I had drunk,
Or emptied some dull opiate to the drains
    One minute past, and Lethe-wards had sunk:
'Tis not through envy of thy happy lot,
    But being too happy in thine happiness, —
        That thou, light-winged Dryad of the trees,
        In some melodious plot
Of beechen green, and shadows numberless,
    Singest of summer in full-throated ease.

The *Ode to a Nightingale* opens with a slow, poignant urgency reaching its deepest depression at "sunk." It is merely by conscious metaphor that one speaks of these first four lines as a "down" or "negative" movement, but the imagery of the lines is so pervasively concerned with specific means and modes of death and oblivion as to deserve the description. At the very outset, however, it should be clear that the powerful negation of these lines and their explicit mention of deadly "hemlock" are part of a poem which is profoundly vital in all its parts. There is no trace of debility in the art even though the ostensible theme may be that of a suicidal swoon.

The low point of "sunk," with its heavy rhymed emphasis, is no sooner reached than the movement and sense shift slowly upwards with "too happy in thine happiness," from the heavy visceral sensations of the first part of the stanza to the delightful visual and auditory life of "melodious plot" and "full-throated ease." This, the first "up" movement, grows with complete probability from "being too happy in thine happiness." The poem is plausibly committed to a swinging between extreme moods by thus referring it to this universal human commonplace.

(I I)

> O, for a draught of vintage! that hath been
>   Cool'd a long age in the deep-delved earth,
> Tasting of Flora and the country green,
>   Dance, and Provençal song, and sunburnt mirth!
> O for a beaker full of the warm South,
>   Full of the true, the blushful Hippocrene,
>   With beaded bubbles winking at the brim,
>   And purple-stained mouth;
> That I might drink, and leave the world unseen,
>   And with thee fade away into the forest dim—

The second stanza sustains the joyous note on which the first ends, carrying joy to sensual excess, and thus naturally reintroducing the note of negation. The joy of the first stanza is associated with the superior senses of eye and ear. Significantly, the second stanza evokes delight by extreme stress on the lower senses of taste and touch, concluding with the vivid Bacchic image of excess in "purple-stained mouth." The same symbol occurs more obliquely in "Joy's grape" in the last stanza of the *Ode on Melancholy*. The frequent recurrence of such themes and images in all the odes is artistically significant, representing, as it does, the achievement of a patterned economy, a possibility of more concise and disciplined achievement than Keats had hitherto had at command. Such recurrence, far from obscuring the individuality of the odes, should lead to an appreciation of their differences.

The very excess of sensual joy in wine and dance leads naturally through the symbol of wine as a means of heightening life to the use of wine as a means of evading life. All the images of the poem act and interact, and re-act in this way, so that to give more than a few hints and examples would be as interminable as it should be unnecessary. "Being too happy in thine happiness" is the ostensible motive of the first or opening "down" movement of the poem. The second "down" movement develops at the end of the second stanza from an analogous excess of joy in sensual life.

(I I I)

Fade far away, dissolve, and quite forget
  What thou among the leaves hast never known,
The weariness, the fever, and the fret
  Here, where men sit and hear each other groan;
Where palsy shakes a few, sad, last gray hairs,
  Where youth grows pale, and spectre-thin, and dies;
    Where but to think is to be full of sorrow
    And leaden-eyed despairs,
Where Beauty cannot keep her lustrous eyes,
  Or new Love pine at them beyond to-morrow.

The third stanza elaborates this second extreme of depression in a climax of gloomy hyperboles. These dramatic hyperboles are the means of stressing the obverse of "Flora and the country green," their ultimate point being reached in the reflection that while Beauty is transient enough, yet the love it stimulates is even more so. This even negates any impulse to give permanence to Beauty. Life is thus completely rejected, since not only is it ugly and harsh,

but its conditions are not altered even by the casual beauty which it
seems to possess.

(I V)

> Away! away! for I will fly to thee,
>   Not charioted by Bacchus and his pards,
> But on the viewless wings of Poesy,
>   Though the dull brain perplexes and retards:
> Already with thee! tender is the night,
>   And haply the Queen-Moon is on her throne,
>   Cluster'd around by all her starry Fays;
>   But here there is no light,
> Save what from heaven is with the breezes blown
>   Through verdurous glooms and winding mossy ways.

The fourth stanza seems to leap upwards with a life which is born
of the conclusive dialectic of the third. Its vitality is feverish, ecstatic, and quite unlike the first "up" movement. Having twice
tasted the poignancy and despair of actuality, and having once
tasted its joy, we are offered an escape, not through drugs or wine,
"But on the viewless wings of Poesy." The sudden introduction of
the life of "fancy" in vinous juxtaposition with "Bacchus and his
pards" is significant, and the significance is underlined in the last
stanza of the ode.

It is of a piece with the vigorous dramatic movement of the poem
that Keats no sooner indicates an escape through the life of art than
he embodies the concept in the warm and vivid life of "tender is the
night," and the following two lines. The insubstantiability of the
faery pageant, its inadequacy as a resource, is suggested by its brief
evocation and the sudden relapse into "actuality":

> But here there is no light,
> Save what from heaven is with the breezes blown.

The lush delicacy of "tender is the night" is a natural transition
from the hectic flight of the first four lines of the stanza. The sudden
change of tone is perfectly adjusted by its appearing to be an

achieved desire, the term of the movement of flight. Similarly, "But here there is no light," with its light stress on "here," is both a contrast with the world of moonlit fancy and a faint echo of "Here, where men sit and hear each other groan." But that grim theme now begins to merge with "verdurous glooms and winding mossy ways."

(V)

> I cannot see what flowers are at my feet,
>   Nor what soft incense hangs upon the boughs,
> But, in embalmed darkness, guess each sweet
>   Wherewith the seasonable month endows
> The grass, the thicket, and the fruit-tree wild;
>   White hawthorn, and the pastoral eglantine;
>   Fast fading violets cover'd up in leaves;
>   And mid-May's eldest child,
> The coming musk-rose, full of dewy wine,
>   The murmurous haunt of flies on summer eves.

It is with this gesture of ineffable ease and delicacy that Keats begins the transmutation of the previous themes of profound revulsion from, and ardent pursuit of, life. The fifth stanza uninterruptedly expands a single moment of "negative capability." After the first two movements from extreme to extreme this stanza is without any strain or striving. The poet does not woo death, life, or art, but is, in a spirit of humility, wooed by nature. "I cannot see . . . but guess," perfectly conveys the abeyance and passivity of sensual life. The phrase "embalmed darkness" reinforces this mode of experience (perfectly linking it with the different but related "drowsy numbness" of the first stanza) by indicating the passivity of both human and subhuman womb-life. After violent waywardness the poet, as it were, plants himself in the spring-time earth, coming to a profound acceptance and understanding of nature. This is not stated, but is realized dramatically. The stanza unfolds in accordance with the "seasonable month" (which, we shall see, is the technical mode of the *Ode to Autumn*), following the order of developing life, and at the same time paralleling the maturing wisdom of the poet. This is the dramatic center of the poem, and it clearly constitutes an equilibrium born of previous conflicts. It is as inevitably right as it is unexpected.

(V I)

> Darkling I listen; and, for many a time
>   I have been half in love with easeful Death,
> Call'd him soft names in many a mused rhyme,
>   To take into the air my quiet breath;
> Now more than ever seems it rich to die,
>   To cease upon the midnight with no pain,
>   While thou art pouring forth thy soul abroad
>   In such an ecstasy!
> Still wouldst thou sing, and I have ears in vain—
>   To thy high requiem become a sod.

"Darkling I listen," beginning the sixth stanza, continues the sensual passivity of the previous one. "Darkling" echoes both "embalmed darkness" in the fifth, and "here there is no light" in the fourth stanza, with its striking notion of "creature of the dark," and is indicative of the extremely close-knit texture of the poem, the merging and remerging of basic themes. The themes developed in the first four stanzas now recur in the last three, with modifications which are related to the stabilization achieved in the fifth. The phrase "half in love" is significant of the new mode, the measure and restraint which is imposed on themes that previously were expressed in extremes. Thus in "with easeful Death" and "mused rhyme" one notes a harmonious conjunction and assimilation of the themes of depression (from the first stanza) and the flight on the "wings of Poesy" (from the fourth). That is, the first "down" movement and the second "up" movement recur together as a new thing.

In an excellent chapter of *Revaluation,* Mr. Leavis makes a passing reference to "easeful Death" in this stanza as a clearly defined mode of nostalgia which expresses Keats' longing for his mother. That longing for "easeful Death" is implicated with such emotion in actual life, few would deny. "To cease upon the midnight with no pain" carries unmistakably the figurative force of a child or lover on the breast of mother or beloved. There is an obvious correlation with the sonnet *Bright Star,* which was written a few days earlier than this ode. Without setting aside this fact, the significance of the phrase is really defined in the poem by its multiple associations with the "embalmed darkness" in the fifth stanza. Thus the mere negative nostalgia of "easeful Death" is strongly modified by its being linked through "soft names" and "quiet breath" with the "negative capability" of the fifth stanza. It is this fact which makes "rich to die" artistically plausible; and, as the last line, "to thy high requiem become a sod," emphatically stresses, it is not physical death that seems "rich" to the poet. In the heavy, rhymed stress on "sod" with all its negative associations of absence, loss, decay, the poet strikes a strong note of rebellion against physical death. This gives us the theme of the seventh stanza.

(V I I)

Thou wast not born for death, immortal Bird!
No hungry generations tread thee down;
The voice I hear this passing night was heard
In ancient days by emperor and clown:
Perhaps the self-same song that found a path
Through the sad heart of Ruth, when, sick for home,
She stood in tears amid the alien corn;
The same that oft-times hath
Charm'd magic casements, opening on the foam
Of perilous seas, in faery lands forlorn.

The sixth stanza having taken up and modified the themes of the first and fourth, the seventh now resumes the themes of the second and third. The grim picture of actual life in the third stanza is seen again for an instant in "No hungry generations tread thee down." It seems not to have been noticed about this line, that it is a very neat statement of the Malthus-Ricardo population theories, which shocked a great many people in the early nineteenth century. "Emperor and clown," "Ruth," and "faery lands" represent widely separated ages which somewhat correspond to the similar evocation of different civilizations in the second stanza: "Flora," "country green," "Provençal," and "Hippocrene." In the second stanza this nostalgic time-sense is expressed with vigorous enthusiasm. Here it is modified both by the "hungry generations" and by the "born for death" theme, which has grown out of the sixth stanza.

Close attention to the development of the stanzas has left little opportunity for comment on their interweaving with the song of the nightingale. An earlier remark about it is paradoxically used in these last three stanzas. In the last line of the sixth stanza "high requiem" and "sod" are strongly counterpointed. The same mode is pursued in the seventh with the "immortal Bird." "Immortal" being used as well in the sense of "glorious" and "imperishably beautiful," gives the whole line some such force as "You were not born to defeat and evasion and nostalgia, but to sing deathlessly." It is only by taking "death" in its simplest physical sense, and thus disregarding its modification by the sixth stanza, that "immortal" offers any difficulty. Its deathless and invariable song is counterpointed with "this passing night" and all the nights that pass over "emperor and clown" and "Ruth" and the medieval knights ("faery lands").

The celebrated "magic casements, opening on the foam Of perilous seas, in faery lands forlorn" reintroduce, but in a new and significant way, the flight on the "viewless wings of Poesy" to the "Queen-Moon" and her "starry Fays," preparatory to the last stanza. Both in the fourth and in the seventh stanzas this flight to an ethereally enchanted "faery land" is explicitly related to the compelling beauty of the nightingale's song. In this stanza, however, the "faery lands" are "forlorn." Just as in the previous stanza the earlier death motif is checked by "sod," so here the unrestrained pleasures of fancy in the fourth stanza are moderated by "perilous" and "forlorn." The tempting baits and lures of the merely aesthetic life have been implicitly repudiated in the profound acceptance of the fifth stanza. Some editors have noted how "forlorn" in this poem seems to echo "desolate" in the fourth stanza of the *Ode on a Grecian Urn*. In the latter poem "desolate" does, indeed, occur, as here, just before the poet makes an explicit repudiation of the merely aesthetic life.

(V I I I)

Forlorn! the very word is like a bell
    To toll me back from thee to my sole self!
Adieu! the fancy cannot cheat so well
    As she is fam'd to do, deceiving elf.
Adieu! adieu! thy plaintive anthem fades
    Past the near meadows, over the still stream,
        Up the hill-side; and now 'tis buried deep
    In the next valley-glades:
Was it a vision, or a waking dream?
Fled is that music:—Do I wake or sleep?

The opening of the eighth stanza almost insists on the delusiveness of the life of fancy. When the poet returns to "actuality" for the third or fourth time in this poem, it is to comment ironically that "the fancy cannot cheat so well As she is fain'd to do, deceiving elf." "Elf" makes explicit the relation between his fanciful view of the nightingale's song and "faery lands forlorn" and "starry Fays." The rather overly rational complications of the judgment on "fancy" is another way of underlining a change of tone. The poem is now, for the first time, at the level of explicit rationality, and it is at this level that the resolution of the conflicting claims of all the other modes of life in the poem is effected.

We are made aware of the basic conflicts of the poem in the first line of the eighth stanza, where there is something utterly paradoxical in "toll me back," as though returning to life were actually death. It is as though in putting away the moods he has elaborately built around the song of the nightingale he were burying his spirit, as though the "sole self" which remains were a mere husk. "To thy high requiem become a sod" is the obverse of this conflict. Only in the eighth stanza it is the "requiem" or "plaintive anthem" which dies and is "buried deep," and Keats who returns to "life." In the fourth and sixth stanzas it is Keats who flees the world or thinks of ceasing "upon the midnight with no pain," and in the eighth it is the nightingale which ceases and Keats who returns: "Fled is that music." The "meaning" of this poem is only to be apprehended in terms of this complex structure and the reverberation and interaction of its delicately modulated themes.

As the song fades and "actuality" presses in once more, it is not, this time, some dramatically visioned phase of life such as is presented in the third stanza, but the world of rational wakefulness. The way in which this is conveyed by the literal accuracy of observation of the movements of the bird is exquisitely right: "Past the near meadows, over the still stream, Up the hill-side." "Do I wake or sleep?" implies the depth of absorption, the exclusive attraction of what has preceded it, and thus betokens an abrupt shift of tone and attention which constitutes the resolution of the tensions.

It seemed best to give rather full consideration to the *Ode to the Nightingale,* and thus to suggest the lines along which the other odes should be read, rather than to deal with them all briefly. There now remains space for only the most general comment on the organization of the *Ode on a Grecian Urn* and the *Ode to Autumn.*

The *Ode on a Grecian Urn* has a central symbol which is much more limited than that of the nightingale. For all that, this ode likewise realizes the dramatic intention of the poet by means of a similar modulation of tones and rhythms which are in strict relation to the modes of contemplating the urn. The ode opens with a slow ritual movement suggesting enrapt gazing. This is suddenly interrupted by a series of abrupt and dramatic questions which convey more than a slight note of doubt and alarm. The note recurs in the fourth stanza as the poet develops the mood of desolation.

There are three basic themes involved in this ode, and they are of equal importance. The first is that of pastoral, with all its implications of rural and romantic peace and beauty. Pastoral offers a conventional escape for hearts "high-sorrowful and cloy'd"; the sophisticated have often cultivated it. The second theme, less explicit, is that of pagan culture under the sentimental aspect of its superiority to the current code—its freedom from complexity and dogma. Significantly, this conventional theme serves Keats' purpose in "discrediting" the urn as an escape; for "what maidens loth" and "that heifer lowing at the skies" strike a grim sacrificial note which is not to be mistaken. The third theme is also nostalgic: the life of aesthetic contemplation offered by the urn. In the artistic organization of the poem they are given alternate stress, and their tensions are relaxed in the last stanza by what can only be called an outright rejection of all three modes of escape.

An interval of but three months separates these odes from the *Ode to Autumn.* Apropos of the remarkable stabilizing function of the fifth stanza of the *Ode to a Nightingale,* it was observed that the stability was achieved not by espousal or rejection of life, nor by affirmation nor negation, but by a mode of being which Keats, himself, called "negative capability." Keats' definition of this phrase is especially relevant to the *Ode to Autumn:* ". . . when a man is capable of being in uncertainties, mysteries, doubts, without any irritable reaching after fact and reason."

Just as in the fifth stanza of the *Ode to a Nightingale* Keats plants himself in the springtime earth, so in the *Ode to Autumn* he seems to have reached fruition. "Ripeness is all" could certainly be its epigraph. There are no superficial conflicts or tensions in this ode. The ideal and the actual are one, and the restless spirit of the poet seems to be completely absorbed by the object of contemplation.

The dramatic movement or action of the poem appears to follow the process of natural growth. The three phases correspond to the three stanzas. Instead, however, of oscillating "up" and "down" movements, there is in this ode a single motion of expanding awareness from vegetable immobility to expressive and vital consciousness. In richly presenting these aspects of created being for immediate enjoyment, Keats makes his most mature comment.

The first stanza is remarkable for the rich suggestions of inner, hidden life and the aura of facts related to gestation. Reinforcing this, the point of view adopted by the poet is from within the cottage. There is here a world of rich organic and tactual awareness, but no suggestion of bodily movement.

The second stanza opens with a vigorous rhythm inviting us to "seek abroad." There is a recurring insistence on physical movement and posture carrying us well beyond the gentle undulating rhythms of the gestation stanza. It is not all motion, of course; for the finest effects concern a delicate indolence of motions which are halted as soon as hinted at.

The last stanza expands into a fully orchestrated expressiveness on the theme of triumphant fruition and fulfilment. Music is the mode, the basic and unifying image of the stanza. Keats reserves the full power of his verse and the full scope of his images of contrapuntal sensation for the realization of autumn. The transience of this beauty does not grieve the poet: Ripeness is all.

The rather willful habit of supposing all Keats' odes to be concerned with escape rather than the rejection of escape has probably been encouraged by the escape of his early death, but even more by reading Keats through the media of his successors, Rossetti, Swinburne, Pater, and Tennyson. These were preoccupied with a dream world, and they were influenced by Keats; but they had only a small share of that artistic toughness of fiber which made Keats finally reject anything less than a total view of his experience. It is just such a totality, the escapes, their attractiveness, their futility, and their rejection, which is the concern of these odes. The odes have no message. They are actions. Conflicts occur in the very nature of the themes, and Keats develops and resolves them dramatically within the limits which they themselves impose.

Coleridge as Artist

⊂⊃ ⊂⊃ ⊂⊃ ⊂⊃ ⊂⊃

"As I BENT my head," wrote Coleridge to Godwin, "there came a distinct, vivid spectrum upon my eyes; it was one little picture—a rock, with birches and ferns on it, a cottage backed by it, and a small stream." The peculiar combination of interests which in Coleridge has served for thirty years to make of him a figure of increasingly contemporary relevance appears in almost any excerpt from his writings or conversation. This note to Godwin is typical of his concern with the poetic vision as a process involved, even "as I bent my head," with ordinary experience. For it was Coleridge as much as anybody who hastened the recognition of the poetic process as linked with the modes of ordinary cognition, and with the methods of the sciences. The very great effort he made to thread the labyrinth of the arts and sciences compelled him to an encyclopedism unapproached since Francis Bacon. For Coleridge was convinced that in the heart of the poetic process was to be found not only the echo of human perception but the Filium Labyrinthi which Bacon sought in vain. Yet even the pursuit of that thread made Bacon's treatise as exciting for Shelley as the greatest poetry.

It is characteristic of Coleridge's encyclopedism, which so many find congenial today, that it locates the arts foremost among human interests as providing the material and the guide for every type of insight and pursuit. Not only the archeologist but the anthropologist and sociologist, equally with the historians and reconstructors

115

of the phases of human culture, repair today to the arts to acquire the disciplines and the techniques necessary for their creative analysis. It has taken a full century to move from the stage of artistic awareness of Edgar Poe to that of Siegfried Giedion. Poe put crime detection on a scientific basis by bringing into play the poetic process of retracing the stages of human apprehension. It is likewise the procedure of Wordsworth's *Prelude* and Sterne's *Tristram Shandy*. And this process of arrest and retracing, which has been consciously followed by poets since the end of the eighteenth century (when used by a cultural historian and analyst like Siegfried Giedion) provides the very technique of empathy which permits intimate insight into the processes and impulses behind products utterly alien to our own immediate experience. In fact, the Coleridgean awareness of the modes of the imagination as producer represents an enormous extension of the bonds of human sympathy and understanding, socially and historically. Coleridge wrote to Wordsworth *On the Night After His Recitation of a Poem On the Growth of An Individual Mind:*

> The truly Great
> Have all one age, and from one visible space
> Shed influence!

This has more than a neo-Platonic doctrinal interest at the present time when the instantaneity of communication between all parts of the world has brought into involuntary juxtaposition the whole diversity of human cultures. What century is it today in Peking or Jerusalem or Moscow? Yet the very speed of communication between these entities so discontinuous in space, time, and experience makes for a simultaneity in which lineal history is abolished by becoming present. Coleridge, a myriad-minded man living in a most tumultuous age, might not have enjoyed our time more than his own, but he was forced to invent a great deal of conceptual equipment which is indispensable to an intellectual of today. And more than any of his contemporaries or successors in the nineteenth century the modes of his apprehension and energizing compel the study and attention of the present generation.

The poetry of Coleridge has suffered from both doctrinaire approval and disfavor so that to avoid such pitfalls in approaching it there is much to be said for a genetic approach to the poetic problems and techniques which in the eighteenth century had preceded his own technical innovations. Writing in *Shelley and the Thought of His Time,* Joseph Barrell laments the split between Shelley's thought and expression: "For there is a vast difference in the manner with which the thought is expressed and in the logic, or way of thought, that the manner implies." So far as manner goes, he continues:

> The Greek way, which is Shelley's way and on the whole the Western way, is to take the reader, or listener, by the hand and lead him step by step from the old position to the new position. It seeks to explain and to demonstrate. Its logic might be described as linear and transitional. . . .
>
> The Oriental way is different. Its logic might be described not as linear but as radial. The recurring statements do not progress, but return to their center as the spokes of a wheel to their hub.

The dichotomy between linear and radial expression is not really as radical as might appear, but it has in such terms as "continuous" versus "discontinuous" or "statement" versus "suggestion" divided the allegiance of poets, critics, and readers from the time of Coleridge to the present. It certainly had much to do with the intellectual divergence between Coleridge and Wordsworth, between Browning and Tennyson, and between Pound and Eliot. In general, it seems to be felt that the Greek way of continuous transition in a poem makes for a habitable world of homely realities, whereas the Oriental way is inhuman in its austere demands of unflagging and unremitting intensity of contemplation and participation. In one case the poet leads us through the labyrinth of his work, and in the other we are left bewildered to multiply variety in an illusory world of mirrors.

In actual fact the quarrel is pointless so far as art goes since both kinds are inevitably dynamic, following the stages of cognition, which are equally the base of religious ritual and human creation. Francis Bacon knew this very well when he divided the modes of human communication into "magistral" and "probative" or popular and esoteric. The Ciceronian delivers knowledge in a concatenated form having regard to its direct reception and retention. The Senecan, on the other hand, is less concerned with the reception and retention of any given body of data than with having the learner experience the actual process by which the data were achieved. The one is concerned with preserving and transmitting an achieved body of truth, the other with maintaining the process by which truth is achieved. This division embroiled the ancient world. In the twelfth century it recurred as the quarrel between St. Bernard and Abelard, between the historical method of the patristic humanists and systematic or scholastic procedure. In the sixteenth and seventeenth centuries it continues as the quarrel between the Ciceronians and the Senecans, the ancients and the moderns. With Newton, however, the balance is upset in favor of the modern or scientific party. And despite the rise of the Hellenists the arts in the main have followed Newton ever since Thomson's *Seasons.*

That is to say that Newton's *Optics* established a correspondence between inner and outer worlds, between the forms and textures of the world and the faculties of perception and intellection, which has affected the practice of every poet and painter since his time. This correspondence once ascertained, it was possible for a Hartley to derive our inner world from the outer or for a Berkeley to indicate that the outer world was the fiat of our perception and creative imagination. This split between "the physics of the Self and the Not-Self," as it is called by Wyndham Lewis in *The Enemy of the Stars,* helps to explain the differences between the early and later Wordsworth and Coleridge as well as the aesthetic quarrel which grew up between them. And it tells much of the story of the impressionists versus the expressionists or symbolists. At the theological level the Hellenic dualist finds the quarrel insoluble on the assumption of the eternity of matter. The Oriental and the Romantic monist simply fuse inner and outer, matter and spirit, seeking an H-bomb formula of annihilation for ego and existence alike. For the Christian there is no problem since he accepts the revelation that the world was made from nothing as well as the dogma of the resurrection of the body. But for the practicing artist there is no point in the quarrel since works of art are not made from ideas or doctrines but, like ourselves, must come into existence by a process which is indifferent to the winds of doctrine. Yet if the artistic process must always be the same the conditions of art and the artist are always changing. Certainly Newton helped to change the circumstances and the matter employed by the artist. The problems faced by Coleridge were of Newton's making.

Until Newton the Senecans had dominated the literary scene from Montaigne to Pascal and from Donne to Pope. Their preoccupation was with the literary techniques for arresting and projecting some phase of the human mind: to arrest in order to project, and to project in order to contemplate. Like the inventors of cinema at the beginning of this century they hit upon the technique of stylistic discontinuity as a means of analyzing or arresting a moment of consciousness. The movie camera takes a thousand still shots in order to capture the aspects of a brief movement. The *style coupé* and the "cutted period" attempted something comparable in the essay and the poem. But to have carried this art further than Pope was probably impossible. At any rate the advent of Newton's *Optics* diverted artistic effort from poetic statement to the use of external landscape as a means of projecting and controlling states of mind under the guidance of two major concepts. The first of these was derived from the study of the visual harmonics of the spectrum which led to a revival of the classic images of the harps of Aeolus and Memnon. If the surfaces of matter were varied prisms for revealing the qualities of light, then the entire visible and audible world could be conceived as a species of visual music. The second concept is related to the first. For, if the external world is attuned to the mind of man then the whole of Nature is a language and the poet is a pontifex or bridger between the two worlds. He conducts the symphony of mind and nature.

The harp and language themes are fused in *Frost at Midnight:*

> . . . so shall thou see and hear
> The lovely shapes and sounds intelligible
> Of that eternal language, which thy God
> Utters. . . .

And in *France: An Ode* the pontifex theme is linked to the harp.

> . . . on that sea-cliff's verge,
> Whose pines, scarce travelled by the breeze above,
> Had made one murmur with the distant surge!
> Yes, while I stood and gazed, my temples bare,
> And shot my being through earth, sea, and air,
> Possessing all things with intensest love. . . .

The poet here is exercising his priestly powers of purifying the wells of existence, exerting his primary imagination which is the agent of all perception, not the secondary imagination which brings art into existence as an echo of the functions of perception.

The world felt as Aeolian harp and as an apocalyptic language, on one hand, and the poet as pontifex or magus, on the other, pretty well sets the stage for all the problems of aesthetics from Thomson, Collins, and Akenside to Coleridge, Keats, and Shelley. These problems, moreover, remain our own. For the work of Yeats, Joyce, and Eliot represents a continuous development of poetic theory and practice along these lines. The artist becomes scientist, hierophant, and sage, as well as the unacknowledged legislator of the world.

Naturally enough, accompanying this hypertrophy of the artistic role in society has come a good deal of bewildered dissent, and it has centered around Matthew Arnold's claim that the business of poetry is in the middle realm of culture or the region of ethical and political teaching. The poet may be pontifex between this world and the next, but our business is to live well in this world. This dilemma is a crux for Coleridge and Wordsworth and helps perhaps to explain their gradual cessation of poetic activity as well as their turning to social and ethical speculation. That this was the way in which the disciples of Coleridge interpreted him is perfectly plain from the activities of John Sterling, Thomas Arnold, and F. D. Maurice. But it is significant that it is not this side of Coleridge which interests the modern student of poetry. When Voltaire approached Congreve as a celebrated poet and was told that the dramatist wished to be considered "only as an English gentleman," he replied that had he thought of Congreve that way he should never have troubled to seek him out. Were Coleridge to tell a young intellectual today that he wished to be considered only as the author of *The Statesman's Manual* he would get the same reply as that given by Voltaire. Mr. Basil Willey's discussion of Coleridge in *Nineteenth Century Studies* sets him in his proper Victorian perspective as the alternative to Bentham. Coleridge represented the movement to reconcile neo-Platonism and Christianity as a means of envisaging social and political institutions *sub specie aeternitatis,* as opposed to the utilitarian functionalists and mechanists for whom the entire fabric of society was unpenetrated by the divine. In this regard, the prose of Mr. Eliot since *The Use of Poetry and the Use of Criticism* (1933) has for the most part been concerned to promote the same point of view. Whereas Mr. Richards, in accord with the work of Lord Russell, has attempted to retain and to assimilate Coleridge's post-Hartleian speculations on aesthetics within Bentham's scheme.

To approach Coleridge's art, however, it is necessary to see him at work amid the technical developments of the poetry of his time. For poetry being concerned with obtaining specific effects must always be seeking new means for these effects amid the constantly changing conditions of culture. For young Coleridge the most immediate and intense poetic experience was obtained from the sonnets of Bowles. For Mr. Eliot the same awakening occurred when reading FitzGerald's *Omar Khayyám.* In each instance there was a very striking technical innovation which, in the particular circumstances of each of these poets, released a chain of consequences. FitzGerald held up to Mr. Eliot the technique of discontinuous vignettes with their endless power of comment and revelation of one another by the mere fact of their harmonic or ironic juxtaposition. Subsequently Mr. Eliot found this paratactic principle embodied in varying modes in all the great art of the world from Homer to Pope. But it was revealed to him by the unlikely FitzGerald. In the same way Coleridge found in the sentimental flaccidities of William Bowles the technique of exploring an arrested moment of emotion by fixing it spatially in a particularized landscape. This technique had already been elaborated in painting, music, and poetry since the later seventeenth century. But by Bowles it was revealed to Coleridge for the first time. Just as the tone of FitzGerald was perhaps an antidote to certain strenuous banalities of the Victorians, so the languid sentiment of Bowles struck Coleridge as tender, natural, and bracing amid the rhetorical posturings of the later eighteenth century. And what pleased him in Bowles he was soon to find more fully in the old ballads and in Wordsworth's *Evening Walk* and *Descriptive Sketches*. What is evident at once from a glance at *An Evening Walk* and *Descriptive Sketches* is the extreme artiness of young Wordsworth. He is a master of every visual and auditory nuance dear to the picturesque school:

> Where falls the purple morning far and wide
> In flakes of light upon the mountain side;
> Where with loud voice the power of water shakes
> The leafy wood, or sleeps in quiet lakes.

Those "flakes of light" were not to be discovered by painters until much later. But already in a poem "written in very early youth" there is the opening line which fixes amid the picturesque techniques the mature vision:

> Calm is all nature as a resting wheel.

That is the master vision of all those "spots of time" for which Wordsworth painfully sought the precise objective correlative in carefully wrought landscapes. It is the key to all his lyrics and even to *The Prelude,* which in order to follow his process of enlightenment has to arrest for contemplation the entire movement of his mind from youth to age:

> The stilly murmur of the distant Sea
> Tells us of silence.

Coleridge gave a good deal of deliberate attention to the forms of the external world, but it is significant that as with Eliot external forms exerted their greatest power upon him through the medium of books. So filtered, the external world became for Coleridge an internal moon-haunted landscape which he could manipulate with the utmost effect. Seen this way, the division of labor which Coleridge and Wordsworth proposed in their project of *Lyrical Ballads* corresponded to the diversity of their native powers. But the aesthetic theory which they largely shared awarded the bays to the poet of the eye and daylight. So that Coleridge could hardly fail to take a desponding view of his own poetry. Since Rimbaud, Mallarmé, Eliot, and Joyce the enormous advantages in scope, learning, and precision of the interior landscape over external landscape have become evident, and the poems of Coleridge have accordingly gained in interest. But it may well have been that for Coleridge his own acceptance of the theory of imagination and perception exemplified in the poetry of Wordsworth was a detriment to the continuance of poetic activity. The theory of language and communication shared by Mallarmé, Valéry, Joyce, and Eliot would have proved as unwelcome to Wordsworth as it might have been inspiring to Coleridge. In *The Use of Poetry and The Use of Criticism* (p. 111) Eliot gives this account of the matter:

> What I call this "auditory imagination" is the feeling for syllable and rhythm, penetrating far below the conscious levels of thought and feeling, invigorating every word; sinking to the most primitive and forgotten, returning to the origin and bringing something back, seeking the beginning and the end. It works through meanings, certainly, or not without meanings in the ordinary sense, and fuses the old and obliterated and the trite, the current, and the new and surprising, the most ancient and the most civilised mentality.

That passage makes a better critical account of *The Ancient Mariner* than perhaps Coleridge or Wordsworth knew how to give as critics. It explains what they were up to in bringing the old ballad rituals and verbal simplicities into juxtaposition with the lyric impulse generated by their study of the aesthetic moment and its attendant landscape.

But Wordsworth the seer had little sense of the auditory dimensions of language which could control great vistas of erudition and collective experience. For the auditory labyrinth is charged with the experience of the past of the race and unites the poet with history in a continuous present. Whereas the poet of the eye is more solitary than social, finding his satisfactions in stylized patterns rather than in the acoustic accumulations of learning and collective insight. It is thus perfectly natural for Coleridge to justify the mode of his poetic activity by an auditory image which Wordsworth would have avoided: "The reader should be carried forward . . . by the pleasurable activity of the mind excited by the attractions of the journey itself. Like the motion of a serpent, which the Egyptians made the emblem of intellectual power; or like the path of sound through the air;—at every step he pauses and half recedes, and from the retrogressive movement collects the force which again carries him onward." The latter comment seems to set the gloss subsequently added to *The Ancient Mariner* in a sufficiently luminous light while retorting to Wordsworth's critique about the discontinuity of the poem.

As poetic practitioners Wordsworth and Coleridge were in agreement about two things—that poetry was concerned with the rendering of an instant of arrested awareness which freed the mind from the clogs of habitual perception, and that a landscape with human figures was the necessary means of achieving this end. The aim was to dislocate the reader into attention not so much by rhythmic or verbal novelty such as Eliot or Auden rely on, as by some startling visual fact which did not distort but reveal nature:

> During the first year that Mr. Wordsworth and I were neighbors, our conversations turned frequently on the two cardinal points of poetry, the power of exciting the sympathy of the reader by a faithful adherence to the truth of nature, and the power of giving the interest of novelty by the modifying colours

of the imagination. The sudden charm, which accidents of light and shade, which moonlight or sunset diffused over a known and familiar landscape, appeared to represent the practicability of combining both.

As for the human figures in these landscapes, "it was agreed that my endeavours should be directed to persons and characters supernatural, or at least romantic; yet so far as to transfer from our inward nature a human interest and a semblance of truth sufficient to procure for these shadows of imagination that willing suspension of disbelief for the moment, which constitutes poetic faith."

Scattered up and down in *The Prelude* and *The Excursion* Wordsworth has a good deal to say about the aesthetic program enunciated by Coleridge, leaving no doubt concerning the reasons for their divergent theories of communication and the poetic process. But because the landscape techniques of neither Coleridge nor Wordsworth have been much studied the point of Wordsworth's polemic seems to have been missed. Although Coleridge had no difficulty in locating the excellence of Wordsworth's poetry, Wordsworth could not but attribute the very virtues of Coleridge's poems to disease:

> I have thought
> Of thee, thy learning, gorgeous eloquence,
> And all the strength and plumage of thy youth,
> Thy subtle speculations, toils abstruse
> Among the schoolmen, and Platonic forms
> Of wild ideal pageantry, shaped out
> From things well-matched or ill, and words for things,
> The self-created sustenance of a mind
> Debarred from Nature's living images,
> Compelled to be a life unto herself . . .
> . . . had we met,
> Even at that early time, needs must I trust
> In the belief, that my maturer age,
> My calmer habits, and more steady voice,
> Would with an influence benign have soothed,
> Or chased away, the airy wretchedness
> That battened on thy youth.

The patronage aside, Wordsworth is here making a technical critique of Coleridge which he knew Coleridge was gloomily disposed to accept. For if the imagination is the very agent of perception, the means of communication between persons and objects in nature, and if the poetic process is an echo of this imagination, then the poet deprived from earliest years of intimate communion with natural objects (poor Coleridge left only to commune with the stars on the slates of Christ's Hospital) is necessarily in an "airy" and undernourished state.

The *Prelude* is a full-dress reconstruction of the rich and glorious stages of sensuous apprehension by which Wordsworth escaped the "airy" fate of Coleridge. Coleridge and the auditory imagination provide the subplot of that portrait of the artist as a great river, the image which recurs when Wordsworth thinks of himself in poetic act. Wordsworth would seem to elect himself to play St. Michael to Coleridge's Lucifer.

> . . . we have traced the stream
> From the blind cavern whence is faintly heard
> Its natal murmur . . . .
> Imagination having been our theme.

Moments of insight in Wordsworth's poetry are explicitly associated with an experience of an arrest in time:

> And, on the shape of that unmoving man,
> His steadfast face and sightless eyes, I gazed,
> As if admonished from another world.
> Though reared upon the base of outward things,
> Structures like these the excited spirit mainly
> Builds for herself; scenes different there are,
> Full-formed, that take, with small internal help,
> Possession of the faculties,—the peace
> That comes with night; the deep solemnity
> Of nature's intermediate hours of rest,
> When the great tide of human life stands still:
> The business of the day to come, unborn,
> Of that gone by, locked up, as in the grave . . . .

Wordsworth was an artist with an intensely educated and sophisticated eye. Coleridge by comparison has an illiterate eye but shows a

cultivation of the auditory powers greatly superior to Wordsworth.
It is a distinction which also separates Joyce and Eliot from Pound.
Wordsworth is the indefatigable watcher thrilling to the dramatic
minutiae and nuances of vision:

> Once again I see
> These hedge-rows, hardly hedge-rows, little lines
> Of sportive wood run wild: these pastoral forms
> Green to the very doors; and wreaths of smoke
> Sent up, in silence, from among the trees!

In his management of external landscape Coleridge is by comparison a botcher but usually he redeems his landscapes with some
auditory touch of magic:

> And watch the clouds, that late were rich with light,
> Slow saddening round, and mark the star of eve
> Serenely brilliant (Such should Wisdom be)
> Shine opposite! How exquisite the scents
> Snatch'd from yon bean-field! and the world so hush'd!

Confronted with the corrupt and artificial labyrinth of the city,
Wordsworth slips into the language of Coleridge and the inner
landscape of "fancy":

> With deep devotion, Nature, did I feel,
> In that enormous City's turbulent world
> On men and things, what benefit I owed
>   To thee . . .
>   . . . more exquisitely fair
> Than that famed paradise of ten thousand trees,
>   .   .   .   .
> A sumptuous dream of flowery lawns, with domes
> Of pleasure sprinkled over, shady dells
> For eastern monasteries, sunny mounts
> With temples crested, bridges, gondolas,
> Rocks, dens, and groves of foliage taught to melt
> Into each other their obsequious hues,
> Vanished and vanishing in subtle chase,
> Too fine to be pursued.

"Too fine to be pursued" would seem to be an echo of Milton's
demonic disputants "in wandering mazes lost." Some lines further

in the same book Wordsworth explains how though he, too, could indulge an oriental fancy, unlike Coleridge, he was blessed with a redemptive grace:

> . . . . 'mid the fervent swarm
> Of these vagaries, with an eye so rich
> As mine was through the bounty of a grand
> And lovely region, I had forms distinct
> To steady me: each airy thought revolved
> Round a substantial centre, which at once
> Incited it to motion, and controlled.
> I did not pine like one in cities bred,
> As was thy melancholy lot, dear Friend!
> Great Spirit as thou art, in endless dreams
> Of sickliness, disjoining, joining, things
> Without the light of knowledge.

Within the intellectual scheme of the late eighteenth century Wordsworth could give himself the airs of a modern working-class intellectual condescending to a millionaire Marxist. As a poet reared in the city Coleridge could have fancy but not imagination. So that exercising his own genius for the interior landscape Coleridge was as one born out of due time. And gratuitously he seems to have accepted his fate as a hopeless barrier to major poetic activity. At least it is worth suggesting this line for further study, that there is something doctrinaire rather than spontaneous and necessary about the stages leading to the decline of his poetic activity. For the future of poetry lay on the path which Wordsworth avoided and that Coleridge was prompted to discontinue even after having discovered the way of the interior landscape in his great poems.

The exterior landscape serves very well for certain states of mind and some areas of experience. But it is necessarily a cumbersome apparatus ill-suited to the variety and compression of the modern city:

> Au cœur d'un vieux faubourg, labyrinthe fangeux
> Où l'humanité grouille en ferments orageux,
>
> On voit un chiffonnier qui vient, hochant la tête,
> Buttant, et se cognant aux murs comme un poëte.

Inspired by Edgar Poe, as Poe was by Coleridge, Baudelaire developed the technique of the interior landscape as a means of revealing the intensities generated by the harsh dissonances, overlayerings, and discontinuities of city life. The picturesque world of Wordsworth, on the other hand, has not proved capable of carrying the complex freight of modern experience nor of assimilating the riches of the collective human past which the modern poet needs to evoke in the midst of city landscapes.

Wordsworth and Coleridge were agreed that the poetic process coincided with the learning process, but Coleridge saw that the formal learning of philology and philosophy was not incompatible with the poetic process. And in this he pointed the way to restoring erudition to the scheme of poetic communication. Writing to Cottle, he said:

> I should not think of devoting less than twenty years to an epic poem. Ten years to collect materials and warm my mind with universal science. I would be a tolerable Mathematician. I would thoroughly understand Mechanics; hydrostatics; optics and Astronomy; Botany; Metallurgy; Fossilism; Chemistry; Geology; Anatomy; Medicine; then the mind of man; then the minds of men, in all. Travels, Voyages and Histories.

This is the full classical program of studies, the *eguklios paideia,* pursued by Vergil, Dante, Chaucer, Spenser, and Milton. In intention, at least, it is recognized as necessary by modern poets like Valéry, Joyce, Pound, and Eliot. And there is the work of Lowes to show how much of this kind of learning went to the making of *The Ancient Mariner,* which is at least a little epic.

Despite the fact that the epyllion or little epic is a classical form which has been used continuously in classical, medieval, and modern times, it has been given little scholarly or critical attention. Most readers might scarcely recognize *The Waste Land* or *Four Quartets* as epyllia. But such is also the form of Hemingway's *The Old Man and the Sea,* a work which readily associates itself with *The Ancient Mariner.* Eliot's intimate mastery of this compact and learned form enables him to point out the debt of Byron to Coleridge in working up a poem like *The Giaour:*

As a tale-teller we must rate Byron very high indeed: I can think of none other since Chaucer who has an equal readability, with the exception of Coleridge whom Byron abused and from whom Byron learned a great deal . . . . Byron's plots, if they deserve that name, are extremely simple. What makes the tales interesting is first a torrential fluency of verse and a skill in varying it from time to time to avoid monotony; and second a genius for divagation. Digression, indeed, is one of the most valuable arts of the story-teller. The effect of Byron's digressions is to keep us interested in the story-teller himself, and through this to interest us more in the story.[1]

If Byron's plots are so simple as scarcely to deserve the name it is because his tales are nature rituals like *The Ancient Mariner. The Giaour* (jour-day) follows the east-west movement of the sun, through the hours of the day and the signs of the zodiac, celebrating the fire principle. Such is presumably the larger pattern of the *Iliad,* whereas the *Odyssey,* like the *Ulysses* of James Joyce, the *Cantos* of Pound, and *The Ancient Mariner* involves the ritual of both sun and moon. As Lowes has shown, Coleridge's great plans for hymns to the sun, moon, and the four elements are reduced to, or realized in, the *Mariner.* This clears up at once the problem of the "motiveless malignancy" of the old navigator in killing the albatross. For the action of the poem is not on the ethical plane of social or political existence, but, like *The Giaour,* concerns a spiritual adventure of ascent. This appears plainly in the commentary of Thomas Taylor, one of Coleridge's favorite writers, on "The Wanderings of Ulysses," as well as in Porphyry's *Cave of the Nymphs.* Porphyry says of the episode of the blinding of the Cyclops who is the natal daemon of Ulysses:

> For it will not be simply, and in a concise way, possible for any one to be liberated from this sensible life, who blinds this daemon, and renders his energies inefficacious, but he who dares to do this, will be pursued by the anger of the marine and material Gods, whom it is first requisite to appease by sacrifices, labours, and patient endurance. . . . Nor will he even then be liberated from labours; but this will be effected when he has entirely passed over the raging sea, and, though still living, becomes so

ignorant of marine and material works as to mistake an oar for a corn-van.[2]

Taylor also comments that whereas in superior souls the natal and essential daemons are one, it is not so in imperfect souls whose natural lot, like that of Ulysses, is cast on the plane of ethical and political striving: "As he is, however, departing from a sensible to an intellectual life, though circuitously and slowly, he is represented in so doing as blinding and irritating his natal daemon. For he who blinds the eye of sense, and extinguishes its light, after his will has profoundly assented to its use, must expect punishment for the deed; as necessary ultimately to his own peculiar good, and the general order of the universe."

The Mariner's natal daemon is the albatross, as is the white whale the daemon of Captain Ahab; and Coleridge was right in saying that the poem had, if anything, too much of the moral in it.

What is relevant here to the art of Coleridge concerns the confessional and digressive character of *The Ancient Mariner.* For it is this confessional and circuitous character which has penetrated not only Byron's tales but the art of *The Ring and the Book,* the novels of Henry James, of Ford Madox Ford, and of Joseph Conrad. It is the pattern of Pound's *Mauberley* and the *Cantos,* and provides the thread to the labyrinth of Eliot's poems from *Prufrock* to *The Cocktail Party.* Seen as movements of ascent or descent, of abstraction or concretion, these works follow the stages of human apprehension and cognition, of purgation and fruition. So that in linking the primary and secondary imaginations as analogous, and as providing the key to the poetic process and pattern, Coleridge would appear as the master of the literary art of our time.

The dislocation of the simple chronology of events is not a whim directed to obscurity, but, as in the wanderings of Ulysses, a fidelity to a higher order of intelligibility. As Conrad put it, it is *that you may see:* the endless circuits and digressions follow the path not of raw events but of the extraction of the significance from events in the order of learning and experience. This is the course of Tiresias, the narrator of *The Waste Land.* And Edward Chamberlayne in

The Cocktail Party (in which there are three cyclopean guardians) having made a decision, sets in motion a machinery that he is as powerless to arrest as the old navigator in *The Ancient Mariner*.

Since many modern readers have complained about the illogical order of symbolist art it is worth stressing the fact that the order of learning and insight is not the order of rational concatenation but of analogical perception. And it is much owing to Coleridge that since Poe and Baudelaire poetry and fiction have largely employed the pattern of the spiritual and intellectual quest rather than that of realistic narrative. Thus, Eliot notes that "Byron developed the verse *conte* considerably beyond Moore and Scott . . . . Byron's verse tales represent a more mature stage of this transient form than Scott's . . . . Scott perfected a straightforward story with the type of plot which he was to employ in his novels. Byron combined exoticism with actuality, and developed most effectively the use of *suspense*." Only suspense is not for thrill but for arrest of movement for contemplation, and to create one of those "spots in time" which permit a flash of intuitive wisdom.

It is plain, in the light of Eliot's remarks, that not only the nineteenth-century verse tale but the short story as handled by Flaubert, Henry James, Joyce, and Hemingway is in debt to nature ritual, of which *The Ancient Mariner* is the great exemplar.

If the development of medieval art was from ritual to romance, the process of art since Coleridge has been from romance to ritual, and *The Ancient Mariner* like its precursor *The Wanderings of Cain* foreshadows *The Waste Land*. In this perspective Eliot's further remarks on *The Giaour* become luminous:

> *The Giaour* is a long poem, and the plot is very simple, though not easy to follow . . . . We subsequently discover that the story of this vendetta—or part of it—is being told by the Giaour himself to an elderly priest, by way of making his confession. It is a singular kind of confession because the Giaour seems anything but penitent, and makes quite clear that although he has sinned, it is not really by his own fault. He seems impelled rather by the same motive as the Ancient Mariner, than by any desire for absolution—which could hardly have been given: but

the device has its use in providing a small complication to the story.

The complications and interruptions are necessary artistically (witness those which impede the narrative of Sweeney in *Sweeney Agonistes*) in order that not just the understanding but the whole man may become involved in response to the developing situation. The few interruptions which Coleridge at first provided for the narrative of the old navigator may well have seemed insufficient for this artistic purpose, and so he may have been led to add the gloss to the poem years later to provide a kind of cosmic chorus. So completed, the poem achieves a kind of continuous parallel between two levels of action, as does Joyce's *Ulysses* in moving simultaneously in modern Dublin and ancient Ithaca. And it is in this same way that Tiresias in *The Waste Land* moves "between two lives."

A great deal more needs to be said and done about the poetic art of Coleridge in relation to his contemporaries and to ourselves. His own development from a poet of rhetorical statement to a master of symbolic ritual prophetically enacts the history of art and poetry of the century which followed him. Seen, moreover, in its full light this development was impossible without the great intellectual labor which is too often supposed to have sterilized his poetic gifts. But it may well have been that, as with Rimbaud, the very magnitude of the change he experienced in his own modes of thought and feeling discouraged further experiment along lines that made such exhausting demands on mind and heart.

NOTES

[1] *From Anne to Victoria,* ed. Bonamy Dobree (1937).
[2] Taylor's translation.

Tennyson and Picturesque Poetry

ᑕᑭ ᑕᑭ ᑕᑭ ᑕᑭ ᑕᑭ

IN HIS *Autobiographies* W. B. Yeats mentions that a great advantage which he enjoyed over his fellows of the Cheshire Cheese was his acquaintance with Arthur Hallam's review of Tennyson's poems (*The Englishman's Magazine,* 1831). Hallam's essay is worth close study. It is a manifesto as decisive in the issues it raises as Wordsworth's Preface to *Lyrical Ballads* or Mr. Eliot's "Tradition and the Individual Talent." In 1895 Yeats found it invaluable as a key to the French symbolists who were puzzling his friends. Had it been understood in 1831 the energies of the Pre-Raphaelites might have found more direct channels to what in English poetry did not occur until the advent of Joyce, Pound, and Eliot.

Hallam's essay suggests that from his meeting with Tennyson at Trinity in 1828 until his death in 1833 his intense aesthetic interests were of the greatest importance to Tennyson's development as a poet. Until 1842 Tennyson seems to have retained Hallam's insights exclusively. Thereafter he began to admit rhetoric and reflection into his verse, wonderfully purging this admixture from the great "Rizpah" of 1880 and from several subsequent poems.

Hallam's aesthetic theory was the result of studying Dante through the poetry of Keats. But the extraordinary precision and elaboration of English impressionist criticism and speculation,

135

which had persisted from the 1780s, was still there to sharpen perception and judgment in 1830. The main effort of speculation had been directed towards landscape painting, for reasons which will be mentioned later on. All the Romantic poets were nurtured in this speculation; but Hallam's essay draws into a sharp focus some of the neglected implications for poetry:

> Whenever the mind of the artist suffers itself to be occupied, during its periods of creation, by any other predominant motive than the desire of beauty, the result is false in art.

Of course, he goes on, there may be states of mind in which thought and reflection are themselves unified by intellectual emotion:

> But though possible, it is hardly probable: for a man whose reveries take a reasoning turn, and who is accustomed to measure his ideas by their logical relations rather than the congruity of the sentiments to which they refer, will be apt to mistake the pleasure he has in knowing a thing to be true, for the pleasure he would have in knowing it to be beautiful, and so will pile his thoughts in a rhetorical battery, that they may convince, instead of letting them flow in a natural course of contemplation, that they may enrapture. It would not be difficult to show, by reference to the most admired poems of Wordsworth, that he is frequently chargeable with this error; and that much has been said by him which is good as philosophy, powerful as rhetoric, but false as poetry.

This passage arrives at once at the twentieth-century controversy over poetry and beliefs. It implies the Symbolist and Imagist doctrine that the place of ideas in poetry is not that of logical enunciation but of immediate sensation or experience. Rhetoric must go, said the Symbolists. Ideas as ideas must go. They may return as part of a landscape that is ordered by other means. They may enter into a unified experience as one kind of fact. They may contribute to an aesthetic emotion, not as a system of demonstration but as part of a total order which is to be contemplated.

So Hallam pronounces in favor of the Cockney School over "the Lakers":

We shall not hesitate to express our conviction, that the cockney school (as it was termed in derision from a cursory view of its accidental circumstances) contained more genuine inspiration, and adhered more steadily to that portion of truth which it embraced, than any *form* of art that has existed in this country since Milton . . . Shelley and Keats were indeed of opposite genius; that one was vast, impetuous, and sublime, the other . . . does not generalize or allegorize nature; his imagination works with few symbols, and reposes willingly on what is freely given. . . . They are both poets of sensation rather than reflection. . . . Rich and clear were their perceptions of visible forms; full and deep their feelings of music. So vivid was the delight attending the simple exertions of eye and ear, that it became mingled more and more with their trains of active thought, and tended to absorb their whole being into the energy of sense. Other poets seek for images to illustrate their conceptions; these men had no need to seek; they lived in a world of images; for the most important and extensive portion of their life consisted in those emotions which are immediately conversant with sensation. . . . Hence they are not descriptive, they are picturesque.

The force of this last antithesis depends on knowledge of the aesthetic developments of the eighteenth century, which are summarized in Christopher Hussey's classic *The Picturesque* (1927). "The picturesque view of nature," says Hussey, "led towards the abstract appreciation of colour and light that in painting marks the work of Turner and Constable." At the end of the epoch of picturesque experiment and exploration there is Cézanne in painting, and Rimbaud in poetry. That is, the impressionists began with sensation, discovered "abstraction," and achieved, finally a metaphysical art. The picturesque begins with work like Thomson's *Seasons,* in the search for significant art-emotion amid natural scenes; and it achieved plenary realization in Rimbaud's metaphysical landscapes —*Les Illuminations.* The early Romantics sought aesthetic emotion in natural scenes; the later Romantics confidently evoked art-emotion from art-situations. The early Romantics ransacked nature, as the Pre-Raphaelites did literature and history, for situations which would provide moments of intense perception. The

Symbolists went to work more methodically. As A. N. Whitehead showed, the great discovery of the nineteenth century was not this or that fact about nature, but the discovery of the technique of invention so that modern science can now discover whatever it needs to discover. And Rimbaud and Mallarmé, following the lead of Edgar Poe's aesthetic, made the same advance in poetic technique that Whitehead pointed out in the physical sciences. The new method is to work backwards from the particular effect to the objective correlative or poetic means of evoking that precise effect, just as the chemist begins with the end product and then seeks the formula which will produce it. Mr. Eliot states this discovery, which has guided his own poetic activity since 1910 or so, in his essay on *Hamlet:*

> The only way of expressing emotion in the form of art is by finding an "objective correlative"; in other words, a set of objects, a situation, a chain of events which shall be the formula of that *particular* emotion; such that when the external facts, which must terminate in sensory experience, are given, the emotion is immediately evoked.

Mr. Eliot is saying apropos of "sensory experience" exactly what Hallam was saying about Shelley and Keats: "They are both poets of sensation rather than reflection." Clearly Hallam is setting them above Wordsworth in tendency rather than achievement. And the tendency which he approves in them is precisely what we have more recently come to consider as the "unification of sensibility." Hallam refused to accept the magnificent rhetoric of Wordsworth as a substitute for such an integral poetry. That such integrity was possible he was sure, because of the poetry of Keats especially. We have the achievement of Joyce, Yeats, Pound, and Eliot to assure us not only that Hallam was entirely right but that Keats had not gone far enough.

What must have been the effect of Tennyson's five years of such conversation and study with Hallam? The volumes of 1830 and 1833 try to surpass Keats in richness of texture and sensuous impact. And "Mariana" is there to prove that the most sophisticated symbolist poetry could be written fifty years before the Symbolists. On a dependent and uncertain temper such as Tennyson's the effect of the death of the vigorous and clear-headed Hallam was not merely that of personal loss. It was more nearly the loss of his poetic insight and his critical judgment.

Hallam's essay goes on to define the kind of poetry which his age demanded, and which Tennyson was later to provide in such abundance:

> Since then this demand on the reader for activity, when he wants to peruse his author in a luxurious passiveness, is the very thing that moves his bile, it is obvious that those writers will be always most popular who require the least degree of exertion. Hence, whatever is mixed up with art, and appears under its semblance, is always more favourably regarded than art free and unalloyed. Hence, half the fashionable poems in the world are mere rhetoric and half the remainder are, perhaps, not liked by the generality for their substantial merits. Hence, likewise, of the really pure compositions, those are most universally agreeable which take for their primary subject the usual passions of the heart, and deal with them in a simple state, without applying the transforming powers of high imagination. Love, friendship, ambition, religion, etc., are matters of daily experience even amongst unimaginative tempers. The forces of association, therefore, are ready to work in these directions, and little effort of will is necessary to follow the artist. For the same reason, such subjects often excite a partial power of composition, which is no sign of a truly poetic organization. We are very far from wishing to depreciate this class of poems, whose influence is so extensive, and communicates so refined a pleasure. We contend only that the facility with which its impressions are communicated is no proof of its elevation as a form of art, but rather the contrary.

Hallam is insisting, just as much later Mallarmé, Eliot, and Valéry were to insist, that in "pure poetry," the poetry of suggestion rather than statement, or poetry in which the statments are themselves suggestions and in which the poetic form is the mode of the creative process itself, the reader is co-creator with the poet; since the *effect* depends on the reader's precision of response, and the poet is himself only another reader of his own poetry. So that Mr. Harold Nicolson shows himself unaware of this class of poetry, which is often present in Tennyson, when he remarks that "of all poets, Tennyson should be read very carelessly or not at all."

When Hallam finally turns to introduce Tennyson, he makes claims which the modern critic is now prepared to accept with little modification:

> Mr. Tennyson belongs decidedly to the class we have already described as Poets of Sensation. He sees all the forms of nature with the "eruditus oculus," and his ear has a fairy fineness. There is a strange earnestness in his worship of beauty which throws a charm over his impassioned song, more easily felt than described, and not to be escaped by those who have once felt it. We think he has more definitiveness and roundness of general conception than the late Mr. Keats, and is much more free from blemishes of diction and hasty capriccios of fancy. He has also this advantage over that poet and his friend Shelley, that he comes before the public unconnected with any political party or peculiar system of opinions. Nevertheless, true to the theory we have stated, we believe his participation in their characteristic excellences is sufficient to secure him a share of their unpopularity. . . .
>
> The features of original genius are clearly and strongly marked. The author imitates nobody; we recognize the spirit of his age, but not the individual form of this or that writer. His thoughts bear no more resemblance to Byron or Scott, Shelley or Coleridge, than to Homer or Calderon, Firdusi or Calidasa. We have remarked five distinctive excellences of his own manner. First, his luxuriance of imagination, and at the same time, his control over it. Secondly, his power of embodying himself in ideal characters or rather moods of character, with such extreme accuracy of adjustment, that the circumstances of the narration seem to have a natural correspondence with the predominant feeling, and, as it were, to be evolved from it by assimilative force. Thirdly, his vivid, picturesque delineation of objects, and the peculiar skill with which he holds all of them *fused,* to borrow a metaphor from science, in a medium of strong emotion. Fourthly, the variety of his lyrical measures, and exquisite modulation of harmonious words and cadences to the swell and

fall of the feelings expressed. Fifthly, the elevated habits of thought, implied in these compositions, and imparting a mellow soberness of tone, more impressive to our minds, than if the author had drawn up a set of opinions in verse, and sought to instruct the understanding rather than to communicate the love of beauty to the heart.

The fact that Tennyson is in great measure a landscape poet led Hallam to define him in 1831 by the then technical term "picturesque." In 1897 Francis Palgrave, another intimate acquaintance, published *Landscape in Poetry from Homer to Tennyson.* It is a poor book, lacking in technical and critical insights, but it makes plain the kind of traditional perspective in which Tennyson set his craftsman's interest in the problem of landscape.

From the first of Thomson's *Seasons* (1726) to the *Lyrical Ballads* of Wordsworth and Coleridge (1798) English landscape art in paint, poetry, and prose had undergone a very great technical development, which was also a growth of awareness at once psychological and naturalistic. Scientific observation and psychological experience met in landscape. Shelley, Keats, and Tennyson, as well as Ruskin and the Pre-Raphaelites, were not only quite conscious of these eighteenth-century discoveries, but set themselves the task of further advance along the same lines.

It might be suggested that landscape offered several attractive advantages to the poets of the mid-eighteenth century. It meant for one thing an extension of the Baroque interest in *la peinture de la pensée,* which the study of Seneca had suggested to Montaigne and Bacon and Browne—an interest which reached a maximal development, so far as the technique of direct statement permitted, in Pascal, Racine, and Alexander Pope. Pope especially deserves study from this point of view since he first developed the couplet to do the complex work of the double-plot of the Elizabethans. He discovered how to make a couplet achieve a symbolic vision. That is, to effect an instant of inclusive consciousness by the *juxtaposition without copula* of diverse and even paradoxical situations or states of mind:

The hungry judges soon the sentence sign,
And wretches hang that jurymen may dine.

The judges are hungry but not for justice; yet there is no suggestion
that they would be better judges if they had dined. The stark con-
frontation of this human condition is enforced by the second line or
"sub-plot" which is parallel but inferior. The suggestion that meat
must hang before it is edible, and that jurymen are merely promot-
ing the proper business of society in seeing that it gets hung is analogous to the vision of society in Swift's *Modest Proposal* and to
Lear's vision on the heath. The couplet in Pope's hands escaped
from the conditions imposed by univocal discourse which had developed in the Cartesian milieu.

But landscape offered a broader and less exacting course for
those who were preoccupied with the new psychological interests on
one hand and with means of evading the new insistence on non-
metaphorical and mathematical statement as the mode of poetry, on
the other hand. With Blake there are many moments when the new
landscape interests and techniques are fused with the wit and paradox of Pope. But his success passed unnoticed until it had been
reduplicated by the Symbolists. Wordsworth, Shelley, Keats, and
Tennyson typically use landscape without the precision and wit
provided by apposition of situation without copula. They achieve
an exclusive rather than an inclusive consciousness.

Looking back over the landscape developments of a century and
more, Ruskin in introducing the Pre-Raphaelites in 1851 summed
up what was a commonplace to Wordsworth in 1798 and also to
Tennyson in 1830:

> The sudden and universal Naturalism, or inclination to copy
> ordinary natural objects, which manifested itself among the
> painters of Europe, at the moment when the invention of print-
> ing superseded their legendary labours, was no false instinct. It
> was misunderstood and misapplied, but it came at the right time,
> and has maintained itself through all kinds of abuse; presenting
> in the recent schools of landscape, perhaps only the first fruits of
> its power. That instinct was urging every painter in Europe at the

same moment to his true duty——*the faithful representation of all objects of historical interest, or of natural beauty existent at the period;* representation such as might at once aid the advance of sciences, and keep faithful record of every monument of past ages which was likely to be swept away in the approaching eras of revolutionary change.

This amalgam of moral duty, aesthetic experience, scientific discovery, and political revolution was first effected in the age of Leibniz, Locke, and Newton; and we are still engaged today in contemplating its unpredictable derivatives. For the moment, and in the arts, the terminus appears as the fascinating landscapes of *Finnegans Wake* and *Four Quartets.* So that, if we take our bearings with reference to this new work it will be easier to assess the intentions and achievement of Tennyson, whose work falls just midway between that of James Thomson and Mr. Eliot. The huge tapestries of the *Wake* are not merely visual but auditory, talking and moving pictures; not just spatial in their unity, but effecting a simultaneous presence of all modes of human consciousness, primitive and sophisticated. Rocks, rivers, trees, animals, persons, and places utter with classical dramatic decorum the kind of being that is theirs. The poet in effacing himself utterly has become a universal Aeolian Harp reverberating the various degrees of knowledge and existence in such a hymn of life as only the stars of Pythagoras were ever conceived to have sung. To this concert there came all the arts and sciences, trivial and quadrivial, ancient and modern, in an orchestrated harmony that had first been envisaged by Joyce's master Stéphane Mallarmé.

Flaubert and Baudelaire had presided over the great city landscape of *Ulysses.* And Mr. Eliot's *The Waste Land* in 1922 was a new technical modulation of *Ulysses,* the latter of which had begun to appear in 1917. The *Quartets* owe a great deal to the *Wake,* as does *The Cocktail Party.* There is in all these works a vision of the community of men and creatures which is not so much ethical as metaphysical. And it had been, in poetry, due to the technical innovations of Baudelaire, Laforgue, and Rimbaud that it was possible to render this vision immediately in verse without the extraneous aids of rhetoric or logical reflection and statement. The principal innovation was that of *le paysage intérieur* or the psychological landscape. This landscape by means of discontinuity, which was first developed in picturesque painting, effected the apposition of widely diverse objects as a means of establishing what Mr. Eliot has called "an objective correlative" for a state of mind. The openings of *Prufrock, Gerontion,* and *The Waste Land* illustrate Mr. Eliot's growth in the adaptation of this technique, as he passed from the influence of Laforgue to that of Rimbaud, from personal to impersonal manipulation of experience. Whereas in external landscape diverse things lie side by side, so in psychological landscape the juxtaposition of various things and experiences becomes a precise musical means of orchestrating that which could never be rendered by systematic discourse. Landscape is the means of presenting, without the copula of logical enunication, experiences which are united in existence but not in conceptual thought. Syntax becomes music, as in Tennyson's "Mariana."

In the landscapes of the *Quartets* as in those of the *Wake* everything speaks. There is no single or personal speaker of the *Quartets,* not even the Tiresias of *Gerontion* and *The Waste Land.* It is the places and things which utter themselves. And this is also a stage of technique and experience achieved by Pound in his *Cantos,* and by St. John Perse, just as it had earlier been reached by Mallarmé in *Un Coup de Dés.* Browning was groping for it in *The Ring and the Book.* One might say that as the effect of Laforgue had been to open Mr. Eliot's mind to the effects of Donne and the Metaphysicals, so the effect of Rimbaud was to make him more fully aware of the means by which Dante achieved a zoning of states of mind through symbolic landscape.

Facing this unrivaled sophistication and self-awareness of metaphysical landscape in modern poetry, it is easier to observe what the eighteenth century was striving for as well as what effects Wordsworth, Coleridge and their successors were interested in obtaining. Hitherto the eighteenth century has been examined in retrospect from Wordsworth and Coleridge rather than from Keats and Tennyson. The Lake poets have often been supposed to have exhausted its potencies and to have settled its problems. Such, however, was not the view of Arthur Hallam and Alfred Tennyson. But looked at now across the work of Cézanne and Rimbaud it takes on a different and more impressive character than has usually been allowed it aesthetically. And today we are far from having explored the speculations of Burke and Blake or even of Knight and Price. What is put forward here as a suggested view of the eighteenth-century attitude to landscape has primarily relevance to what became Tennyson's idea of the function of landscape in poetry. For Tennyson, while accepting much of Wordsworth, certainly differed from him in important respects.

It is plain, for example, that Tennyson did not agree with the author of *The Prelude* in expecting an automatic amelioration of the human condition from the workings of external landscape on passive childhood, youth, and age. Tennyson could see very little valuable truth in Wordsworth's program for the recovery of a terrestrial paradise. He had many reasons for thinking it what Wordsworth incredulously queried in the preface to *The Excursion:*

> A history only of departed things,
> Or a mere fiction of what never was?

Then Wordsworth takes up the great eighteenth-century theme:

> For the discerning intellect of Man,
> When wedded to this goodly universe
> In love and holy passion, shall find these
> [i.e. "Paradise and groves"]
> A simple produce of the common day.
> I, long before the blissful hour arrives,
> Would chant in lonely peace the spousal verse
> Of this great consummation:—and, by words
> Which speak of nothing more than what we are,
> Would I rouse the sensual from their sleep
> Of death, and win the vacant and the vain
> To noble raptures; while my voice proclaims
> How exquisitely the individual Mind to the external world

Is fitted, and how exquisitely too —
Theme this but little heard of among men —
The external World is fitted to the Mind;

the notion of this preestablished harmony between the individual mind and the external world is the key to the eighteenth-century passion for landscape. Wordsworth naturally underrates the degree to which this "theme" was rehearsed among men from 1730 onwards, if only because anybody tends to be least aware of the decades immediately before his own time. They are taken for granted, as known. For by then the civilized world had much recovered from the dismay felt by Pascal and his contemporaries at the vision of an infinity of worlds, and had begun to speculate on the possible psychological nexus between man and a geometrically perfect universe. They turned from reflection on man's wretched insignificance to the thought of his sublimity of comprehension, by a simple reversal of the telescope.

Swift spotted the human vanity in the workings of this psychological mechanism and spoofed it at once in *Gulliver's Travels,* but without disturbing the course towards which things were shaping. For it was to be in the main a century of simple psychological mechanisms which were not to break down until Malthus and Darwin had shifted attention to the biological level. It was Leibniz who, as Professor Lovejoy suggests, translated the cosmological and mathematical views of his time into psychological terms. The hierarchy of creatures in his monadology "is defined primarily in psychological rather than morphological terms; it is by the levels of consciousness which severally characterize them, the degrees of adequacy and clarity with which they 'mirror' or represent the rest of the universe, that the monads are differentiated."

As soon as Newton had added to this view the proof that the universe which we (or rocks, trees, flowers) mirror is a marvel of automatic precision, the road is clear to Wordsworth's therapeutic idea of the educational power of the external world. For it was not enough to know that the mind of man is exquisitely fitted to the external world. It was also necessary to be sure that the external world was exquisitely harmonious with itself. It naturally follows for the early Wordsworth and Coleridge that the best mirrors of the radiant universe of life are those simple, spontaneous natures who have received the least admixture of social artifice and corruption. For it is the necessary operation of traditional society to implant within our natures "a universe of death." It has been not uncommon to accept not only this phrase from *The Prelude* but Wordsworth's poetic as expressive of a revulsion from the Newtonian world of science. Professor Willey, for example, says that Wordsworth's "more positive beliefs, those by which he appears in reaction against the scientific tradition, were built up by him out of his own poetic experiences . . . to animize the 'real' world, the 'universe of death' that the 'mechanical' system of philosophy had produced, but to do so without either using an exploded mythology or fabricating a new one, this was the special task and mission of Wordsworth."

But neither Wordsworth nor Tennyson rejected science as presenting a "universe of death." For if they had done so there would have been no predominance of landscape in their aesthetics, and, most pertinently, there would have been none of Tennyson's celebrated "accuracy" of observation and description, which, of course, can be matched in the painters and in poets like Barnes and Hopkins. Rather, in their view, science and poetry were near twins, of which poetry was a little the elder. And *The Prelude* passage (Book xiv) not only locates the "universe of death" as a product of divided aims, selfish passions, mean cares, and low pursuits, but goes on to contrast it with that which moves with light and life informed,

Actual, divine, and true.

It is the objective world observed by science and mirrored by simple, loving souls which Wordsworth sets over against the toyshop of vanities that is the soul of man, sensual and dark, under the regime of social custom and private egotism.

The study and discipline of the passions had from the time of Aristotle's *Rhetoric* been a branch of that art. It was the business of the orator to enlist the passions for political ends; and the function of literature was to enlarge, purge and order the passions for the exercise and solace of the good life. Dr. Johnson was simply expressing this view when he said of Richardson that "he teaches the passions to move at the command of virtue." It is important for a grasp of the meaning of landscape in the eighteenth century to see that traditional politics and literature were, in contemporary opinion, being supplanted by science. Men took readily to the notion that the disordered passions of the human heart might be restored to their pristine integrity by the automatic and unconscious operation of landscape on the passive mind—especially when a Newton had guaranteed the exquisite mathematical order of the external world.

The first published essay of Edmund Burke was his ironical *Vindication of Natural Society* (1756), which ridicules the deistic doctrines of Bolingbroke while appearing to utter them. Burke built no political hopes on the new idea that a true social harmony would be born of the direct operation of external nature on the passions of men. Nor could he accept the deistic verdict on human history as an artificial pageant of blood and butcheries perpetrated by "a few, mad, designing, or ambitious priests." But he was too intelligent a man of his time not to have made psychology the ground of his inquiry into the origin of our ideas of *The Sublime and The Beautiful.* For that age was committed by its science to the testing of art and external nature as a school of the affections, with landscape art, in particular, cast in the role of teacher of men. The artifice and guile of traditional oratory, art and politics, were to be supplanted by the practice of the contemplation and recollection of the external creation which speaks directly to the human heart.

That Burke's treatise had the greatest effect on the later eighteenth century is admitted by historians. Its influence on Coleridge and Poe, and through them on Baudelaire and the Symbolists, still deserves to be traced very carefully. For its speculations on the nature and effect of landscape art serve to unify the development of poetry from James Thomson to the present. It is in this treatise that are to be found the definitions of "state of mind" in art, of "emotions of the mind," of aesthetic emotion, objective correlative, and of the relation between beauty and melancholy as used later by Coleridge, Poe, and Baudelaire. Burke arrived by a single stride at the position that the cognitive process was also the creative process. And it is that awareness in Cézanne and Mallarmé, as later in Joyce and Eliot, which produced the doctrine and practice of "significant form" in modern art. That this same notion of form was apprehended by Arthur Hallam is plain in the passage already quoted from him concerning Tennyson's *fusion* of objects in the medium of a predominant emotion. Hallam could have had this from Coleridge, but he knew Burke directly.

From the dream of universal social therapy and regeneration which Wordsworth and Coleridge had at first accepted as a necessary consequence of submission of the heart to the pure messages of the external world, Coleridge awakened with his *Dejection: An Ode* in 1802. The Aeolian lute in his window, type of the poet and the faithful medium of the voices of the external world, now tells him not of the enchantment of a prospective Elysium, but of torture, Devil's yule, and

> of the rushing of an host in rout,
> With groans of trampled men . . . .

If Shelley perhaps persisted in the cosmic optimism, Keats did not. He knew the beauty of the natural order, and the beauty of art, but also the human

> Weariness, the fever, and the fret
> Here, where men sit and hear each other groan . . . .

There had been not only the wreck of the French Revolution, but the vision of the "hungry generations" in the doctrine of Malthus and the first fruits of the industrial towns to digest by this time. There had come the end of the notion of the external universe as a great clock which could order the inner passions of those who fed their minds on landscape in a wise passiveness. Nature was soon to be officially accepted as "red in tooth and claw," and the age of private enterprise to get under way. Biological automatism was ready to take over educational and political theory after a century of psychological automatism. Byron, however, was the appointed spokesman of disenchantment with the Newtonian sleep, which had sealed the spirits of the landscape idolators, when he proclaimed himself "a link reluctant in a fleshly chain." He was not in the least charmed by the great deist doctrine that "I live not in myself but I become portion of that around me." And he gave a cue and a credo to the new race of aristocratic dandies from Lytton to Disraeli, Poe, Baudelaire, and Wilde. They took up again the burden of individual consciousness which had been systematically relinquished in the first landscape era. And it is this which links them to the Augustans. The young Tennyson was a bohemian devotee of Byron. The young Arnold was a dandified gentleman, whose muse deserted him with his dandyism. It is hard to see how there could have been any nutriment for the development of Wordsworth's poetic sensibility along his first lines in a milieu that had suddenly abandoned Newton and cosmic automatism. Faced with an equally dramatic reversal of milieu, W. B. Yeats remade himself as a poet. Wordsworth instead settled down to edit his own work.

It was in this milieu that Tennyson was shaped as a poet. His predecessors, expecting to be made whole, had immersed themselves in a cosmic landscape bath certified by Newton. His contemporaries had begun to suspect that the bath was poisoned. His successors, such as Hardy, were sure it was.

When the eighteenth century plunged into the cosmic landscape it was consciously and scientifically seeking to reunite itself with primal energies from which it felt remote. The dim past, the age-old face of the earth, the primitive, the childlike, the pastoral were alike landscapes in which the sophisticated sought to merge themselves. But this merging was also, for civilized men, an act of symbolic suicide, a willful extinction of personality. So that there is over the eighteenth century both the light of natural reason and a cloud of intense melancholy, which led the French to call eighteenth-century England the "land of spleen and suicide." (Karl Polanyi's *The Great Transformation* traces the effect of the Newtonian and deist doctrines of cosmic harmony on the idea of a self-regulating market in land, labor, and capital. Quite unaware of the artistic parallels, Polanyi's work is yet of the greatest interest for aesthetics.) Similar ambivalence attends nineteenth-century England but for opposite reasons. It was the reawaking of the individual ego after the self-forgetful plunge into landscape that produced both the social optimism and the personal melancholy which Tennyson reflects. To have awakened in the lap of a trusted Nature that now seemed diseased and malignant brought on a new suicidal gloom which the century never resolved or dissipated.

If this were just a question of the "history of ideas" there would be little excuse for pursuing it in connection with Tennyson. But the interest in landscape had, from the time of Claude and Poussin in the seventeenth century, been closely associated with the new science. So that when landscape was no longer supported by Newtonian physics for Coleridge and Keats, it was reinforced by botany, biology, and geology for Tennyson, Ruskin, and the Pre-Raphaelites. Science remained as an important prop for interests which were primarily aesthetic. But unlike the later Hopkins and Cézanne, Tennyson and the Pre-Raphaelites were unable to achieve the intensity of contemplation which led to the metaphysical breakthrough of that later art. They remained picturesque. That is, they devoted themselves to the means of prolonging the moment of aesthetic emotion or of arrested experience, and failed to accept such moments as the thread through the labyrinth of cognition. They substituted immediate feeling and emotion for the process of retracing.

Tennyson began, and, for the most part, remained at the very interesting Constable level. Hopkins, pursuing "inscape," as Joyce did "epiphanies," broke through to the life which restored body and solidity to art in an existential vision that is truly metaphysical:

It is the forged feature finds me; it is the rehearsal
Of own, of abrupt self there so thrusts on, so throngs the ear.

But, thoroughly trained in the picturesque school, Tennyson never fails to compose his larger pictures with the utmost care for the texture and placing of objects (and words as objects), light, and shade. So that the enjoyment of his best poetry calls for the most patient and alert attention. The derision which was once shed indiscriminately on his "accuracy" and his flag-waving reflects a recent period when, for various reasons, it was thought that art could be taken at the gallop. We are not likely to repeat that mistake. But Tennyson now deserves to be reread and revalued with the aid of recovered reading ability. And it will be the Tennyson of the precise ear and eye who will provide the most unexpected and persistent enjoyment.

The gallery of pictures which is "The Palace of Art" is a recreation of the "worlds" discovered by painters like Wilson, Turner, Danby, and Martin. They are not just descriptions of scenes or paintings but immediate impressionistic evocations of situations in which it is the state of mind of the protagonist that is central, situations which as in Maturin's tales, present "those struggles of passion when the soul trembles on the verge of the unlawful and the unhallowed." So that each brief vista is an objective correlative for a moment of concentrated awareness:

> One seem'd all dark and red—a tract of sand,
> And someone pacing there alone,
> Who paced forever in a glimmering land
> Lit with a low large moon.

Tennyson is here practicing the art of compression which Mr. Eliot carried even further in such effects as

> Madame de Tornquist, in the dark room
> Shifting the candles, Fraulein von Kulp
> Who turned in the hall, one hand on the door.

This concentration, which requires the utmost precision of eye, of phrase, and rythm, Tennyson never ceased to exercise. "Mariana" is a triumph of the sustaining of such concentration; and "Oenone" is only less successful because of the admixture of the narrative flashback which Tennyson could never handle. But in "The Voyage of Maeldune" (1881) he solved the problem by only appearing to narrate. It is because of his habitual definition of a moment of awareness in terms of objective landscape that Tennyson found his strength in the short poem such as the sections of *In Memoriam* tend to be. And his longer poems are always risky expansions of these moments, as is plain in the *Idylls of the King*. But the short tale in verse, of which Crabbe was the master Tennyson admired, never ceased to tempt him.

It is in this matter of the landscape or episode which defines and concentrates an intense experience, that Tennyson both inspired and surpassed Rossetti, Morris, and the Pre-Raphaelites. Browning, too, was, in a more dramatic mode, concerned with rendering the intense "immortal moment" which unified a lifetime of awareness. And Proust, the student and admirer of Ruskin, also lavished his art on the expansion of the "immortal moment." Staying close to the lyric mode in which he was so great a technician, Tennyson impresses many today as more successful because less tempted merely to decorate and comment on an experience which commonly eludes us in Browning and the Pre-Raphaelites when they fail to "force the moment to its crisis." At his frequent best he never departs from the critical insights that Hallam arrived at concerning rhetoric, Wordsworth, and the slackening effect of intellectual comment.

But the best of Wordsworth is also landscape in the picturesque mode, and "The Solitary Reaper" is not unrelated in theme and technique to "La Figlia che Piange." Modern criticism with its tools ready for the anatomy of verbal wit and dramatic ambiguities will have to go to school to the painters again before it can do justice to the variety and skill of conscious landscape art in prose and poetry after Thomson. Modern verbal criticism finds itself equally mute before Dante's visual art and that of Spenser. Spenser was, inevitably, a master of the picturesque poets from Thomson to Tennyson. Music would appear to be a resource of the poet seeking visual and plastic effects with words—much more so than in the case of the kinesthetic and dialectical verbal drama of a Donne or Hopkins. For subtleties and ambivalence of mood are managed less by tropes than impressionistic devices. "She was a phantom of delight" is, for example, a triptych of condensed impressions which rival a cinematic rapidity and nuance. And so it is with the best of the Romantics. Looked at with the camera eye "The Ancient Mariner" or "Resolution and Independence" seem to be immediately contemporary with ourselves. The Romantics had nothing to learn from cinema. It is rather cinema that can learn from them.

If anybody ever had and consciously cultivated a movie-camera eye it was Tennyson. But if one asks what it was of landscape art that the Romantics and the Victorians did not achieve, it must be replied, *le paysage intérieur* which had to wait for Baudelaire, Laforgue, and Rimbaud. It was this discovery that gave the later poets and painters alike, the power to be much more subjective and also more objective than the Romantics. For all their skill in discovering and manipulating external-nature situations by which to render states of mind, the Romantics remained tied to the object when they wished only to present it as a point from which to leap to another kind of vision. So they repeatedly bog down in reflection just at the moment when they are ready to soar. They could not discover the technique of flight. It would be interesting to inquire how far the cessation of the poetic activity of Wordsworth and Coleridge was connected with this technical frustration. By means of the interior landscape, however, Baudelaire could not only range across the entire spectrum of the inner life, he could transform the sordidness and evil of an industrial metropolis into a flower. With this technique he was able to accept the city as his central "myth," and see it as the enlarged shape of a man, just as Flaubert did in *The Sentimental Education,* Joyce in *Ulysses,* and Mr. Eliot in *The Waste Land.* (It is noteworthy that the English novel also preceded English poetry in the management of the city as "myth." Dickens was the first to make London a character or a person. And James and Conrad in their different modes preceded Joyce and Eliot in assimilating the urban to the stuff of poesy.) Moreover, the technique of inner landscape not only permits the use of any and every kind of experience and object, it insures a much higher degree of control over the effect; because the arrangement of the landscape is the formula of the emotion and can be repeatedly adjusted until the formula and the effect are in precise accord. Whereas the romantic poet and painter was much more dependent on the caprices of external nature, sketching as Ruskin says of Turner, "the almost instantaneous record of an *effect* of colour or atmosphere taken strictly from Nature. . . ." The Romantic and picturesque artists had to take advantage of accidents. After Baudelaire there is no need for such accidents. The picturesque artists saw the wider range of experience that could be managed by discontinuity and planned irregularity, but they kept to the picturelike single perspective. The interior landscape, however, moves naturally towards the principle of multiple perspectives as in the first two lines of *The Waste Land,* where the Christian Chaucer, Sir James Frazer, and Jessie Weston are simultaneously present. This is "cubist perspective" which renders, at once, a diversity of views with the spectator always in the center of the picture, whereas in picturesque art the spectator is always outside. The cubist perspective of interior landscape typically permits an immediacy, a variety and solidity of experience denied to the picturesque and to Tennyson.

But the Romantics and Victorians, lacking this comprehensive and elastic technique, were compelled to remain "nature" poets whether they liked it or not. They were certainly conscious of having new "art-emotions," but they were unable to achieve art-conditions for them and so continued to use external nature as a vehicle for art-emotions. It was the science of their time that taught them to like nature, just as it is the science of our time that has freed us from their particular kind of bondage to external nature. For it is, perhaps, a mistake to regard nature as the subject matter of the Romantics. They wanted not just to see it but to see through it; and failing that they made it an objective correlative for states of mind that are independent of it.

The Aesthetic Moment in Landscape Poetry

⊂⊃ ⊂⊃ ⊂⊃ ⊂⊃ ⊂⊃

MY SUBJECT, the indispensability of landscape as a technique for managing the aesthetic moment in poetry, grows out of my recent study of Tennyson and landscape. In that essay, I indicated some of the Leibnitzian and Newtonian influences in bringing about the eighteenth-century concern with psychology and landscape and concluded that the central difference between romantic or picturesque poetry and modern symbolist poetry was that whereas the landscape poets from Thomson to Tennyson were engaged in manipulating an external environment as a means of evoking art emotion, after Poe, Baudelaire, and Rimbaud, the symbolists turned to the manipulation of an interior landscape, a *paysage intérieur,* as the means of controlling art emotion or of exploring the aesthetic moment. This amounted to a considerable revolution— from natural conditions for art emotion to art conditions for art emotion. I shall try to clarify this proposition.

In his essay "On Going Forth by Day," Frank Budgen tried to explain Joyce's later techniques in the *Wake* as follows.

> The worst of writing about *Finnegans Wake* is that all our words are wrong. Story is wrong, of course, for a story is one thing happening after another along a one-way time street, coming from and going to some place, whereas *Finnegans Wake* is going

nowhere in all directions on an every-way roundabout with infiltrations from above and below. On every page Joyce insists upon this all-time dream-time by every device of suggestion and allusion and by a continual modification and cancellation of all-time words.

Mr. Budgen's excellence as a Joyce critic is closely associated with his knowledge as a painter. As early as *Ulysses* he saw that Joyce's manipulation of language depended typically on a plastic feeling for words as things, which in juxtaposition released new entities. With Joyce, words syntactically ordered to statement yielded to words as pantomime, as ballet, and especially as static landscape. Mallarmé, in his *Coup de dés,* had preceded Joyce in establishing the printed page as a symbolist landscape able to evoke the most ephemeral incident and, simultaneously, the most remote cycles of time. For Mallarmé, as for Joyce, the minutest, as well as the most esoteric, features of the alphabet itself were charged with dramatic significance, so that he used the word and the printed page as do the Chinese, for whom landscape painting is a branch of writing.[1]

Mallarmé had been led to this technique by an aesthetic analysis of the modern newspaper, with its static inclusiveness of the entire community of men. But the newspaper, not so much a cross section as a vivisection of human interests, stands, as I have shown elsewhere, behind *Ulysses,* with its dateline Thursday, June 16, 1904. The shape of *Ulysses* is that of the city presented as the organic landscape of the human body. The shape of the *Wake* is the same, save that the landscape of the human mind and body is presented more intimately and under a much greater diversity of forms, landscape taking over even the functions of "character." What Mallarmé and Joyce exploit in landscape technique is its power of rendering an inclusive consciousness in a single instant of perception. Not even Rimbaud's *Illuminations* had pushed this technique as far as they did. And for that reason it is well to begin with them and to proceed backward, as in detective fiction, to reconstruct the motives and the steps which led to what is popularly regarded as a crime against art, taste, and common sense.[2] If we can establish what happened, it is often unnecessary to explain why it happened. Some who are alarmed by the features of discontinuity in modern art might be surprised to discover, for example, that those who re-established discontinuity as an artistic principle in the eighteenth century did so in the name of democracy. The art of Fielding, like that of Scott and Dickens, is strictly "picturesque" in achieving social inclusiveness by means of discontinuous perspectives. Social panoramas, if they are to include more than one level of society, must exploit techniques of juxtaposition or discontinuity. So that what the Elizabethan drama achieved by the device of the double plot, the novel and poetry managed to do by taking over the methods of the landscape painters. Beginning with Thomson's *Seasons* the poets appropriated landscape as a means of evoking and defining states of mind. And in so doing they were conscious of reverting to some features of the Spenserian picturesque which Donne and the metaphysicals had tended to discredit. The eighteenth-century picturesque poets and artists were not only conscious of affinities with Spenserian landscape but also, as is well known, of the congeniality of many aspects of Gothic art. Perhaps too much stress has been placed on the view of the Gothic revival as an escape from the drabness of life in the new industrial towns. Certainly this view takes no account of the basic technical resemblance between the Gothic and the new picturesque art. For Gothic architecture, sculpture, and painting achieved their peculiar encyclopedic inclusiveness by means of the same discontinuous juxtapositions that were reintroduced in the later eighteenth century. And for Ruskin, Gothic was exciting and relevant, not as an archaic form, but as a model for revolutionary activity in art and society.

There is a passage in *Modern Painters* which brings all these matters to a focus, and it is hard not to suppose that in 1874 Arthur Rimbaud did not study it very carefully before beginning his last work, the *Illuminations:*

A fine grotesque is the expression, in a moment, by a series of symbols thrown together in bold and fearless connection, of truths which it would have taken a long time to express in any verbal way, and of which the connection is left for the beholder to work out for himself; the gaps, left or overleaped by the haste of the imagination, forming the grotesque character.[3]

What follows not only provides a description of Rimbaud's procedure in his landscapes but also affords an extraordinary anticipation of the salient techniques of *Ulysses* and the *Wake:*

> . . . the grotesque . . . springing as it does from any tendency to playfulness in minds highly comprehensive of truth; and being also one of the readiest ways in which such satire or wit as may be possessed by men of any inferior rank of mind can be for perpetuity expressed . . . it is an infinite good to mankind when there is full acceptance of the grotesque, slightly sketched or expressed; and, if field for such expression be frankly granted, an enormous mass of intellectual power is turned to everlasting use, which, in this present century of ours, evaporates in street gibing or vain revelling; all the good wit and satire expiring in daily talk (like foam in wine,) which in the thirteenth and fourteenth centuries had a permitted and useful expression in the arts of sculpture and illumination, like foam fixed in chalcedony. It is with a view . . . to the reopening of this great field of human intelligence, long entirely closed, that I am striving to introduce Gothic architecture into daily domestic use; and to revive the art of illumination, properly so-called, not the art of miniature-painting in books, or on vellum, which has been ridiculously confused with it; but of making writing, simple writing, beautiful to the eye, by investing it with the great chord of perfect colour, blue, purple, scarlet, white, and gold, and in that chord of colour, permitting the continual play of the fancy of the writer in every species of grotesque imagination, carefully excluding shadow; the distinctive difference between illumination and painting proper, being, that illumination admits *no* shadows, but only gradations of pure colour . . . the abstract, shadeless hues . . . are eminently fitted for grotesque thought.[4]

On the one hand, Ruskin saw in this kind of abrupt symbolic juxtaposition the means to great compression, and on the other the extreme of democratic inclusiveness of experience and taste. Similarly, there is on one hand Mr. Eliot's oft-expressed preference for an illiterate audience, and on the other hand, Joyce's habit of ransacking the pulps and comic books for the materials of his art. Earlier than Mr. Eliot or Joyce, Mallarmé, pointing to the intimate connection between the ultimate artist and nature, insisted that fragments of the great work were constantly being written by the many who are as Nature to the hero-artist.[5]

Whether Rimbaud got his idea for *Illuminations* from Ruskin or not, there is no question but that the French had for several decades recognized the priority and pre-eminence of English picturesque techniques in paint and letters. And Rimbaud spent the year 1874 in London looking at pictures and reading in the British Museum. Moreover, the specific technical advance made in *Illuminations* is precisely the one recommended by Ruskin in this passage. It consists in a shift from exterior to interior landscape. Coleridge had arrived at the perception of interior landscape in the *Ancient Mariner* and then had faltered. Tennyson approached it in *Mariana* (admired and translated by Mallarmé) and then receded. Rimbaud was the first to occupy and to exploit the new ground discovered by Coleridge, Tennyson, and Ruskin.

The passage from Ruskin began with a reference to the *moment* in which the grotesque achieved its revelation of a complex consciousness. The doctrine of the aesthetic "moment" has a continuous history from the eighteenth century to the present, and a brief sketch of its development may serve to illuminate and unify a considerable diversity of practice in landscape painting and picturesque poetry. Often noted from Montaigne onward is the growing interest in the anatomy of states of mind which in Giambattista Vico reached the point of stress on the importance of reconstructing by vivisection the inner history of one's own mind. A century separates Vico's *Autobiography* and Wordsworth's *Prelude,* but they are products of the same impulse. Another century, and Joyce's *Portrait* carries the same enterprise a stage further. Vico generalized the process as a means of reconstructing the stages of human culture by the vivisection and contemplation of language itself.

It was a Jesuit contemporary of Vico's, Père de Caussade (1675–1751), who was, perhaps, the first to insist on the doctrine of the moment in his famous phrase "The Sacrament of the Present Moment." At least he is regarded today by masters of ascetical theology as having been the first to have done so.[6] However, the practitioners of Zen Buddhism have long had a doctrine of this sort concerning the momentary and unexpected transport from the realm of time to eternity,[7] which has played an important role in the poetry of Mr. Eliot. A Zen moment is reputed to present us in an instant of time with a landscape strange, yet familiar, showing us the original face of our being, as it were, in the landscape of our birthplace.[8] It is not likely that the Buddhist doctrine had any direct European influence before Schopenhauer. But in Schopenhauer it is stated in an essay which was a favorite with the symbolist poets: "On the comparative place of interest and beauty in works of art." [9] Art emotion is intellectual emotion, says Schopenhauer: "Thus we perceive that beauty is always an affair of *knowledge,* and that it appeals to the *knowing subject,* and not to the *will;* nay, it is a fact that the apprehension of beauty on the part of the subject involves a complete suppression of the will." Improper art arouses some appetite or other. It arouses *interest.* Accordingly Schopenhauer argues that the only form for true art is landscape.

> Neither does the quality of interest often attach to masterpieces of descriptive poetry. Father Homer lays the world and humanity before us in its true nature, but he takes no trouble to attract our sympathy by a complexity of circumstance, or to surprise us by unexpected entanglements. His pace is lingering; he stops at every scene; he puts one picture after another tranquilly before us, elaborating it with care. We experience no passionate emotion in reading him; our demeanour is one of pure perceptive intelligence. . . . This is all still more true of Dante, whose work is not, in the proper sense of the word, an epic, but a descriptive poem. The same thing may be said of the four immortal romances: *Don Quixote, Tristram Shandy, La Nouvelle Heloïse,* and *Wilhelm Meister.* To arouse our interest is by no means the chief aim of these works; in *Tristram Shandy* the hero, even at the end of the book, is only eight years of age.

It was partly to Schopenhauer that the symbolists owed their peculiar insistence on the aesthetic experience as an arrested moment, a moment in and out of time, of intellectual emotion for which in their poems they sought the art formula by retracing the stages of apprehension which led to this moment.

But from the mention of *Tristram Shandy* it is also plain that Schopenhauer recognized in Sterne not only a great landscape artist but also a master analyst of the arrested moment of aesthetic consciousness. Sterne's playful dalliance with such moments needs no illustration. He vivisected them and retraced them until his work was freed from that sort of improper interest which Schopenhauer and the symbolists deplored. To take a widely divergent example, the journals of John Wesley show him to have had a detached scientific interest in the moment of religious conversion. Even when inducing this moment from the pulpit in thousands of feverish enthusiasts, he stood calmly noting the phenomena with the eye of an experimentalist.[10] The poetry of Wordsworth, however, is in itself a sufficient testimony to the eighteenth-century obsession with the privileged moment of heightened awareness presented to the inward eye as a landscape. In such moments we see into the life of things, yet are detached from them. Wordsworth's attitude to these moments also displays the aloof temper of the experimentalist, but by symbolist standards he was greatly given to diffusing and dissipating the moment by rhetorical comments. And it was the conscious effort of Keats, Tennyson, and the pre-Raphaelites to render the moment more immediately. However, it is with Rossetti's translation of Dante's *Vita Nuova* that the study of the aesthetic moment takes on the character which it presents in the work of Pater, Hopkins, Yeats, Pound, Joyce, and Eliot.

Analyzing the means and effects of Giorgione, Pater says:

> The sudden act, the rapid transition of thought, the passing expression—this he arrests. . . . Now it is part of the ideality of the highest sort of dramatic poetry, that it presents us with a kind of profoundly significant and animated instants, a mere gesture, a look, a simile, perhaps—some brief and whole concrete moment—into which, however, all the motives, all the interests and effects of a long history, have condensed themselves, and which seem to absorb past and future in an intense consciousness of the present. Such ideal instants the school of Giorgione se-

lects, with its admirable tact, from that feverish, tumultuously coloured world of the old citizens of Venice—exquisite pauses in time, in which arrested thus, we seem to be spectators of all the fulness of existence, and which are like some consummate extract or quintessence of life.[11]

If there were time, it would be interesting to illustrate how the Beatrician moment as understood by Rossetti and Pater is modified in Browning's doctrine of the "immortal moment." Browning abandons the cognitive and metaphysical side of the experience in favor of its importance as a moment of ethical choice and assertion. Tennyson at his lyric best remains faithful to the purely aesthetic clairvoyance of the moment as a cognitive fact. Of course, Tennyson and Rossetti alike were consciously in debt in this matter to Keats's art and doctrine of negative capability.[12]

I will venture to state what appears as a radical distinction between the moment in the pre-Raphaelites and Yeats, on one hand, and in Pound, Joyce, and Eliot, on the other. Because the aesthetic moment was recognized as an experience of arrest and detachment, the pre-Raphaelites sought to prolong it in the work of art by means of dreamy somnambulist rhythms and motifs. Their atmosphere of languorous romantic melancholy was the accidental result.[13] Essentially they were aiming at intensity and the hard gem-like flame. And the work of the early and later Yeats divides according to the means adopted rather than the end envisaged. Hopkins was, perhaps, the only pre-Raphaelite who reached an approximate solution of the problem before 1900 by using both landscape and the dramatic voice in unison. But from the point of view of Joyce, Pound, and Eliot this could only be a partial solution. For them the aesthetic moment was, like the band of the spectrum, an affair of zoning. As Mallarmé stated the matter: "The poetic act consists in seeing suddenly that an idea fractions itself into a number of motifs equal in value, and in grouping them; they rhyme." [14] In other words, Mallarmé discovered that the aesthetic moment of arrested cognition can be split up into numerous fractions which can be orchestrated in many discontinuous ways. Contemporary with

Mallarmé, Theodor Lipps was elaborating the same perception about the laws of the visual and auditory imagination. And the doctrines of Lipps were aired in London before 1914 by T. E. Hulme. The pre-Raphaelites never arrived at this power of aesthetic fission which established suggestion in place of statement and gave rise to the symbolist landscapes of Joyce, Pound, and Eliot. But for the pre-Raphaelites the moment resisted analysis, and they fell back on subject matter as a means to achieve intensity. They tended to select for presentation special moments in the lives of people colorful in history or romance—moments invested with a lifetime of significance, and the result too commonly was the forcible feeble of "the Gypsy's Warning."

Rossetti's Dante studies were not nearly so intense as those of Joyce, Pound, and Eliot.[15] He did not penetrate the secret of the *dolce stil nuovo* as based on the learning process itself. Helped by Rimbaud and Mallarmé, Joyce arrived quickly at the formula of the aesthetic moment and its attendant landscape as consisting in a retracing of the stages of ordinary apprehension. The poetic process he discovered and states in *Stephen Hero* is the experience of ordinary cognition, but it is that labyrinth reversed, retraced, and hence epiphanized.[16] The moment of arrested cognition achieves at once its stasis and epiphany as a result of the reconstruction of the stages of ordinary apprehension. And every moment of cognition is thus a Beatrician moment when rendered lucid by a retracing of its labyrinth. Dante implies all this in the Beatrician moment of the *Vita Nuova,* but the pre-Raphaelites had accepted it at the relatively banal level of psychological impressionism. The Beatrician, or sacramental, moment when analyzed as a spectrum band yields the entire zoning of the hierarchized scenes and landscapes of the *Commedia,* as Charles Williams has shown in *The Figure of Beatrice.* As the eighteenth century recovered some of the techniques of the Middle Ages through their own development of the picturesque, so Joyce, Pound, and Eliot recovered the secret of the *dolce stil nuovo* through the prismatically arranged landscapes of Rimbaud and Mallarmé. And this secret consists in nothing less than a fusion of the learning and the creative processes in the analysis and reconstruction of the aesthetic moment of arrested awareness.

This peculiar fusion of the cognitive and the creative by an act of retracing the stages of apprehension was arrived at by Joyce as a result of the prior discovery for the technique of fission of the moment of aesthetic awareness. And landscape plays an indispensable role in every stage of both fission and fusion. In art as in physics fission preceded fusion.

NOTES

1 A. C. Moorhouse, *Writing and the Alphabet*, London, 1946, p. 59.

2 T. E. Hulme on space-thinking in *Speculations* will lead the student back through Hartmann and Lipps on these questions. Lipps is of special importance for an understanding of Joyce, Pound, and Eliot: "The simple clang represents to a certain extent all music. The clang is a rhythmical system built up on a fundamental rhythm. This fundamental rhythm is more or less richly differentiated in the rhythm of the single tones." Theodor Lipps, *Psychological Studies*, 2d ed., tr. by H. C. Sanborn, Baltimore, 1926, p. 223. This should be considered in relation to Mallarmé's text given later in this paper. It is exactly what Pound meant by "Imagism": "An 'Image' is that which presents an intellectual and emotional complex in an instant of time. . . . It is the presentation of such a complex instantaneously that gives us that sense of sudden liberation; that sense of freedom from time limits and space limits; that sense of sudden growth, which we experience in the presence of the greatest works of art." *Pavannes and Divisions*, New York, 1918, p. 96.

3 Everyman Ed., III, 91.

4 *Ibid.*, p. 96.

5 Robert Cohn, *Mallarmé's Un Coup de dés: an Exegesis*, New Haven, 1949, p. 79.

6 Jean Pierre de Caussade, S.J., *On Prayer*, tr. by Algar Thorold, introd. by Don John Chapman, London, 1949, p. xix.

7 D. T. Suzuki, *Introduction to Zen Buddhism*, New York, n.d., p. 47.

8 Clearly related to the moment of Zen Buddhism are the Japanese Noh plays, each of which embodies a primary human relation or emotion, a single intense emotion elevated by intensity and purity of treatment. The direct influence of this drama on Yeats and Pound is well known.

9 Schopenhauer, *Complete Essays*, tr. by T. Bailey Saunders, New York, 1942.

10 R. Knox, *Enthusiasm*, London, 1950, p. 452.

11 "The School of Giorgione," *Fortnightly Review*, XXVIII (1877), 535–536.

12 It is easy to see the connection of this doctrine with the art of Proust and Virginia Woolf. Clive Bell shows why Frith's "Derby Day" has no claim to be art in Pater's sense (*Art*, London, 19, pp. 16–18). But an understanding of the art of Joyce, Pound, Eliot, and Wyndham Lewis depends on seeing why they modified Pater's doctrine and depreciated the aims of Proust and Woolf.

13 D. S. McColl's *Nineteenth Century Art* (Glasgow, 1902) opens with an important statement on landscape, science, and art. His analysis of Burne-Jones (pp. 142ff.) and "the romantic world that had been gathering vision in literature and that spilled over into painting with Rossetti and Millais" is relevant to the present discussion.

14 *Oeuvres complètes*, Paris, 1945, p. 365.

15 Apart from Pound's *Spirit of Romance* (London, 1912) and Mr. Eliot's several essays on Dante, I know only of Charles Williams' *The Figure of Beatrice* (London, 1943) where technical study is given to Dante's way of managing the moment in terms of landscape.

16 See my "Joyce, Aquinas, and the Poetic Process," *Renascence, Fall*, 1951.

On Pope's *Dunciad*

⊂⊋ ⊂⊋ ⊂⊋ ⊂⊋ ⊂⊋

Pope's Dunciad *indicts the printed book as the agent of a primitivistic and Romantic revival. Sheer visual quantity evokes the magical resonance of the tribal horde. The box office looms as a return to the echo chamber of bardic incantation.*

In 1683–84 there appeared in London by Joseph Moxon, *Mechanick Exercises on the Whole Art of Printing*. The editors point out (p. vii) that "it put in writing a knowledge that was wholly traditional," and that Moxon's book "was by forty years the earliest manual of printing in any language." Like Gibbon in his retrospect of Rome, Moxon seems to have been animated by a sense of print as having reached a terminus. A similar sentiment inspires *The Tale of a Tub* and *The Battle of the Books* by Dean Swift. But it is to *The Dunciad* that we must turn for the epic of the printed word and its benefits to mankind. For here is the explicit study of plunging of the human mind into the sludge of an unconscious engendered by the book. It has been obscured to posterity, in keeping with the prophecy at the end of Book IV, just why literature should be charged with stupefying mankind, and mesmerically ushering the polite world back into primitivism, the Africa within, and above all, the unconscious. The simple key to this operation is that which we have had in hand throughout this book—the increasing separation

169

of the visual faculty from the interplay with the other senses leads to the rejection from consciousness of most of our experience, and the consequent hypertrophy of the unconscious. This ever-enlarging domain Pope calls the world "of Chaos and old Night." It is the tribal, non-literate world celebrated by Mircea Eliade in *The Sacred and the Profane*.

Martinus Scriblerus in his notes to *The Dunciad* reflects on how much more difficult it is to write an epic about the numerous scribblers and industrious hacks of the press than about a Charlemagne, a Brute, or a Godfrey. He then mentions the need for a satirist "to dissuade the dull and punish the wicked," and looks at the general situation that has brought on the crisis:

> We shall next declare the occasion and the cause which moved our Poet to this particular work. He lived in those days when (after providence had permitted the Invention of Printing as a scourge for the Sins of the learned) Paper also became so cheap, and printers so numerous, that a deluge of authors cover'd the land: Whereby not only the peace of the honest unwriting subject was daily molested, but unmerciful demands were made of his applause, yea of his money, by such as would neither earn the one, or deserve the other; At the same time, the Liberty of the Press was so unlimited, that it grew dangerous to refuse them either: For they would forthwith publish slanders unpunish'd, the authors being anonymous; nay the immediate publishers thereof lay sculking under the wings of an Act of Parliament, assuredly intended for better purposes.[1]

Next he turns (p. 50) from the general economic causes to the private moral motivation of authors inspired by "Dulness and Poverty; the one born with them, the other contracted by neglect of their proper talents. . . ." In a word, the attack is on applied knowledge as it manifests itself in "Industry" and "Plodding." For authors inspired by self-opinion and the craving for self-expression are driven into "setting up this sad and sorry merchandise."

By means of the agglomerate action of many such victims of applied knowledge—that is, self-opinionated authors endowed with Industry and Plodding—there is now the restoration of the reign of

Chaos and old Night and the removal of the imperial seat of Dulness their daughter from the City to the Polite world. As the book market expands, the division between intellect and commerce ends. The book trade takes over the functions of wit and spirit and government.

That is the meaning of the opening lines of the first editions of the poem:

> Books and the man I sing, the first who brings
> The Smithfield Muses to the ears of Kings.

It seemed quite unnatural to the "polite world" of the time that decision-making and kingly rule should be accessible to popular authors. We no longer consider it odd or revolting to be ruled by people for whom the book of the month might appear quite respectable fare. Smithfield, where Bartholomew Fair was kept, was still a place for book-peddling. But in later editions Pope changed the opening:

> The mighty Mother, and her Son, who brings
> The Smithfield Muses to the ear of Kings.

He has encountered the public, the collective unconscious, and dubbed it "the mighty Mother," in accordance with the occultism of his time. It is Joyce's "Lead kindly Fowl" (foule, owl, crowd), which we have seen earlier.

As the book market enlarged and the gathering and reporting of news improved, the nature of authorship and public underwent the great changes that we accept as normal today. The book had retained from manuscript times some of its private and conversational character, as Leibnitz indicated in his evaluation. But the book was beginning to be merged in the newspaper, as the work of Addison and Steele reminds us. Improved printing technology carried this process all the way by the end of the eighteenth century and the arrival of the steam press.

Yet Dudek in *Literature and the Press* (p. 46) considers that even after steam power had been applied to printing:

English newspapers in the first quarter of the century, however, were by no means designed to appeal to the whole population. By modern standards they would be considered too dull to interest more than a small minority of serious readers. . . . Early nineteenth century newspapers were run largely for the genteel. Their style was stiff and formal, ranging between Addisonian gracefulness and Johnsonian elevation. The contents consisted of small advertisements, of local affairs and national politics, especially of commercial news and long transcriptions of parliamentary reports . . . the best current literature was noticed in the newspapers. . . . "In those days," Charles Lamb recalled, "every morning paper, as an essential retainer to its establishment, kept an author, who was bound to furnish daily a quantum of witty paragraphs. . . ." And since the divorce between the language of journalism (journalese) and the literary use of language had not yet been brought about, we find in the eighteenth and early nineteenth century that some of the principal men of letters contributed to the newspapers or made a living by writing.

But Pope peopled his *Dunciad* with these very figures, for his perceptions and criticisms were not personal or based on a private point of view. Rather he was concerned with a total change. It is significant that this change is not specified until the fourth book of *The Dunciad,* which came out in 1742. It is after introducing the famous classics master, Dr. Busby of Westminster school, that we hear the ancient and especially Ciceronian theme concerning the excellence of man (IV, 11. 147–50):

> The pale Boy-Senator yet tingling stands,
> And holds his breeches close with both his hands.
>   Then thus. "Since Man from beast by Words is known,
> Words are Man's province, Words we teach alone."

Earlier * we had noted the meaning of this theme for Cicero who regarded eloquence as an inclusive wisdom harmonizing our faculties, unifying all knowledge. Pope is here quite explicit in citing the

* Cf pp. 95–104 of *The Gutenberg Galaxy,* Toronto, 1962. The reference notes the effect of the Ciceronian concepts of rhetorical eloquence and wisdom on the medieval schoolmen. [Ed. note]

destruction of this unity as deriving from word specialism and denudation. The theme of the denudation of consciousness we have followed continuously throughout the Renaissance. It is also the theme of Pope's *Dunciad*. The Boy-Senator continues:

> When Reason doubtful, like the Samian letter,
> Points him two ways, the narrower is the better.
> Plac'd at the door of Learning, youth to guide,
> We never suffer it to stand too wide.
> To ask, to guess, to know, as they commence,
> As Fancy opens the quick springs of Sense,
> We ply the Memory, we load the brain,
> Bind rebel Wit, and double chain on chain,
> Confine the thought, to exercise the breath;
> And keep them in the pale of Words till death.
> Whate'er the talents, or howe'er design'd,
> We hang one jingling padlock on the mind:
> A Poet the first day, he dips his quill;
> And what the last? a very Poet still.
> Pity! the charm works only in our wall,
> Lost, lost too soon in yonder House or Hall.

Pope has not received his due as a serious analyst of the intellectual *malaise* of Europe. He continues Shakespeare's argument in *Lear* and Donne's in the *Anatomy of the World:*

> 'Tis all in pieces, all coherence gone,
> All just supply and all relation.

It is the division of sense and the separation of words from their functions that Pope decries exactly as does Shakespeare in *King Lear*. Art and science had been separated as visual quantification and homogenization penetrated to every domain and the mechanization of language and literature proceeded:

> Beneath her foot-stool *Science* groans in Chains,
> And Wit dreads Exile, Penalties and Pains.
> There foam'd rebellious *Logic* gagg'd and bound,
> There, stript fair *Rhet'ric* languish'd on the ground;[2]

*The new collective unconscious Pope saw as the accumulating
backwash of private self-expression.*

POPE HAD A very simple scheme for his first three books. Book I
deals with authors, their egotism and desire for self-expression and
eternal fame. Book II turns to the booksellers who provide the con-
duits to swell the tides of public confession. Book III concerns the
collective unconscious, the growing backwash from the tidal wave
of self-expression. It is Pope's simple theme that the fogs of Dulness
and new tribalism are fed by the printing press. Wit, the quick interplay among our senses and faculties, is thus steadily anesthetized
by the encroaching unconscious. Anybody who tried to get Pope's
meaning by considering the content of the writers he presents would
miss the needed clues. Pope is offering a formal causality, not an
efficient causality, as an explanation of the metamorphosis from
within. The entire matter is thus to be found in a single couplet (I,
11. 89–90):

> Now night descending, the proud scene was o'er,
> But liv'd, in Settle's numbers, one day more.

Print, with its uniformity, repeatability, and limitless extent,
does give reincarnate life and fame to anything at all. The kind of
limp life so conferred by dull heads upon dull themes formalis-
tically penetrates all existence. Since readers are as vain as authors,
they crave to view their own conglomerate visage and, therefore,
demand the dullest wits to exert themselves in ever greater degree
as the collective audience increases. The "human interest" newspaper is the ultimate mode of this collective dynamic:

> Now May'rs and Shrieves all hush'd and satiate lay,
> Yet eat, in dreams, the custard of the day;
> While pensive Poets painful vigils keep,
> Sleepless themselves to give their readers sleep.[3]

Of course, Pope does not mean that the readers will be bored by the products of sleepless poets or news writers. Quite the contrary. They will be thrilled, as by seeing their own image in the press. The readers' sleep is of the spirit. In their wits they are not pained but impaired.

Pope is telling the English world what Cervantes had told the Spanish world and Rabelais the French world concerning print. It is a delirium. It is a transforming and metamorphosing drug that has the power of imposing its assumptions upon every level of consciousness. But for us in the 1960s, print has much of the quaint receding character of the movie and the railway train. In recognizing its hidden powers at this late date we can learn to stress the positive virtues of print but we can gain insight into the much more potent and recent forms of radio and television also.

In his analysis of books, authors, and markets, Pope, like Harold Innis in *The Bias of Communication,* assumes that the entire operation of print in our lives is not only unconscious but that for this very reason it immeasurably enlarges the domain of the unconscious. Pope placed an owl at the beginning of *The Dunciad,* and Innis entitled the opening chapter of *The Bias of Communication* "Minerva's Owl"; "Minerva's Owl begins its flight only in the gathering dusk. . . ."

Aubrey Williams has a fine treatment [4] of the second *Dunciad* of 1729 in which he quotes Pope's own words to Swift:

> The Dunciad is going to be printed in all pomp. . . . It will be attended with *Proeme, Prolegomena, Testimonia Scriptorum, Index Authorum,* and Notes *Variorum.* As to the latter, I desire you to read over the text, and make a few in any way you like best, whether dry raillery, upon the style and way of commenting of trivial critics; or humorous, upon the authors in the poem, or historical, of persons, places, times; or explanatory; or collecting the parallel passages of the ancients.

Instead, that is, of a mere individual book attack on Dulness, Pope has provided a collective newspaper format and much "human interest" for the poem. He can thus render the plodding industry of

Baconian applied knowledge and group toil with a dramatic quality that renders, yet irradiates, the very Dulness he decries. Williams points out (p. 60) that the reason why "the new material attached to the poem has never been adequately defined is due, I think, to the assumptions most critics and editors have made: that the notes are to be taken at the level of history, and that their main purpose is to continue the personal satire in a prose commentary."

The last book of The Dunciad *proclaims the metamorphic power of mechanically applied knowledge as a stupendous parody of the Eucharist.*

THE ENTIRE FOURTH book of *The Dunciad* has to do with the theme of *The Gutenberg Galaxy,* the translation or reduction of diverse modes into a single mode of homogenized things. Right off (ll. 44–5), this theme is rendered in terms of the new Italian opera.

> When lo' a Harlot form soft sliding by,
> With mincing step, small voice, and languid eye;

In the new chromatics, Pope finds (ll. 57–60) the all-reducing and homogenizing power that the book exercises on the human spirit:

> One Trill shall harmonize joy, grief, and rage,
> Wake the dull Church, and lull the ranting Stage;
> To the same notes thy sons shall hum, or snore,
> And all thy yawning daughters cry, *encore.*

Reduction and metamorphosis by homogenization and fragmentation are the persistent themes of the fourth book (ll. 453–6):

> O! would the Sons of Men once think their Eyes
> And Reason giv'n them but to study *Flies!*
> See Nature in some partial narrow shape,
> And let the Author of the Whole escape:

But these were the means by which, as Yeats tells us:

> Locke sank into a swoon;
> The Garden died;
> God took the spinning jenny
> Out of his side.

The popular mesmerism achieved by uniformity and repeatability, taught men the miracles of the division of labor and the creation of world markets. It is these miracles that Pope anticipates in *The Dunciad,* for their transforming power had long affected the mind. The mind now afflicted with the desire and power to climb by sheer sequential additive toil:

> Why all your Toils? Your Sons have learn'd to sing.
> How quick Ambition hastes to ridicule!
> The Sire is made a Peer, the Son a Fool.

Then follows a decisive passage of explicit comment (ll. 549–57) on the Gutenberg miracles of applied knowledge and human transformation:

> On some, a Priest succinct in amice white
> Attends; all flesh is nothing in his sight!
> Beeves, at his touch, at once to jelly turn,
> And the huge Boar is shrunk into an Urn:
> The board with specious miracles he loads,
> Turns Hares to Larks, and Pigeons into Toads.
> Another (for in all what one can shine?)
> Explains the *Seve and Verdeur* of the Vine.
> What cannot copious Sacrifice attone?

Pope deliberately makes the miracles of applied knowledge a parody of the Eucharist. It is the same transforming and reducing power of applied knowledge which has confounded and confused all the arts and sciences, for, says Pope, the new *translatio studii* or transmission of studies and disciplines by the printed book has not been so much a transmission as a complete transformation of the disciplines and of the human mind as well. Studies have been translated exactly as was Bottom the Weaver.

How closely Pope's progress of Dulness over the earth conforms to the concept of *translatio studii* can be seen easily if lines 65–112 of Dunciad III are compared to this statement of the historic theme by an English humanist of the fourteenth century, Richard de Bury: "Admirable Minerva seems to bend her course to all the nations of the earth, and reacheth from end to end mightily, that she may reveal herself to all mankind. We see that she has already visited the Indians, the Babylonians, the Egyptians and Greeks, the Arabs and the Romans. Now she has passed by Paris, and now has happily come to Britain, the most noble of islands, nay, rather a microcosm in itself, that she may show herself a debtor both to the Greeks and to the Barbarians." [5]

And Pope in making Dulness the goddess of the unconscious is contrasting her with Minerva, goddess of alert intellect and wit. It is not Minerva but her obverse complement, the owl, that the printed book has conferred on Western man. "However ill-fitting their heroic garb," Williams remarks (p. 59), "one at last finds the dunces invested with uncivilizing powers of epic proportions."

Supported by the Gutenberg technology, the power of the dunces to shape and befog the human intellect is unlimited. Pope's efforts to clarify this basic point have been in vain. His intense concern with the *pattern* of action in his armed horde of nobodies has been mistaken for personal spite. Pope was entirely concerned with the *formalistic pattern* and penetrative and configuring power of the new technology. His readers have been befogged by "content" obsession and the practical benefits of applied knowledge. He says in a note to Book III, l. 337:

Do not gentle reader, rest too secure in thy contempt of the Instruments for such a revolution in learning, or despise such weak agents as have been described in our poem, but remember what the *Dutch* stories somewhere relate, that a great part of their Provinces was once overflow'd, by a small opening made in one of their dykes by a single *Water-Rat*.

But the new mechanical instrument and its mesmerized and homogenized servants, the dunces, are irresistible:

In vain, in vain, —The all-composing Hour
Resistless falls: The Muse obeys the Pow'r

She comes! she comes! the sable Throne behold
Of *Night* Primaeval, and of *Chaos* old!
Before her, *Fancy's* gilded clouds decay,
And all its varying Rain-bows die away.
Wit shoots in vain its momentary fires,
The meteor drops, and in a flash expires.
As one by one, at dread Medea's strain,
The sick'ning stars fade off th'ethereal plain;
As Argus' eyes by Hermes' wand opprest,
Clos'd one by one to everlasting rest;
Thus at her felt approach, and secret might,
Art after *Art* goes out, and all is Night.
See skulking *Truth* to her old Cavern fled,
While the Great Mother bids Britannia sleep,
And pours her Spirit o'er the Land and Deep.
She comes! she comes! The Gloom rolls on,
Mountains of Casuistry heap'd o'er her head!
Philosophy, that lean'd on Heav'n before,
Shrinks to her second cause, and is no more.
Physic of *Metaphysic* begs defence,
And *Metaphysic* calls for aid on *Sense!*
See *Mystery* to *Mathematics* fly!
In vain! they gaze, turn giddy, rave, and die.
Religion blushing veils her sacred fires,
And unawares *Morality* expires.
Nor *public* Flame, nor *private,* dares to shine;
Nor *human* Spark is left, nor Glimpse *divine!*
Lo! thy dread Empire, chaos! is restor'd;
Light dies before thy uncreating word:
Thy hand, great Anarch! lets the curtain fall;
And Universal Darkness buries All.[6]

This is the Night from which Joyce invites the Finnegans to wake.

NOTES

[1] *The Dunciad* (B), ed. James Sutherland, p. 49.

[2] *Ibid.,* IV, ll. 21–4.

[3] *Ibid.,* IV, ll. 91–4.

[4] *Pope's Dunciad* by Aubrey Williams, p. 60.

[5] *Ibid.,* p. 47.

[6] *The Dunciad* (B), IV, ll. 627–56.

Part Three

Scenario for the American Dream

"I want History to jump on Canada's spine with sharp skates."
—LEONARD COHEN

In a Canadian Broadcasting Corporation radio talk (May 29, 1967) called "Canada: a Borderline Case," McLuhan spoke of Canada's future role as a frontier nation. "Frontier" meant two things: first of all, Canada is inescapably, geographically on the border of the United States, as the frontier of the United States in a way. As the U.S. becomes more and more world-oriented, McLuhan argued, Canada is able to help make the U.S. experience available, both to the world at large and to Americans themselves. The second meaning of "frontier" is more abstract. McLuhan spoke of the DEW line as a kind of electronic frontier, a borderline of data and information. Both senses of "frontier" or "border" had an especially apt cogency in 1967, Canada's centennial year, the year of Expo, when the Montreal fair drew all the civilizations of the globe into one conglomerate, aggregate, corporate artifact. What people posit themselves, where they think they are, materially and spiritually, is expressed through the medium of play at a World's Fair. Canada was, in 1967, on the frontier for the whole world.

181

It is this advantage of perspective which has always made Canadians keen critics of American life. Americans are immersed in their own experience, absorbed in it, as a swimmer is involved in water. We never, as McLuhan points out, see the element we are immersed in. It was a Canadian, Dr. R. M. Bucke, who first recognized Walt Whitman's genius, and it was a Canadian professor who anticipated the Melville "revival" during the last quiet decade of Melville's life. They had the advantage of perspective, of being on the border.

In a sense, artists are creators of counterenvironments. They provide society with analogical models which enable them to escape from their unconscious immersion in their environment. So also with critics. They are the last frontiersmen.

Hence, this last cluster of essays, on the American literary and cultural milieu, is not only further evidence of McLuhan's continuing interest in literature *per se,* but is also evidence of this advantage of perspective.

For example, he saw the complex fabric of the Southern tradition as a *quality*. This subtle distinction in awareness could only have come from someone who was immersed neither in that tradition nor in the Northern tradition, which would have shaped his judgment by the angle of that vision, by a whole other set of prejudices and assumptions. "The Southern Quality" is his most ambitious attempt to trace the "ancient quarrel" between rationalism and humanism to, respectively, the North and the South, with especially close attention to literary manifestations.

"Edgar Poe's Tradition" is essentially a closer, more narrow application of the same perspective. As McLuhan put it:

> . . . Poe's achievements are to be understood in the light of a great tradition of life and letters which he derived from the South of his day. This tradition has been a continuous force in European law, letters, and politics from the time of the Greek sophists. It is most conveniently referred to as the Ciceronian ideal, since Cicero gave it to St. Augustine and St. Jerome, who in turn saw to it that it has never ceased to influence Western society.

Poe, therefore, freed from the narrow critical strictures of doctrinaire *a priori* critical assumptions (obsessed with the "abnormal," the "morbid," etc.), can be seen as a political writer, as perhaps the only American writer of his time who was firmly and deeply involved in the American tradition.

Finally, in a closely reasoned essay, McLuhan provides the schematic network which underlies the literary phenomena of Poe and the South. The flippant graffiti *McLuhan reads books* becomes, at last wryly literal. The "Ciceronian ideal" of eloquent wisdom finds cogent existence once again in our time.

The Southern
Quality

❧ ❧ ❧ ❧ ❧

THERE IS A sense in which at least literary and artistic discussion
may benefit from the advent of the atom bomb. A great many trivial
issues can now, with a blush, retire from guerrilla duty and literary
partisans can well afford to cultivate an urbane candor where previously none had been considered possible. Perhaps Malcolm Cowley's recent appraisal of William Faulkner * may be viewed as a
minor portent of even happier events to come. *La trahison des
clercs* may come to an end since the atom bomb has laid forever the
illusion that writers and artists were somehow constitutive and di-
rective of the holy *zeitgeist*. In colossal skyletters the bomb has
spelt out for the childlike revolutionary mind the fact of the abdica-
tion of all personal and individual character from the political and
economic spheres. In fact, only the drab and deluded among men
will now seek to parade their futility and insignificance in public
places. This is more than the very vigorous and very human egotism
of artists and writers is prepared to swallow. It was one thing to
indulge in the lyrical megalomania of being a "revolutionary"
writer when mere political affiliation absolved one from a too
strenuous artistic discipline and assured reputation and audience.
How easy it was then to concoct or to applaud a plastic or poetic

* *The Sewanee Review*, Summer, 1945.

185

bomb designed to perturb the unyielding bovines, and, at the same time, to feel that the metaphysics of human welfare were being energetically pursued.

It is quite another thing to look around today. The destructive energy postulated by the revolutionaries is here, and it is vastly in excess of any available human wisdom or political ingenuity to accommodate it. Of course, Marx had always pointed to the revolutionary process as technological rather than political or literary. His austere concept of "man" and the universe was rigorously monistic and technological—a perfect expression of the cynical sentimentality of an era. Like the affirmations of Calvin and Rousseau those of Marx are rooted in the negation of the human person. But technology hath now produced its masterpiece. The Brick Bradford brains of modern laboratory technicians, the zanies of big business, fed on the adventures of Tarzan and detective thrillers, have finally given adequate physical form to the romantic nihilism of nineteenth-century art and revolution. Every human cause has now the romantic charm of a "lost cause," and the irrelevance of proposed human ends is only equaled by the likelihood of the annihilation of human beings. Even the "lost" cause of the South begins to assume intelligible and attractive features for a great many who formerly assumed that it was more fun to be on the side of the big battalions. In fact, the "Southern cause" is no more lost than that of the present-day left-wingers, whose literary production, for that matter, has been dependent on the creative effort of men like Hopkins, Eliot, and Yeats, whose own allegiance was in turn given to the seemingly most forlorn of causes.

Perhaps the point of this can best be illustrated by the case of Henry James, whose current vogue is by no means related to a commensurate improvement in the general level of literary discrimination. A primary postulate of James' world is that it enjoys an enormous material ascendancy with its consequent euphoria. Correlative with the elaborate and tenuous sensibility of his created world there is the even more elaborate structure of abstract finance, and the ethereal technology which that finance called into being.

Wherever this abstract structure exists and triumphs James can manipulate his puppets, for both are completely inter-animated. It is no accident, of course, that in this area feminine life should be dominant and luxuriant, and masculine beings timid and meager. It is a big, safe nursery world on its material side. There are no financial worries. (Almost everybody in his novels is a tourist, forever engaged in a pilgrimage not from this world to the next but from one part of the Old World to the next.) But the moment James steps beyond the confines of this abstract materialism, as he did once, he is helpless. The eye of the "restless analyst" grows dull and evasive. It sees nothing. Gone are all familiar and, to him, indispensable groupings of human motives and energies. It does James no harm to smile at his chapters on the South in *The American Scene*. They force him to show his hand, a very strong hand, though not so strong as he thought it.

Henry James belonged to a society suffering from the last stages of elephantiasis of the will. In fact, he could bear to contemplate only its peripheral products—dominant women and effete men. The pivotal figures of the Jamesian *ethos* are never obtruded in his work—the morbid tycoons whose empty and aimless wills served a power-appetite as lovely as a tapeworm's. This is not for a moment to suggest that James is complacent about these remote figures. His composure in the presence of the diabolical, his "quiet desperation," produces the maximum tension in his work—its co-ordinates are clearly theological, delicacy of nervous constitution being both the means and sign of grace. (The eighteenth century had earlier substituted lacrymose sensitivity for sectarian religious enthusiasm.) And yet, that society was riddled with negation and timidity. A philosophy of action is always bankrupt of thought and passion, and "nothing is more timid than a million dollars." Against the lurid background of such an *ethos* there is *bathos* rather than *pathos* emergent in Lambert Strether's exhortation in *The Ambassadors* ". . . it doesn't much matter what you do in particular, so long as you have your life. If you haven't had that what *have* you had? . . . Live, live!" A society held together by a tense will and evasive bustle can never produce a life-style with all that implies of *passion*. It can and does produce abundant tourists, museums, and houses like museums. And with these James is completely at home.

For, after all, a "business civilization" (a contradiction in terms), with its elaborate subterfuges and legal fictions, produces equally intricate and subtly aimless characters. Such a society requires endless action and hence *motivation* of its members. And *character* is strictly constituted by motive. *Passion* constitutes character only negatively. The "lover the madman and the poet" only become characters in the degree to which the ruling passion conflicts with another passion, or with some rational end. Likewise, *passion* makes for the tragic in art and life just as *character* tends toward satire, comedy, and the play of manners. The sharp division between these two worlds is, for example, the heart of *Wuthering Heights*—the Earnshaw-Linton clash being an analogue of the modern world's intolerance of passion, thus forcing passion into the monstrous outlaw forms which occur in Faulkner, as well as in the Brontës. As Lockwood symbolically says to Mrs. Dean, who is the narrator of *Wuthering Heights,* when she tries to put him *into* the story: "I'm of the busy world and to its arms I must return. Go on. Was Catherine obedient to her father's commands?"

Passionate life does not produce subtle characters. Heathcliff is less complex than Edgar Linton. And the nature of simply agrarian society, for example, is such as to produce men who are primarily passionate in the strict sense. They understand the severe limits of mere human motives and habitually *feel* the fatality of the larger forces of the life that is in them as well as outside them. A sense of the ineluctible dominates the memories and loyalties of such a people. Character in passionate societies is consequently simple, monolithic, and, when occasion requires, heroic. There is unconscious irony, therefore, in James' stricture: "I caught the wide-eyed smile of the South, that expression of temperamental felicity in which shades of character, questions of real feature, other marks and meanings, tend always to lose themselves." This hardly exhausts the passions of the South, but it provides a comment on James' own characters. Had they chosen to live passionately, the restless analyst would not have been interested in them. When James' world did try, with its head, to go passionate and dithyrambic, D. H. Lawrence took over. But not even Lawrence could make a Heathcliff of Edgar Linton. Passion obliterates differences rather than makes them, as the Civil War illustrates. Witness the removal of deep economic and class divisions, both sectional and political, as a result of that conflict. And the primarily non-introspective and passionate character of Southern life speaks from every product of Southern writers. At the same time that this passion defines the Southern writer it baffles the Northern critic, who is of purpose all compact. But this to arrive too quickly at the problem.

To the merely rationalist and revolutionary mind of the social "planner" or engineer there is never any way of grasping the nature of politics or of art. Rilke makes the same point as Eliot in "Tradition and the Individual Talent": "Add to this that neither can I in any respect imagine the artist, obedient, patient, fitted for slow development as he is, among the insurrectionists." However, the true traditionalist will always agree with the revolutionary on the facts. But only the traditionalist can be radical. He isn't content merely to cut the shrubbery into new shapes. The *essential* impatience and rebellion of the New England mind disqualifies it for political and artistic functions, so that the defection of Henry James and T. S. Eliot was a trauma necessary to the preservation of their talents. It was not primarily the meager texture of the American scene which attached them to the English aristocracy and the Anglican Church. On the other hand, it is worthy of prime consideration that the Southern man of letters, while always feeling a considerable affinity for English and European tradition, has never felt any need to expatriate himself either in the nineteenth or twentieth century. Whereas the Northern writer in the twenties was engaged, as Malcolm Cowley says, in discovering that "people in Dijon and Leipzig and Edinburgh were not very different from people in Zenith and Gopher Prairie"; and while he was spending his main energies in defying the old lady from Dubuque, the Southern writer on the other hand was not tortured by this need for revolt. One reason for this striking divergence of attitude may be indicated by an observation of W. B. Yeats. The quality which he isolates and contemplates in his own experience is variously present in all Southern writing of the present day, just as clearly as it is absent in the world of Henry Adams and Henry James:

> Considering that Mary Battle received our thoughts in sleep, though coarsened or turned to caricature, do not the thoughts of the scholar or hermit, though they speak no word, or something of their shape and impulse, pass into the general mind? Does not the emotion of some woman of fashion, pass down, although she speak no word, to Joan with her Pot, Jill with her Pail and, it may be, with one knows not what nightmare melancholy to Tom the Fool? . . . Was not a nation, as distinguished from a crowd of chance comers, bound together by this interchange among streams or shadows; that Unity of Image, which I sought in national literature, being but an originating symbol?
>
> From the moment when these speculations grew vivid, I had created for myself an intellectual solitude, most arguments that could influence action had lost something of their meaning. How could I judge any scheme of education, or of social reform, when I could not measure what the different classes and occupations contributed to that invisible commerce of reverie and of sleep, and what is luxury and what necessity when a fragment of old braid or a flower in the wall paper may be an originating impulse to revolution or to philosophy?

It would be easy to show an identical awareness with this of Yeats in *The Fathers, So Red the Rose, Night Rider,* or a dozen more novels. It is the theme of Donald Davidson's *Attack on Leviathan,* and it is the product of a profound political and social passion—a common attitude to a common experience. Behind this passionate vision there is, of course, a major human tradition which did not originate in the South, any more than the totally non-political and "theological" solitude of the characters of Henry James is rooted in a tradition that originated in New England.

To grasp the implications of this passage from Yeats, as of the preceding one from Rilke, is to see the specific disease of modern "politics." Whereas Yeats passionately and humbly sets himself to watch and listen for the hints and promptings of a corporate wisdom far richer than his merely individual perception can invent, the social planner arrogantly identifies his own impulses and perceptions with social good. Contrast with Yeats' awareness of the nature of culture the *ad hoc* note of Van Wyck Brooks when he says that we need "a race of artists profound and sincere" who will bring us "face to face with our own experience and set working in that experience the leaven of the highest culture." That Kaltenborn tone would be recognized anywhere as that of a pedagogic engineer. Moral fervor is made a substitute for patient thought and perception, and good intentions become the excuse for enslaving men for their own good. Perfectly analogous with Brooks' engineer-culture is Sinclair Lewis' proclamation in his Nobel Prize speech: The aim of the American writer should be "to give to the America that has mountains and endless prairies, enormous cities and lost far cabins, a literature worthy of her vastness." The pulps have taken care of that order.

As Guizot put it: "Even the best revolutionaries have a vain confidence in themselves, and in all they think and all they desire, which urges them to rush head foremost along the path they once have chosen. . . . Modesty is a great light; it keeps the mind open and the heart ready to listen to the teachings of truth." And it is precisely this kind of intellectual modesty which is to be found disseminated throughout the social comments of Southern men of letters, a freedom from that note of political rectitude and absolutist contempt for the person which is inherent in the "progressive," for whom things and persons are just so much energy to be harnessed for virtuous purposes.

Just how much of the latent insurrectionist and moral aggression of the social planner lurked in the make-up of Henry James emerges amusingly in his contact with the South. In his tour he has never once to make his perpetual Northern complaint about "the air of hard prosperity, the ruthlessly pushed-up and promoted look worn by men, women and children alike." On the contrary: "I was to find myself liking, in the South and in the most monstrous fashion, it appeared, those aspects in which the consequences of the great folly were, for extent and gravity, still traceable." In other words James senses some dangerous depravity in his own admiration for the cultural vestiges of an alien and defeated nation—the "great folly" being the presumption of a people in having established a mode of life distinct from the North. It is as though a too successful missionary were for a moment to see a commercialized China through the eyes of a Coomaraswamy. But complacency soon returns. James had a basic respect for success which could never forgive failure. The Southern cause was in his eyes *predestined* to fail. Therefore it was damned.

Something must be said at this point to place the divergent traditions of North and South in a wider historical frame, if only to relax some of the factional tensions which develop whenever representatives of these dissenting parties begin discussion. Something of the scope of the human issue is finely caught in Tate's poem "Aeneas at Washington." The Civil War and the Trojan War merge:

> Stuck in the wet mire
> Four thousand leagues from the ninth buried city
> I thought of Troy, what we had built her for.

It is no mere attempt to glamorize the defeated South by hinting that Negro slavery was like the rape of Helen, a wrong avenged by an army backed by superior force and calculating guile. It is rather Tate's very Southern feeling for the mysterious unity of history and art alike, which blends these events. Homer's Greeks are actually endowed with the prosaic virtues and vices of the active life. The Trojans are given all the sympathetic qualities of dignity, pathos, and romance. The wrath of Achilles is a passion which is first turned against the Greeks and then against the Trojans. This passion which is the decisive force and the dramatic pivot of the poem, when omitted alike by the medieval versions and by Shakespeare in *Troilus and Cressida,* provides a remarkable analogue of Civil War itself.

But what is important, for the moment, is Tate's sense of the historical dimensions of the Southern attitude. (It occurs equally in John Peale Bishop's "The Burning Wheel.") A merely commercial society (like Carthage) has no historical sense and leaves few traces of itself. (In his research into the origins of American technology Sigfried Giedion was astonished to encounter an almost total absence of records or models of early activity in major industries. Ford, for example, while spending millions on his museum, had no records of the initial *production* process of his firm.) Jefferson, on the other hand, shows, like Aristotle, a strong historical sense concerning the material and intellectual factors which govern the development of societies. William Gilmore Simms, well in advance of the Civil War, displays an historical perspective and even nostalgia for the early South Carolina, that South which frankly and often too boastfully claimed for itself the glory that was Greece and the grandeur that was Rome. A perfectly justified insistence, however, on direct connection with the taproot of classical humanism and Ciceronian *humanitas* and eloquence occurs in every kind of Southern writing from the time of William Byrd of Westover to the present.

Now these claims were never made in the North. Moreover, the reason why New England never laid claim to Ciceronian and Erasmian humanism is abundantly clear from the evidence gathered by Perry Miller in *The New England Mind*. The author of *Jurgen* feels historical affinities of life-style which enable him to move easily and unchallenged among classical myths and medieval legends with a sense of continuity and contemporaneity which is marred only by a self-protective whimsy. But Henry Adams' gropings around Chartres, "stirring the cold breasts of antiquity" with worshipful awe, provide merely the spectacle of artificial respiration. However, this is a sight entirely acceptable to the academic mind when it would simulate a passionate perception which it cannot feel. In a word, Perry Miller's research presents us with a dialectical mind in seventeenth-century New England, just as John Dewey represents the same mind today. Two things most important for an understanding of the quarrel between North and South are not shown by Miller: first, the violent European opposition of the humanist to the dialectical mind in the sixteenth and seventeenth centuries; and, second, the age-old quarrel between these minds in fifth-century Athens, twelfth-century France, and fourteenth-century Italy. This is not the place to provide such an historical picture. But were the New England mind as capable of perceiving its own roots in the dialectics of Abelard and Ockham (striving to settle the problems of metaphysics, theology, and politics as though they were problems in logic) as the South has been able to feel and to focus its own forensic tradition of Ciceronian humanism, then some qualifying modesty might have got into the dispute a great deal earlier.

In short, the trouble with the New England mind has always been its ignorance of its own history. It has always assumed that it was Mind *per se* rather than the fractious splinter of scholastic tradition that it is. Once Ramus had welded Ockham's theories into a tool of *applied* theological controversy, he and his followers laid about them heartily. Ramus was strictly interested in the fray, not the weapon. However, that dubious weapon was the main intellectual equipment that the Cambridge divines brought to Harvard during the time when James I and Charles I had made life intolerable for them by favoring the patristic or humanist party at Cambridge.

The tool of Ramistic scriptural exegesis proved very destructive of Scripture, naturally; for it was rationalistic and nominalistic. That is, it *made* all problems logical problems and at the same time destroyed *ontology* and any possibility of metaphysics, a fact which accounts for the notorious anemia, the paralyzing skepticism of New England speculation. Already in the seventeenth century Harvard had designated *technologia* as the true successor of metaphysics—an absurdity, with all the practical consequences, which is piously perpetuated at this hour by Dewey and his disciples. For this mind there is nothing which cannot be settled by *method*. It is the mind which weaves the intricacies of efficient production, "scientific" scholarship, and business administration. It doesn't permit itself an inkling of what constitutes a social or political problem (in the Burke or Yeats sense) simply because there is no *method* for tackling such problems. That is also why the very considerable creative political thought of America has come only from the South— from Jefferson to Wilson.

For the Ciceronian program of education, as outlined in the *De Oratore* of Cicero (and no less in the *Courtier* of Castiglione), looks primarily to man in his social and political aspect. In fifth-century Greece this had been the aim of the Sophists, whose work we know through the hostile medium of Plato. Cicero received it *via* the great Stoic tradition, and having consolidated and exemplified it, provided the Church Fathers with their charter of Christian education which held the field undisputedly until the time of Anselm and Abelard in the eleventh and twelfth centuries. (It is only recently that Gilson has shown that until the twelfth century the tradition of classical humanism is unbroken, unabridged, and unchallenged in the Church.) Scholastic theology was the anomalous innovation, not the characteristic mode of Christian theology.

Against this background, the humanistic reaction of a John of Salisbury or a Petrarch against what they called the barbaric dialections (the Goths and Huns of the Sorbonne) is, like the similar reaction of Erasmus, Colet, More, the reassertion of the central classical and Christian humanism against an upstart party of vermiculate disputationists. Unfortunately for simplicity of subsequent retrospect, the two intellectual parties in theology (the humanists or patrists and the schoolmen) were not split in accordance with the Protestant-Catholic divisions. Both Protestant and Catholic camps were in turn divided. Each had its partisans of patristic and scholastic theology. (The *ratio studiorum* of the Jesuits attempted to combine both modes.)

The great dispute within the Anglican Church under Elizabeth was over this question. And it was of the greatest possible significance for the cultural and political future of North America that the patristic party finally won out in the Church of England—a victory celebrated by the sudden flourishing under royal patronage of patristic eloquence in Andrewes, Donne, Crashaw, Taylor, and

King. This victory finally settled English Public School education in the Classical grooves of linguistics, history, and manners, and just at the time when the Episcopal Church early gained social and political predominance among the planters. The Ciceronian program of education, because of its social prestige and utility, was readily accepted by all—even by the Presbyterians who in the North pursued very different modes.

Wherever this classical and forensic education spread, it carried with it the full gentlemanly code of honor, dignity, and courtesy, since that was inseparable from the reconstituted program as it was propagated by Castiglione, Sidney, and Spenser. It was no mere archeological revival. It had the full vitality of medieval chivalry and courtly love in every part of it. However, seventeenth- and eighteenth-century England saw such a powerful upsurge of the trading spirit that its gentlemanly code was swiftly modified. Dueling, obviously, is not compatible with commercial equipoise, nor middle-class comfort. In the South there was very little of the trader's self-abnegation about personal honor, and no curtailment of the full Renaissance flavor of the gentlemanly code. In fact, with the strong Celtic complexion of Southern immigration (Scotch-Irish) there was, if anything, an intensification of the cult of personal honor and loyalty to family and patriarch.

In such a society, uniformly agrarian, possessing homogeneity of education and population, the aristocratic idea was democratic. It is obvious, for example, that Jefferson's concept of democracy would have every man an aristocrat. The prevalence in all classes and places of the aristocratic idea was, of course, out of all proportion to the number of planters who could incarnate it with any degree of effectiveness. It certainly got into Whitman. But there need be no mystery about how a small yeoman farmer could overnight, almost, blossom out as an aristocratic planter. It was altogether less superficial and comic than the way in which Thomas Arnold of Rugby plausibly transmogrified the sons of grocers, mechanics, and patent medicine quacks into haughty young bloods. The vigor of the aristocratic idea in the nineteenth-century South probably explains how Poe, alone of his age, forecast the effect of the machine on the forms of human life, on the very notion of the person.

One main condition of aristocratic life was present in the South and not in the North—personal responsibility to other human beings for education and material welfare. (A Carnegie or a Ford, like a bureaucracy, molds the lives of millions without taking any responsibility.) Perhaps even more decisive, at any time or place, in the creation of the aristocrat is *absence of private life*. To live always in the presence of family and family servants subtly changes the most average of beings. Formality becomes a condition of survival. Moreover, to represent one's family first and oneself second in all social intercourse confers a special impersonal character on human manners and actions. A social code will always emerge very swiftly under such conditions. And where there is a code, all classes will share and interpret it for themselves in the way in which Yeats has shown in the passage quoted earlier. Striking evidence of this occurs in Faulkner's *Light in August*. Joe Christmas the octoroon lives and dies by a code which is never mentioned but which is perfectly defined by his own *tenue* as well as by his relations with the other characters in the novel. Clearly an "outlaw" only because he lives among lawless folk—that is, among men and women of endless conniving, average confusion, ordinary egotism, and avocation—he acquires by his detachment and suffering a weird dignity in his full acceptance of fatality. No shadow of mediocrity, vulgarity, or self-pity ever falls on him. He judges nobody, but all the rest are judged by his proximity.

> He nothing common did or mean
> Upon that memorable scene.

In a world of private lives, skeptical ambitions, and cynical egotisms, the aristocrat or the man of passion is helpless. In a world of merely material appetites his role is to suffer. That is why the world portrayed in the novels of the South is one of violence, passion, and death. Joe Christmas is a genuine symbol in the proper sense of being occasioned by an actual and particular spiritual condition—

not just a Southern but a universal human condition today. And this power of symbol-making is not possible for those who conceive of the inner life as being in a perpetual state of flux. For they are incapable of separating spiritual from physical objects. By a rigorous contemplation of his own local experience, Faulkner has moved steadily towards universal statements.

Probably no more discriminating evocation of all the facts of such a society has ever appeared than *The Fathers* of Allen Tate. In that novel the dominant character of George Posey (peripheral Southerner of unstable poise), who had "the heightened vitality possessed by a man who knew no bounds," explains more than a library of sociological investigations:

> I should say that the Poseys were more refined than the Buchans, but less civilized. I never saw a letter written by George Posey; he must have written letters, but I cannot imagine them. In the sense of today nobody wrote personal letters in our time: letters conveyed the sensibility in society, the ordered life of families and neighborhoods. George Posey was a man without people or place; he had strong relationships, and he was capable of passionate feeling, but it was all personal and disordered, and it was curious to see them together: the big powerful man of action remained the mother's boy. What else could he have been? What life was there for him in the caverns of the Posey house? What life was there for him outside it? That was what, as I see it, he was trying to find out.

The Ciceronian ideal reaches its flower in the scholar-statesman of encyclopedic knowledge, profound practical experience, and voluble social and public eloquence. That this ideal was perfectly adapted to agrarian estate-life with its multiple legal problems and its need for direct (republican) political representation is obvious to anybody who has considered the South. Moreover, within such a society, literary ability is quite naturally drained off into legal and political channels, to say nothing of highly developed social conversation. So that in assessing the intellectual quality of such a life one is obliged to turn to semi-public documents and the correspondence of people like Washington and Jefferson.

But since the defeat of the South it may be asked whether the Ciceronian program has any further relevance. That question is usually put in a hostile manner by people who regard Ciceronian humanism as inseparable from feudalism or slavery. One abrupt way to answer it would be to say that whereas the Ciceronian humanism of the South represented the main current of European and Western culture, the technology of the North (with its epiphenomenal art and *belles lettres*) was built on the most destructive aberration of the Western mind—autonomous dialectics and ontological nominalism. The fact of the matter is that one phase of the Civil War is being fought over again in the North today. President Hutchins is merely the most vociferous member of a large party which is embattled against the dialectics and educational technology of John Dewey and Sidney Hook. All the old features of the quarrel have re-emerged. Hutchins wants education for citizenship in a limited society, whereas Dewey wants education for a functional absolutist society—absolutist because the society rather than the person is constitutive of value. Hutchins wants encyclopedic training; Dewey wants training in methods and techniques—know what *vs.* know how. That the "cause of the South" is quite independent of geography needs no urging.

An answer to the question about the value of traditional Southern life and education could, however, to some extent be based on a scrutiny of present-day letters in the South. If some quality or characteristic excellence has emerged in current Southern letters not to be duplicated elsewhere, some testimony or exploration of human experience not attempted by others, then some sort of "answer" to the hostile critic will have been given. For the historian's question —what the South was—is included in the question: what is Southern literature today?

Meanwhile, it is worth pondering the plight of many Southern writers whose works are hooted, or admired for the wrong reasons, in Northern journals. In this respect the position of the Southern writer is not unlike that of an Irish writer forty years ago. When a Galway country editor saw in a London paper that an Irishman had just produced a book about the people of Galway in which at last even the Irish might see the irremediable if picturesque depravity of their stubborn race, with its impractical and morbid brooding over the wrongs done by Cromwell, then the Galway editor would denounce the Irish traitor to his readers. All Irish writers were soon hated in Ireland as wretches who had sold the misery and poverty of people for a price in the Sassenach market. It was partly this which made Joyce so bitter about the old sow that eats her own farrow. But in the present condition of the centralized publishing and marketing of books in New York and London there is no escape from this stultifying situation. What is more natural than that provincial newspaper editors should be more concerned about what a Northern critic says than what he himself thinks about a Southern book? The Northern critic holds in abeyance his habitual moral aggression just as long as he feels sure that a Wolfe, a Caldwell, or a Faulkner is ripping up the South in a manner which squares with Northern convictions.

It has already been suggested that the Southern writer does not feel impelled to technical experiment as other writers simply because he doesn't think of art as a means to *épater les bourgeois*. For good or ill he has never been of the ardent Kreymborgs and Millays who

lust uncomforted
To kiss the naked phrase quite unaware.

The South, on the other hand, may be said to have confronted Philistia in 1861.

Again, letters in the South enjoy a degree of autonomy not envisaged by those who have pitched their wares into the cause of revolt. Literature is not there conceived of as "an inferior kind of social will" as in *Axel's Castle*. In fact, it may be one weakness of Southern writers as writers that they are so concerned with living their own lives that they resist that absorption and annihilation which is expected of the modern writer. The gentlemanly code in a Byron works also in a Thomas Wolfe to produce a rebellious man but a conventional artist. Moreover, the Southern writer shares most of his experience with the majority of Southerners, who never have heard of him—there is not the split between educated and "uneducated" which occurs in an atomized industrial community. In conversation, the Southerner delights to report, without condescension, the fine remarks and shrewd perceptions of quite illiterate folk. But the main reason for this solidarity is the universal acceptance of a passionate view of life. Not only is there no fatal division between educated and uneducated, but there is not the familiar head-heart split of the North, which became glaring in Europe and England in the eighteenth century. The South escaped that because it had no sizable urban trading class until after the Civil War. So it has been able to preserve to a degree the integrity of thought and feeling much as we find it in Conrad and the Russian novelists of the nineteenth century, with whom recent Southern novelists have a strong affinity.

The passionate and tragic sense of life as opposed to the life of multiple and divergent purposes is already discernible as a basic life-style long before the Civil War, as the work of Poe strongly testifies. The ominous sense of fatality which was already haunting that life comes out in all his work, and nowhere more strangely than in "The Man Who Was Used Up," which may have inspired Ransom's "Captain Carpenter." And today the moral aggression of *Uncle Tom's Cabin* has been more than canceled by the great popularity of *Gone with the Wind* in the North. Even so crude a work as Margaret Mitchell's caught something of the style and passion of the South in a way which compelled a wide response. The power of a life-style to mold future imagination and life is incalculable where the spectacle of mere brute power is stupefying. The chivalric South, it has been said, wanted the whole horse, whereas the North wanted only to abstract the horsepower from the horse.

But the huge material achievement of a Boulder Dam evokes another kind of "passion" which it may be well to look at here. There is the passion of a civilized person for whom action is repugnant or unthinkable unless the whole man is involved; and there is the passion or suffering of the little sub-men, the Hollow Men, of Dos Passos, Fitzgerald, and Hemingway. In all the Civil War novels, whether Young's, Tate's, Stribling's, or Faulkner's, the characters are full-size, social beings, because in 1860 men still counted. Not only war but the causes of war, and the problem of evil, both in individuals and societies, are frankly faced. So the South met physical destruction but never felt spiritual defeat at all. However, spiritual defeat came to the North within a few decades. The characters of Hemingway are men of pathos in the limited sense only—they are pitiable, clownlike dwarfs. Their actions have no context. They go to wars they don't understand. Their love is despair. Their speech is little more than a grunt or a *haussement des épaules*. There is no problem of evil and no tragedy in this world because there is no human dignity nor responsibility.

It is the same in Fitzgerald. We are not given any workaday motives or actions in *The Great Gatsby* because it is, in its way, a novel of passion. There is no introspective analysis. But the figures are Hansel-and-Gretel-like. Pathetic, irresponsible waifs, subjects of the Emperor of Ice Cream, whose little interlude of life is played out on the Great Rock-Candy Mountain. One thinks of Gershwin's "Do, do, do what you done- done- done before, baby" as being at the same level as Fitzgerald's "gold-hatted, high-bouncing lover." Ironically, the little sub-men of the great cities best express their own sense of helplessness by means of Negro music. While ostensibly setting about the freeing of the slaves, they became enslaved, and found in the wailing self pity and crooning of the Negro the substitute for any life-style of their own. They destroyed or rejected the best things in the South and took the worst. Even the characters of Erskine Caldwell are free at least from self-pity. Contrast the pseudo-innocence of the people of Hemingway and Fitzgerald with the frank perception of Faulkner:

> She was a waitress . . . she was slight, almost childlike. But the adult look saw that the smallness was not due to any natural slenderness but to some inner corruption of the spirit itself: a slenderness which had never been young. . . .

One of the most persistent naïvetés of Northern criticism of the South has concerned the Southern representation of genuine human evil and tragic violence. It has been supposed again and again that this feature of Southern literature was not a vision of human life but just the natural result of a bad conscience about impenitent Negro-baiting or general political backwardness. That is part of the legacy of Rousseau in the doctrinaire North. As Philip Rahv says of Henry James, he "was always identifying his native land with innocence and "simple human nature,' an idea which his European critics have not found it easy to swallow." There is never any historic sense any more than there is any innocence, where this illusion of innocence prevails. A passage from Faulkner's *Absalom, Absalom!* may help us to see the contrast:

> It was a summer of wistaria. The twilight was full of it and of the smell of his father's cigar as they sat on the front gallery after supper until it would be time for Quentin to start, while in the deep shaggy lawn below the veranda the fireflies blew and drifted in soft random—the odor, the scent, which five months later Mr. Compson's letter would carry up from Mississippi and over the long iron New England snow and into Quentin's sitting-room at Harvard, (It was a day of listening) too— the listening, the hearing in 1909 mostly about that which he already knew, since he had been born in and still breathed the same air in which the church bells had rung on that Sunday morning in 1833 and, on Sundays, heard even one of the original three bells in the steeple where descendants of the same pigeons strutted and crooned or wheeled in short courses resembling soft fluid paint-smears on the soft summer sky.

To this as exegesis one may append Tate's remark: "The Southerner can almost wish for his ease the Northern contempt for his kind of history; he would like to believe that history is not a vast body of concrete fact to which he must be loyal, but only a source of mechanical formulas." For the pragmatist there can be no question of a passionate and loyal contemplation of history. For him it is explicitly an armory from which he draws the weapons to advance whatever conviction he may, at the moment, entertain.

Why has it never occurred to anybody to consider the reason why every Southern novelist is a teller of tales? This is true not only of Poe, Simms, and of even Mark Twain, but of Katherine Anne Porter, Mildred Haun, Andrew Lytle, Ellen Glasgow, John Peale Bishop, Robert Penn Warren, William Faulkner, Caroline Gordon, T. S. Stribling, Stark Young, and James Branch Cabell. The tale is the form most natural to a people with a passionate historical sense of life. For in the tale, events march on, passing sometimes over and sometimes around human lives. Individual character is interwoven with the events but is subordinate. That is why the Southern novel is, at first glance, so very deficient in the portrayal of human character. As Lacy Buchan, the narrator of *The Fathers,* says: "I have a story to tell but I cannot explain the story. I cannot say: if Susan had not married George Posey then Susan would not have known Jane Posey and influenced her." This sense of the fatality and impersonality of events would be upset at once by elaborate character analysis. Instead of sharply defined motives, therefore, and clear-cut frames around people, their individual potential, the charge of spiritual energy that is in them, is indicated from time to time as the narrative proceeds. "He was a hatchet-faced, impassive young man, quite honest—said my father—of the small-farming class for generations: if he never entered our front door, we never entered his simply because we were not wanted." The impersonal social code which permits a formal expression of inward emotion makes it quite pointless for people to interpret one another constantly, as they do in most "realistic" novels. There is thus in the Southern novel a vacuum where we might expect introspection. (It is quite pronounced even in *Huckleberry Finn.*) The stress falls entirely on slight human gestures, external events which are obliquely slanted to flash light or shade on character. Thus John Erskine notes that a sharp difference between the scouts of Cooper and Simms is that Cooper insists that the success of his scouts is dependent on skill and character whereas Simms makes the success of his a matter of happy circumstances, irresistible as Cuchullain's luck. There is a world of difference in life-style here which holds for all Southern writers. The work of Thomas Wolfe, for example, partakes fully of this character, except that in his experience the impersonal attitude born of formalized social symbols, which finally left each person entirely locked up in his own passionate solitude, was intolerable:

> He understood that men were forever strangers to one another, that no one ever comes really to know anyone, that imprisoned in the dark womb of our mother, we come to life without having seen her face, that we are given to her arms a stranger, and that, caught in the insoluble prison of being, we escape it never, no matter what arms may clasp us, what mouth may kiss us, what heart may warm us. Never, never, never, never, never.

Wolfe has all the passion without any of the formal means of constraint and communication which make it tolerable. He was a Southerner by attitude but not by tradition. Thus he stretches himself dramatically over that abyss of personalism which is the negation of every civilized agreement and effort. The same can be said of the frantic puppyism of the early Byron. But Byron had the energy and luck to achieve a quite impersonal poise, finally; and Wolfe might very well have done the same, in time. By contrast, in Stark Young, emotional intensity focuses sharply in the shape of a house, a room, or the movement of hands. "They were long hands, white and shining. . . . As a child I used to watch her hands and used to think she lit the candles by merely touching them." There is nothing here for the analytical mind to seize on. Here is rather the "skill of the interior mind to fashion dignity with shapes of air." Once the social symbol of an interior order of intense personal life has been evoked for contemplation, the writer passes on without comment. Mr. Young's deep sympathy with Italian society (one recalls his fine appreciation of Duse) is as natural as Bishop's for France or Andrew Lytle's for Spain. It is clear that De Soto, the Conquistador in *At the Moon's Inn,* is no mere historical figure but the symbol of some personal and contemporary pressure: "We went for days and weeks at a time lacking any society, and what we had was of men of our own calling, silent and contemplative men given at moments to passionate action."

The teller of tales like these may provide a great deal of conventional description, as a Lytle or a Faulkner does. Description of physical environment is after all of prime importance to the author of passionate narrative whether Scott or Poe, Wordsworth in "Michael," or Twain in *Huckleberry Finn*. It is a major means of controlling emotional response, as the first page of *A Farewell to Arms* illustrates. In Southern writing external nature is usually a major actor or player in the narrative, as for example the heath in Hardy, the sea in Conrad, or the river itself in *Huckleberry Finn*. But for all that, the Southern story-teller takes a great deal for granted in his readers. He assumes a large stock of common experience and a set of basic attitudes which make the surface simplicity of Southern fiction rather deceptive. The surface complexity of Henry James is less difficult in a way, because James is forever explaining everything. One has merely to be patient. That is because his people are elaborately motivated *characters,* not men of passion. There is really no paradox in the fact that intensely self-analytical and introspective people are the ones for whom endless action is the only catharsis, while passionate natures are not at all self-analytical yet seem to be broodingly contemplative and lazy. In *The Beast in the Jungle* James has finally this to say of the life-long esthetic calculations of John Marcher: "No passion had ever touched him. . . . He had seen *outside* of his life, not learned it within, the way a woman was mourned when she had been loved for herself; . . . he had been the man of his time, *the* man, to whom nothing on earth was to have happened."

In contrast, Caroline Gordon's *Aleck Maury, Sportsman* says at the end of his life:

> "I sat there until nearly midnight and during those four or five hours I engaged, I imagine, in more introspection than in all the rest of my life put together. I knew suddenly what it was I had lived by. . . . I had known from the first that it was all luck; I had gone about seeking it, with, as it were, the averted eyes of a savage praying to his god. . . . *Delight* . . . I had lived by it for sixty years. I knew now what it was I had always feared: that this elation, this delight by which I lived might go from me. . . .

Well, it had gone and it might never come again. . . . When I awoke in the morning—and I believe this is the strangest thing that has ever happened to me—I had a plan. . . . I would set myself definite problems. . . ."

Passion at an end, Aleck, as it were, becomes a "Yankee" overnight. Tate refers to this sort of planned, lost life:

> Think of tomorrow. Make a firm postulate
> Of simplicity in desire and act
> Founded on the best hypotheses;
> Desire to eat secretly, alone, lest
> Ritual corrupt our charity.

The whole history of this Northern confusion is in a line or so of Anderson's "The Egg": "She was a tall silent woman with a long nose and troubled grey eyes. For herself she wanted nothing. For father and myself she was incurably ambitious." A more viciously disintegrating formula is unimaginable.

What has been said so far may serve as a means to get a reader into some intelligible relation to Southern literature. However, it cannot properly be said to be an introduction to the numerous writers themselves. The reason for stressing what all Southern writers have in common, rather than their individual notes and idioms, has been to draw attention to the nature of that civilized tradition in which they all share. That is why it may not be amiss to conclude these observations by pointing out some further interests shared by Southern writers as a result of their passionate attitude to life. In none of them is there any discernible effort to evade the very unpleasant limits and conditions of human life—never any burking the fact of evil. Perhaps Wolfe is, in this respect, least satisfactory of all:

> Health was to be found in the steady stare of the cats and dogs, or in the smooth vacant chops of the peasant. But he looked on the faces of the lords of the earth—and he saw them wasted and devoured by the beautiful disease of thought and passion. . . . The creatures of romantic fiction, the vicious doll faces of the movie women, the brutal idiot regularity of the faces in the ad-

vertisements, and the faces of most of the young college men and women, were stamped in a mould of enamelled vacancy, and became unclean to him.

The sense of belonging to a great chain of persons and events, passive yet responsible, is everywhere in Faulkner: "I seem to have been born into this world with so few fathers that I have too many brothers to outrage and shame while alive and hence too many descendants to bequeath my little portion of lust and harm to at death. . . ." Likewise in John Peale Bishop:

> This is my blood, my blood that beats
> In blithe boys' bodies
> And shall yet run (O death!)
> Upon a bright inhabited star.

Equally in T. S. Stribling: "Through what obscure channels his blood had flowed since that distant hour in his father's barn. . . . It was like strangling a python at night . . . the chain of wrongs and violences out of which his life had been molded. . . ."

"Blood" is, of course, a symbol as well as a fact in Southern writing. It is intensely related to the loyalty to historical fact, tradition, family, name. As Cabell says: ". . . one trait at least the children of Lichfield share in common. We are loyal. We give but once; and when we give, we give all that we have." Symbolically associated with this passionate blood loyalty in all Southern fiction goes its disease—the shadow of incest, the avarice of the affections, as St. Thomas calls it. While it may suggest great Ph.D. possibilities, it is actually very complex and, artistically, symbolical. In no instance is it sentimentally exploited, as in Ford, the dramatist. Rather, in Tate, Stribling, and Faulkner, it is incidental to the tragic fatality of the larger theme.

Inseparable from the profound acceptance of the destiny of one's blood and kin goes a contemplation of death which pervades all Southern writing. It goes always with the passionate contemplation of transient beauty, as in the light poise of Ransom's "Blue Girls":

> For I could tell you a story which is true;
> I know a lady with a terrible tongue,

Blear eyes fallen from blue,
All her perfections tarnished—and yet it is not long
Since she was lovelier than any of you.

The conqueror worm haunts Cabell's *Jurgen:*

> Nessus tapped with a forefinger upon the back of Jurgen's hand.
> "Worm's-meat! this is the destined food, do what you will, of
> small white worms. This by and by will be a struggling pale cor-
> ruption, like seething milk. That too is a hard saying, Jurgen. But
> is a true saying."

Finally, there is basic in any tradition of intellectual and social passion a cult of feminine beauty and elegance. A feeling for the formal, civilizing power of the passionate apprehension of a stylized
feminine elegance, so obvious in Southern life and letters, stems
from Plato, blossoms in the troubadours, Dante, and the Renaissance Platonists, and is inseparable from the courtly concept of life.
There is a strong secular vein in this tradition, despite its affinity
with some forms of Christian mystical expression, which was ex-
cluded entirely from that branch of scholastic speculation which
flourished in New England. Perhaps no further explanation of the
bearings of this matter need be given than to say that in this, as in so
many things, Southern writers are at one with Yeats in his vision of
things:

The cloud-pale unicorns, the eyes of aquamarine,
The quivering half-closed eyelids, the rags of cloud or of lace,
Or eyes that rage has brightened, arms it has made lean,
Give place to an indifferent multitude, give place
To brazen hawks. Nor self-delighting reverie,
Nor hate of what's to come, nor pity for what's gone,
Nothing but grip of claw, and the eye's complacency,
The innumerable clanging wings that have put out the moon.

Edgar Poe's
Tradition

❋ ❋ ❋ ❋ ❋

POE IS MUCH in need of an evaluation which will relate him to the American culture and politics of his day, for Poe was the only American man of letters in the nineteenth century who displayed, unequivocally, a mode of awareness at once American and cosmopolitan. That is to say, Poe felt his time, but none the less wrote with a sense of the past in his bones. He objectified the pathetic cleavages and pressures of the age in a wholly unprovincial way. When he died in 1849 there was no writer in England or America who was not, in comparison with him, exploiting a merely local awareness and a merely local response to the psychological tensions of the time. However, the organization of his sensibility, with its dislocations and inadequacies, is never derivative but authentic and firsthand. Thus he and Byron are in the same tradition, but he is not Byronic.

The problem here is not to evaluate Poe's work in relation to the often vital, but always provincial, New England products. But it is evident that Poe's writing had a fitness, an immediacy of impact, and a relevance to European consciousness wholly unlike that of Emerson, Hawthorne, or even Henry James. Indeed, everything about Poe (including his strikingly symbolic private life) was strictly relevant to the problems of his age. And this faculty for

211

relevance confers on him that air of infallible aesthetic efficiency which makes integral the man and the writer. He has no loose ends. He left no unfinished experiments. He uttered himself.

The erudition of Lowell and Longfellow was not his, but neither did he partake of their vagueness and uneasy professorial eclecticism. They read and ruminated while he was seizing with the gusto of pre-ordained certitude on facts, symbols, images, and ideas which became the vehicles of his sensibility. However, Poe's equipment was far from flimsy. He read widely, and with the intensity of the craftsman. Moreover, he had the craftsman's contempt for verbiage masquerading as expression. Poe's literary criticism was the best of his time in America, simply because his own artistic discipline had given him an infallible eye and ear for whatever had been born of a sincere and vital sensibility in immediate contact with its own age. Mr. Hervey Allen says that time has confirmed all of Poe's judgments save his condemnation of Carlyle. Nothing, however, could be more to Poe's credit (and in this one can see the nature of the superiority he enjoyed over Emerson) than his easy penetration into the provincial confusions and over-emphasis of the great Calvinistic mystagogue.

Beside Poe, Emerson is in many ways a mere local sage. For Poe's tones and accents are those of a man conscious of possessing a European and cosmopolitan heritage. Poe cannot be understood apart from the great Byronic tradition (which extends at least back to Cervantes) of the aristocratic rebel fighting for human values in a sub-human chaos of indiscriminate appetite. It is no mere accident that Poe, like Byron, won a European recognition denied to such a great but autochthonous sensibility as Wordsworth's.

I propose here to suggest how Poe's achievements are to be understood in the light of a great tradition of life and letters which he derived from the South of his day. This tradition has been a continuous force in European law, letters, and politics from the time of the Greek sophists. It is most conveniently referred to as the Ciceronian ideal, since Cicero gave it to St. Augustine and St. Jerome, who in turn saw to it that it has never ceased to influence

Western society. The Ciceronian ideal as expressed in the *De Oratore* or in St. Augustine's *De Doctrina Christiana* is the ideal of rational man reaching his noblest attainment in the expression of an eloquent wisdom. Necessary steps in the attainment of this ideal are careful drill in the poets followed by a program of encyclopedic scope directed to the forensic end of political power. Thus, the *doctus orator* is, explicitly, Cicero's sophistic version of Plato's philosopher-king. This ideal became the basis for hundreds of manuals written by eloquent scholars for the education of monarchs from the fifth century through John of Salisbury and Vincent of Beauvais, to the famous treatises of Erasmus and Castiglione. (*The Prince* of Machiavelli stems from a totally distinct tradition of scholastic speculation, though it still tends to be confused with the Ciceronian tradition.)

The encyclopedic ideal of "Renaissance man" was consciously and explicitly that of Cicero's orator, whether exemplified in a fourteenth-century Italian humanist, or a sixteenth-century Spenser, Sidney, or in Shakespeare's *Hamlet* or *Henry V*. This meant that the new gentry were educated along the aristocratic-forensic lines of Cicero's *De Oratore,* as anybody can determine from considering the ingredients of gentlemanly education in any European country of the sixteenth century. So far as America is concerned, this was a fact of decisive importance, since Virginia, and the South in general, was to receive the permanent stamp of this Ciceronian ideal. This is the highly practical and gentlemanly ideal in which knowledge and action are subordinated to a political good. It is thus no accident that the creative political figures of American life have been molded in the South. Whether one considers Jefferson or Lincoln, one is confronted with a mind aristocratic, legalistic, encyclopedic, forensic, habitually expressing itself in the mode of an eloquent wisdom. This is a fact of the utmost relevance to the understanding of Poe, as we shall see.

To focus the facts about Poe, it is necessary to understand a tradition wholly alien and repugnant to him, namely that of New England. The reader of Mr. Perry Miller's *The New England Mind* will know what is meant when it is said that New England is in the scholastic tradition, and profoundly opposed to "humanism." Briefly, the theocratic founders of Harvard and rulers of New England were Calvinist divines, fully trained in the speculative theology which had arisen for the first time in the twelfth century—the product of that dialectical method in theology which is rightly associated with Peter Abelard. Unlike Luther and many English Protestants, Calvin and his followers were schoolmen, opposed to the old theology of the Fathers which Erasmus and the humanist-Ciceronians had brought back to general attention after the continuous predominance of scholastic theology since the twelfth century. To the humanists nobody could be a true interpreter of Scripture, a true exponent of the *philosophi Christi,* who had not had a full classical training. So Catholic and Protestant schoolmen alike were, for these men, the "barbarians," the "Goths of the Sorbonne," corrupting with "modernistic" trash (the schoolmen were called *moderni* from the first) the eloquent piety and wisdom of the Fathers. (The Fathers were called the "ancients" or *antiqui theologi.*) [1]

It need hardly be said that this alignment of traditions throws a startlingly vivid light on the relations between learning and religion in the sixteenth century, which subsequent stages of the original quarrel have obscured. In fact, it means nothing less than this: that from Petrarch to Ramus the violent quarrels about the relative claim of different sorts of learning originated in the conflicting claims of grammar and dialectics to be the exclusive method in theology. The sectarian fogs which, from the beginning, involved the basic intellectual struggles of the Renaissance, have likewise prevented American historians from seeing clearly the most important intellectual fact about America—the fact that, geographically separated for the first time in their age-old struggle, there exist, profoundly entrenched in this country, the two radically opposed intellectual traditions which have been warring since Socrates turned dialectics against the rhetoric of his Sophist teachers. Socrates turned from rhetoric to dialectics, from forensics to speculation and definition, raising the issue which pitted Plato and Aristotle against their formidable rival Isocrates, and which pitted the forensic Cicero against Carneades and the Stoics. The same quarrel as to whether grammar and rhetoric, on the one hand, or dialectics, on the other, should have precedence in organizing the hierarchy of knowledge is the key to an understanding of the Renaissance from the twelfth to the seventeenth centuries. Just when the quarrel, both within the Catholic Church and outside it, was reaching its term, representatives of both parties in the quarrel migrated to America. The schoolmen went to New England, the quasi-humanist gentry to Virginia. (At this time, moreover, the Anglican Church had, with the accession of the patristic and Ciceronian James I, suddenly thrown its weight against the Calvinist party, in favor of the eloquent divines of humanist bent. That is why Andrewes and Donne were able to get royal approval for their patristic rhetoric and grammatical theology. Anyhow, this fact contributed indirectly to directing Southern education along classical-Ciceronian lines.)

Harvard, then, originated as a little Sorbonne, where in 1650 the scholastic methods of Ockham and Calvin, as streamlined by Petrus Ramus, were the staple of education. Logic and dialectics were the basis of theological method, as of everything else at Harvard. Here rhetoric was taught, not for eloquence, but in order to teach the young seminarian how to rub off the cosmetic tropes of Scripture before going to work on the doctrine with dialectical dichotomies. Ramus taught a utilitarian logic for which he made the same claims as pragmatists do for "scientific method." In fact, Peirce, James, and Dewey could never have been heard of had they not been nurtured in the Speculative tradition of the scholastic theologians Calvin and Ramus.[2]

This helps greatly to explain a most puzzling fact—namely, that New Englanders have felt a perennial congeniality for one strand of French culture. (This is also true of Scotsmen, and for the same reasons.) French universities, that is to say, saw to it that part of France remained scholastic. And Descartes is unthinkable without the Schoolmen (especially the Ockhamists), as Pierre Duhem and Etienne Gilson have demonstrated. Thus, not in spite of Calvinism but because of it, the New Englander finds himself able to communicate with part of European culture. It is not otherwise that we can account for that rich cross-fertilization of seemingly distinct cultures, which occurred when Henry James and T. S. Eliot came into contact with France. Superficially, however, there could be no greater anomaly than that of two provincial Puritans returning English letters to the main channels of European culture.

Poe's ??

But what of Pope's affinities with France? If the Calvinistic, scholastic, and academic New Englander has natural roots in the Cartesian traditions of academic France, so has the Ciceronian South maintained relations with Ciceronian and encyclopedist France. For one main current of French letters in the seventeenth century is that of Cicero—an eloquent wisdom politically inspired, and based on universal learning. Whether it is Bossuet and Corneille or Voltaire and Diderot, one has to deal with the forensic, political eloquence of a great tradition whose well-defined roots can easily be examined in the schools of that age. Thus, the American South naturally finds a congenial milieu in France of the eighteenth century—the France of the encyclopedists who rebelled against Descartes. These men proclaimed the Ciceronian origins of their aristocratic republicanism in the very name they bear. And Erasmus, More, Bacon, Swift, Bolingbroke, Burke, or Voltaire would have alike approved the linguistic and forensic program which Jefferson drew up for his university.

Poe must now be focused in relation to this dichotomy of European and American culture. Thus, merely to mention *The Autocrat at the Breakfast Table* is to summon up a type of man and a type of writing which are antithetical to Poe's mode of being. The New England *ethos* naturally finds its highest level of expression in the scholastic man, and the result is that the New England professor is autocratic. There is no social life co-extensive with him, nor one able to embody and criticize his thought and actions. Brought up amidst this social nudity and pedagogical earnestness, T. S. Eliot confronted the situation directly in "Tradition and the Individual Talent." Here it was that he exploded the heresy of "self-expression," of "message," and of artistic isolation and futility, which had found such congenial soil in New England. On the other hand, vividly aware of the defects of his immediate social environment, Poe is yet naturally and unaffectedly cosmopolitan. Because he understood profoundly the nature of his artistic dependence on that society, he was its vigorous and unremitting critic, scrutinizing its dress, its manners, its reading, its furniture and science; and he utilized these things as the basic materials of his prose. For he is the master of a prose whose lucidity and resilience are unmistakably owing to a society in which good talk is common.

All his life Poe fought with eloquence and versatility of learning to maintain serious standards in current literature, to extend the scope of American letters, and to banish parochial habits of mind. To the end he maintained the need and practicality of a critical review which would transform the taste of society at large. Thus, unlike the New England academicians and recluses, Poe was the man of letters in society. He was not professorial but professional—in the forensic tradition of Dr. Johnson and Macaulay.

This is not the place in which to proceed to a careful study of Poe's writings in relation to his tradition. However, the kind of importance which essentially social and political problems have in an understanding of his work must be indicated briefly. For it was from the experience of the Virginia of his day that Poe was able to project those symbols of alienation and inner conflict which won the immediate assent of Baudelaire himself. (Baudelaire was also an aristocratic dandy, and his devotion to Silver Age and patristic rhetoric has implications which relate him decisively to the Ciceronian tradition which has been described.) That Baudelaire should have hailed Poe as he did has a meaning totally unlike that which belongs to the recognition of Emerson by Carlyle. To appreciate the full significance of this event remained for us to discover today; for English poetry had to wait another seventy years for T. S. Eliot finally to incorporate Baudelaire's sensibility and eloquence. No more striking testimony could be asked for Poe's central location in European tradition. And yet he won that place by the uncompromising integrity with which he dealt with his local American experience. While the New England dons primly turned the pages of Plato and Buddha beside a tea-cozy, and while Browning and Tennyson were creating a parochial fog for the English mind to relax in, Poe never lost contact with the terrible pathos of his time. Coevally with Baudelaire, and long before Conrad and Eliot, he explored the heart of darkness.

Within this perspective of deep-lying cultural dichotomy it becomes possible for the critic to show that "the heart of darkness" for Byron, Baudelaire, and Poe is quite distinct from what it is for Hawthorne and Melville. Evil is a fact, perhaps the most important fact, in the New England consciousness. But the evil which Poe and Baudelaire experienced had very different roots from that of the North. It is the evil which led Byron to evoke endless Satanic heroes as objective correlatives in his poems, the evil, not of Calvinistic depravity, but of the split man and the split civilization. The psychological exploration of uneasy conscience as carried on by Hawthorne or Melville could only regain contact with European consciousness after James and Eliot had visited the founts of French culture. But Poe lived in a community which had never breached its relations with the original traditions of its culture. And let us remember that these traditions were, long before the sixteenth century, strongly antipathetic to those which were brought to New England.

Considering this cultural dichotomy now in a new perspective, it is possible to approach even closer to a solution of a major Poe problem: Why is Poe essentially preoccupied with symbols and situations of horror and alienation? Or it can be put this way: Why did the split consciousness of an aristocratic-seigneurial society express itself in symbols of Satanism, sadistic horror, of fear, violence, and desolation? Byron, Baudelaire, and Poe are here together in a literary tradition which stretches back at least to Cervantes, and which is much alive today, even in such degenerate forms as crime fiction with its, significantly, dandified sleuths.

Without considering Corneille and Racine, the matter is obvious

enough in Milton's Satan, and even more in the cult of literary
diabolism associated with that Satan in the eighteenth and nineteenth centuries. The issues are strikingly defined by Marvell in his
Horatian Ode, where he explains how the aristocratic ideals of
noble being have been swept aside by the vulgar Cromwell, whose
genius is for destructive action rather than for harmony of thought
and feeling. Tradesman Richardson offers an obvious incarnation
of the same conflict in his *Clarissa Harlowe.* This time it is from the
"Cromwellian" point of view. Thus Lovelace, the prototype of the
aristocratic villain, provides us with the pattern of the Byronic hero
and the villain of Victorian melodrama, to say nothing of Dupin,
Sherlock Holmes, Lord Peter Wimsey, Rhett Butler, and the Hollywood pantheon. The characteristic pose is that of the man "beautiful but damned," the man who scorns the ignoble conventions and
petty, calculating bustle of commercial society. This man is wholly
alienated from society, on one hand, and feared and admired by the
commercial members of society, on the other hand. The entire conflict is perfectly dramatized in the relations between Edgar Poe and
his guardian, John Allan. John Allan secretly admired Poe quite as
much as Richardson revered Lovelace. Allan despised himself in
the presence of Poe, and Poe in turn pitied and scorned him.

A figure of great interest, who can best be seen in relation to what
has here been said of Poe, is Whitman. Many people have mistaken
him for another variety of Thoreau or the noble savage of the frontier. Actually, as Sidney Lanier very clearly saw and explained long
ago, Whitman is an inverted Byronic dandy. His tradition is that of
the aristocratic and political South. He has nothing in common with
the dons of New England. The inverted Byronic dandyism of Whitman is evident enough as soon as one applies the cipher of reversal.
Put uncritical embrace of all social facts in place of fastidious scorn
and withdrawal. Put pose of noble and omnivorous yokel for pose
of satiated aestheticism of the worldling. Put tones of "barbaric yawp
over the roofs of the world" for the elegant scorn of a Byronic hero
excoriating mankind from a midnight crag. Put boisterous adoles-
cent athleticism for the world-weary *flaneur,* and the pattern is

complete. That is why Whitman was so eagerly accepted by the aesthetes who had only to make one simple adjustment—that of reversal—in order to fraternize with him. Perhaps this also explains his very considerable failure to convince us of his own sincerity. He is *faux naif*. He is often like a man flapping his arms and stamping his feet to restore circulation. More important than this implied valuation is the fact that America's political poet belongs to the aristocratic Southern tradition, a representative of the Ciceronian and forensic ideal of an eloquent wisdom.

Without at present pursuing this theme further, it can be maintained that whereas Poe's art is political, in that its vehicle and dramatic organization concern those symbols which express a basic split in society and personality, the art of Hawthorne, Melville, and James is wholly non-political in its concern with the lacerations of the merely individual conscience—even when this conscience is typical of a certain type of community. For the fact which confronts this individual conscience is, finally, not political dislocation but the theological problem of moral deprivation. Distinct from this type, and within the coordinates of a thoroughly rational sensibility, Poe brought morbidity into focus, gave it manageable proportions, held it up, not for emulation, but for contemplation.

In his own fashion, then, Poe had as great a working faith in civilization as Jefferson himself, and by defining and projecting the inner emotional drama of his time he probably did as much as Jefferson to energize American life. For there is intense vitality in his "morbidity."

NOTES

1 The best published account of the ancient quarrel between the grammatical and dialectical methods in theology is in R. P. McKeon's paper, "Renaissance and Method," *Studies in the History of Ideas,* vol. III.

2 R. M. Weaver ("The Older Religiousness in the South," *Sewanee Review,* Spring, 1943) provides a good deal of incidental documentation for the present paper. He contrasts the speculative, New England theology with the practical, "political" piety of the South. The work of Werner Sombart, on the economic plane, makes the same point: Scholastic philosophy and theology

provided the indispensable viewpoint and technological abstraction which brought about the rise of industrial capitalism. The Southern resistance to technology and industry is inherent, just as the Northern passion for machinery and bureaucracy is inherent in age-old but divergent intellectual traditions. H. J. Ford (*Rise and Growth of American Politics*, pp. 141–142) makes the same contrast between political views of North and South.

An Ancient
Quarrel in
Modern America

❀ ❀ ❀ ❀ ❀

*Hutchins and Adler — Sophists, Grammarians, and
Dialecticians — Cicero vs. John Dewey —
South vs. North — Athens to Chicago*

THE BATTLE OF the books has broken out again. The splenetic in-
terchanges of educators and scholars, beside which the wrath of
Achilles or the ire of Republicans against the New Deal is a puerile
business, are shrieking across the no-man's land of the curriculum.
Hutchins, Adler, and Van Doren have made commando raids deep
into enemy territory, and the rage of the immobilized battalions of
standard and progressive education is uttering itself in howls
against them as "reactionary," "obscurantist," "metaphysical,"
"unscientific."

Hutchins and Adler are news. Education is news. The great
books are talked about, and the "great man's fat book club"
(euphemism for "the fat man's great book club") numbers some
prominent Chicago millionaires in the adult education division of
the University of Chicago. Even the most innocent of bystanders

223

might suppose that Hutchins has "got something" when he sees Midas and Croesus arriving for class with notebook in hand. The ancient Sophists promised to teach men how they could acquire wealth. What does Mr. Hutchins tell those who have already acquired it?

Viewed as an episode in a dispute which began in ancient Athens, the present quarrel over the Chicago program becomes not only more interesting but more intelligible. I shall state briefly what seems to me to be the origin and history of this quarrel before proceeding to fill in the outline with a few facts which will enable the reader to investigate the business more completely than it can be shown here.

The end of education as described by Hutchins is the making of the citizen. The citizen is rational man equipped for social and political life by means of encyclopedic (non-specialized) training in the arts and sciences (the great books program). Special skill in the arts of reading and writing are paramount. The citizen must be fluent, even eloquent, on all subjects. The citizen must know all things which concern the welfare of the group.

The opponents of Hutchins, whether scientists, progressive educationalists, positivists, or experimentalists,[1] are all agreed in a specialist notion of human activity. Scientific knowledge and method are the ultimate bases of social and political authority for men like Professor Dewey.[2] Liberals like Alexander Meiklejohn working with Rousseau's basic assumption that the state is a moral person conclude that "Teacher and pupil are not isolated individuals. They are both agents of the state."[3]

Education as conceived by the liberal opponents of Hutchins is more concerned with making the individual useful to the state than with making the individual potentially a ruler of himself and of the state. Whereas Hutchins' program would make every citizen a potential ruler, the "liberals" conceive rather of the individual as a technologically functional unit in the state. Meiklejohn employs the analogy of the individual as a note in the musical score of society, whereas Hutchins thinks of each person as a complete musical work. Again, Hutchins adopts the classical view of man as a rational animal and hence a political animal. The state from this point of view is an association of autonomous persons. Opposed to this, a conventional representative of nineteenth-century social thought, such as Dewey or Meiklejohn, regards the collectivity as the basic thing. The individual has no nature which is not conferred on him by the collectivity. Man is not a rational animal.

Behind this contrast in basic postulates between Hutchins and his opponents there is a long history. What makes the explanation of the conflict rather difficult is the fact that while the position of Hutchins is recognizably that of Isocrates and Cicero, the position of men like Dewey is not like that of Plato and Aristotle. Nevertheless, I think it can be shown that Dewey and the experimentalists are *lineally descended* from Plato and Aristotle via William of Ockham and Peter Ramus. My explanation of the modern quarrel is in terms of the old quarrel between the grammarians and rhetoricians on one hand and the dialecticians on the other hand. It is the quarrel begun by Socrates against the Sophists, from whose ranks he came. However, the Church Fathers, notably St. Jerome and St. Augustine, made Ciceronian humanism basic training for the exegetist of Scripture. Patristic humanism subordinated dialectics to grammar and rhetoric until this same quarrel broke out afresh in the twelfth century when Peter Abelard set up dialectics as the supreme method in theological discussion. Abelard's party was opposed by the great Ciceronian humanist John of Salisbury, whose *Metalogicus,* as the name implies, was aimed against the logicians, who were called the Schoolmen, or *moderni.*[4]

After four centuries of triumphant dialectics, the traditional patristic reaction, heralded by Petrarch, had gathered sufficient head under Erasmus to supplant a scholasticism weakened from within by bitter disputes. But by many channels—mathematical, philosophical, theological, and scientific—dialectics has persisted. Particularly strong was the scholastic current in New England in the seventeenth and eighteenth centuries where the influence of dialectics through Calvinistic theology made of Harvard a little

Sorbonne. Meantime, the southern states had received a class of small English gentry which had been reared in the Ciceronian encyclopedism that was then standard training in all the secularized schools and colleges of England. Humanistic, legalistic, forensic, southern education has followed Ciceronian lines to this day, as the case of an eminent Kentuckian such as Robert Hutchins illustrates. On the other hand, the North has followed scholastic lines, showing more concern for abstract method and technology than for the *res publica.* It is no accident that nearly all American political thought is Southern. In short, the cultural cleavage of North and South reflects the broad divisions of the age-old quarrel between Socrates and the Sophists in the past and between science and "the great books program" in the present.[5]

Referring to Plato's account of Hippias of Elis, M. Robin observes: "He was an encyclopaedic virtuoso of the picturesque type produced by the Italian Renaissance." [6] My problem is to sketch in the historical facts which made it possible for a Greek Sophist to become the ideal of Renaissance humanist education. By so doing it is possible to highlight the significance of, and the opposition to, the great books program. The Sophists advertised for pupils by promising wealth and power, and they demonstrated their verbal and dialectical skill at great festivals. They gave oratorical displays on all the themes of art, science, and philosophy. To manipulate this encyclopedic knowledge it became necessary to organize it around basic "commonplaces" or *loci* of argument; and in order to retain this knowledge "Hippias' system of mnemonics was of great importance." [7] Naturally, the Sophists made logic subordinate to rhetoric or persuasion, since their end was political. And this it was which raised against them the opposition of Socrates, Plato, and Aristotle, who were all agreed that dialectics should control rhetoric, that knowledge was superior even to prudential action.[8]

It is unfair to suppose that the Sophists were merely cynical power and money gluttons. They claimed also to teach the means to wisdom; for wisdom, as well as eloquence, was thought by them, as by Cicero, to be the by-product of erudition. It was this claim which most annoyed Plato and against which he directs his dialectical refutations in the *Gorgias* and elsewhere.[9] (I think that this is admittedly the claim of the Chicago program also.) But Plato and Aristotle were far from successful in severing rhetoric from wisdom. Isocrates proved a most formidable exponent of the doctrine that eloquence and wisdom are one, and he compelled Plato and Aristotle to make practical compromises.[10]

It is necessary to spend some time in showing how this identity of eloquence and wisdom enters into the work of Cicero, since he, more than any other individual, was responsible for the concepts of humanism which prevailed in the twelfth, the sixteenth, or the twentieth centuries. He who would understand how in the thought of Jefferson, Woodrow Wilson, or in the great books program, all knowledge is subordinated to the development of political prudence, must understand the nature and influence of Cicero. When this is seen it is easy to define the opposition which always rises against the Ciceronian program from the camps of technology, science, or philosophy.

The origin of this important claim for the inseparable character of eloquence and wisdom would seem to lie in the familiar doctrine of the Logos, which may be supposed to have arisen with Heraclitus.[11] Society is a mirror or speculum of the Logos, as, indeed, are the external world, the mind of man and, above all, human speech. Society, ideally the cosmopolis or perfect world state, claimed the devotion of every virtuous man. And just as Zeno considered wisdom or prudence "not only as the first of the virtues, but as the foundation of all," so political prudence is the noblest sphere in which to exercise this virtue.[12] The Stoics deduced from this doctrine the corollary that "The bond of the state is the Logos (*ratio atque oratio*)." [13]

Viewed from the standpoint of the doctrine of the Logos, man is distinguished from the brutes by speech, and as he becomes more eloquent he becomes less brutish.[14] As he becomes less brutish he becomes more wise. There is thus no conflict between eloquence and wisdom; and since eloquence is the means to political power, the great orator, the great statesman, and the great philosopher are one and the same.[15] Boccaccio could hail Petrarch as "him whose heart was the abode of the Muses, and the sanctuary of philosophy and eloquence." [16]

If there is one word which is oftener used by Cicero, or one which better describes his position than another, it is *humanitas*.[17] When we speak of the humanities today as opposed to technology, the physical sciences, or highly specialized disciplines such as logic, we mean what Cicero and Scipio meant: "Scipio . . . introduced into Roman society the atmosphere of Stoicism, known as *humanitas:* this included an aversion to war and civil strife, an eagerness to appreciate the art and literature of Greece, and an admiration for the ideals depicted by Xenophon, of the ruler in Cyrus, and of the citizen in Socrates." [18] For Cicero the complete orator, the *doctus orator,* is the ideal philosopher, ruler, citizen.[19] Moreover, "whatever the theme, from whatever art of whatever branch of knowledge it be taken, the orator, just as if he had got up the case for a client, will state it better and more gracefully than the actual discoverer and the specialist." [20]

Just precisely what is implied in this last statement can best be found in the pioneer investigation done by M. Marrou on the education and work of St. Augustine.[21] Even earlier, de Labriolle had shown how the encyclopedic equipment of the classical grammarian who was competent to give an explication of a poet [22] was likewise required by the exegetist of Scripture.[23] Confronted with the inexhaustible riches of a passage of Scripture, St. Augustine wishes for an ideal theologian who combines all the virtues of Quintilian's grammarian and Cicero's orator: *O utinam doctissimum aliquem, neque id tantum, sed etiam eloquentissimum . . . de hoc ambo (de vi et potentia animae) interrogare possemus!* [24]

St. Augustine, who was the educator of the entire Middle Ages, was himself just this sort of writer. He wrote treatises on the liberal arts. He had become acquainted with the beauty of philosophy by reading the *Hortensius,* the lost treatise of Cicero. There was no eloquence without philosophy in St. Augustine. He also became an historian in the best tradition in his *De Civitate Dei;* and his *De Doctrina Christiana* is the charter of Christian education, laying down a Ciceronian basis for all teaching in the next centuries.[25]

After this brief indication of the opposition of Plato and Aristotle to the ideal of knowledge subordinated to the service of action or political prudence, followed by a reference to Cicero's consolidation of the political ideal, and the way in which Cicero's program became the basis of patristic humanism, it remains to sketch quickly the subsequent stages of this development.

The cultivation of rhetoric and eloquence in the Middle Ages was primarily for exegesis and homiletics, but increasingly it became associated with the law faculties.[26] The authoritative statement of L. J. Paetow will clarify the confused notions which are generally held on these subjects: "There is abroad a generally erroneous notion about religious instruction in the Middle Ages. Any close inspection of the work of medieval schools reveals the rather startling fact that they offered extremely little religious instruction. It is equally surprising to find that theology was taught in comparatively few universities of the Middle Ages, whereas a faculty of law was lacking in not a single one of them." [27]

An important fact for the history of the Ciceronian tradition is that grammar and rhetoric (everything we today know as "humanism") were not supplanted by dialectics in Italy as they were in France, Germany, and England. Italy's great legal tradition kept grammar and rhetoric in the foreground, so that there is nothing strange in the fact that Petrarch got his literary training at the Bologna law school.[28] However, most of the Italian monks who would ordinarily have been studying Cicero and Quintilian at Monte Cassino and such places, had gone off to Paris to study logic. Thus Petrarch's complaint about the state of classical studies in Italy at this time was well founded.[29]

Thus the Goths and Huns of learning (of whom Petrarch and Erasmus never tire to speak) were the logicians of the Sorbonne and Oxford. The logicians were the *moderni.* The humanists called themselves the *antiqui theologi,* because they were sponsoring the revival of the old patristic methods in exegesis against the new speculative and systematic theology.[30]

In traversing so many centuries with a view to setting up finger-posts for those interested in the ancient quarrel of rhetoric and dialectics, only the sketchiest methods are feasible. I must now assume that the existence, at least, of this quarrel between human-ism and something which has been variously designated as "scho-lastic philosophy," "dialectics," and the "scientific spirit," has been indicated. For the purpose of rounding off the paper it is necessary to observe that stage of the battle which occurred in the sixteenth century, since every historian of modern literature and thought is accustomed to take his bearings from that century. No more im-pressive evidence of the continuity of the "Ciceronian" tradition could be given here than that of L. K. Born in his preface to Eras-mus' *Education of a Christian Prince*. Discussing the numerous manuals of this class, he says: "That there is a continuous line of succession at least from the time of Isocrates with his *Ad Nicoclem* to the twentieth century is beyond question." [31] The *Gargantua* of Rabelais is likewise a treatise on humanistic education for the prince just as much as More's *Utopia,* Castiglione's *Courtier,* Ascham's *Scholemaster,* and Spenser's *Faerie Queene*.[32]

As one reads the early eighteenth-century Byrd of Westover [33] one is in contact with a Ciceronian humanist who began every day with reading in Greek and Latin, a man whose training was legalis-tic and whose interests were political. "For some reason," says L. B. Wright, "Southern colonists were less introspective . . . than their contemporaries in New England." [34] The reason for this dichotomy lies in the divergent education of the two sections of America. Whereas the Southerner pursued the linguistic and legalis-tic learning of sixteenth-century humanism, the New Englander was nourished on logic and speculative or systematic theology.[35] Whereas the Southerner had the practical political and social bias of the Renaissance gentleman and tended to study letters and law, the New Englander was absorbed in the most recondite theological problems of human depravity, grace, foreknowledge, and free will.

The stages by which he made the transition from high theology to high finance have been analyzed in R. H. Tawney's classic *Religion and the Rise of Capitalism*.[36]

Without proceeding into the kind of detail possible only in a book, I have done what I could to suggest that behind the immediate controversy about the great books program lies not only the basic cleavage of American culture but a quarrel whose roots are in ancient Greece. Between the speculative dialectician and scientist who says that "the glory of man is to know the truth by my methods," and the eloquent moralist who says that "the bliss of man is good government carried on by copiously eloquent and wise citizens," there need be no conflict. Conflict, however, will inevitably arise between these parties when either attempts to capture the entire education of an age or a country. It would seem to be a matter of distributing time for these studies. The Ciceronian, particularly in a democracy, could reasonably have charge of all education until graduation from college (whether that occurs at eighteen or twenty-one). Intimate association with the scientific spirit, whether inculcated by logic and dialectics or by the physical sciences, can very well afford to be postponed to the stage of graduate study. It would seem, however, that some knowledge of the history of the present dispute would serve to diminish the fog and the passions aroused at present, and would substitute some light for much heat. Of course, no human difficulties ever seem inevitable to the historical gaze. Reasonable inquiry would deprive us of that major distraction from boredom which is invariably sought in hasty accusation and warm rejoinder where both parties raise convenient inconsequence to the level of an intellectual virtue.

NOTES

[1] The attack of Sidney Hook on the Hutchins–Van Doren program puts the objections of the experimentalist camp in the conventional way. ("God, Geometry, and the Good Society," *Partisan Review* [Spring, 1944] 161–167).

[2] Sidney Hook: *John Dewey* (New York, 1939), 155, 175, 220. "The pro-

cess and method of constructing goods is the only thing that can be called *the* good." (180).

3 *Education Between Two Worlds* (New York, 1942), 279. On p. 84 Meiklejohn shows that not the individual but the state is personal. Hence all men have their freedom not in their own natures but in and from and by the state.

4 Basic for an understanding of how the classical disciplines were focused for subsequent centuries is *Saint Augustin et la Fin de la Culture Antique* by H. I. Marrou (Paris, 1930). Lectures given by Etienne Gilson at the University of Toronto (1939–40) traced the Ciceronian tradition to the time of Erasmus, explaining the precise nature of the quarrel between the rhetoricians and dialecticians from the twelfth century onwards. The quarrel between Abelard and St. Bernard, between Petrarch and the Huns of the Sorbonne, between Erasmus and the Schoolmen, between Swift and the "moderns," is basically the same quarrel.

5 The curious way in which this dichotomy illuminates the work of Poe in contrast to the work of the New England *literati* I have tried to show in "Edgar Poe's Tradition" (*Sewanee Review,* Winter 1944, 24–33).

6 Léon Robin, *Greek Thought and the Origins of the Scientific Spirit* (London, 1928), 136. Cf. Werner Jaeger's *Paideia* (New York, 1939), 294.

7 Robin, *op. cit.* (see note 6), 139.

8 Robin, 143. Since everybody is familiar with the claims of Socrates and Plato for dialectics, I give here the less well-known text of Aristotle from the *Topics* (101a). Dialectics "has a further use in relation to the ultimate bases of the principles used in the several sciences. For it is impossible to discuss them at all from the principles proper to the particular science in hand, seeing that the principles are the *prius* of everything else: . . . dialectic is a process of criticism wherein lies the path to the principles of all inquiries." (Trans. of W. A. Pickard-Cambridge.)

9 Richard Robinson, *Plato's Earlier Dialectic* (New York, 1941), 73–74.

10 W. Rhys Roberts, *Greek Rhetoric and Literary Criticism* (New York, 1928), 46. Cf. Cicero's *De Oratore* 3. 35, and *Orator* 51. 172.

11 The best account is that of E. V. Arnold in *Roman Stoicism* (Cambridge, 1911), 37 *et passim.*

12 *Ibid.,* 275.

13 *Ibid.,* 306. Cf. Jaeger, *op. cit.* (see note 6), 274, 318, 323.

14 *De Oratore* 1. 8.

15 It was not until the time of Seneca that the Stoics turned their back on the world and abandoned the burdens of political office, Arnold, *op. cit.* (see note 11), 116.

16 T. Campbell, *Life of Petrarch* (second ed., London, 1843), vol. II, 315.

17 *De Oratore* 2. 37. One of the most interesting things in the *De Oratore* is Cicero's history of philosophy (3. 15–23). His aim is to show how it came about that Socrates and the rest could ever have claimed that there was any separation between eloquence and wisdom. Cicero says this began as a division of the heart and head. Francis Bacon repeats these arguments from Cicero in his *Novum Organum* (1. 63–88). Both Cicero and Bacon evaluate arts and knowledge in utilitarian or political terms.

18 Arnold, *op. cit.* (see note 11), 381.

19 *De Oratore* 3. 25.

20 *Ibid.*, 1. 12. Quintilian (2. 21) gives a lengthy development and illustration of this position. This ideal dominated the humanism of the Renaissance as can be seen in Castiglione's *Courtier,* Elyot's *Governour,* and in such Shakespearean portraits as Hamlet and Henry the Fifth. See especially the latter play, Act I, sc. i. Early Christian piety sculpturally represented *Christus orator.* (Christopher Dawson, *The Making of Europe* [New York, 1938], 64.)

21 H. I. Marrou, *op. cit.* (see note 4), 11ff.

22 Quintilian 1. 4. 6; 2. 1. 4–7.

23 Pierre de Labriolle, *History and Literature of Christianity* (New York, 1925), 6.

24 *De Quantitate Animi,* Migne, *Patrologia Latina,* vol. xxxii, c. 1075. Book vi of Clement of Alexandria's Miscellanies contains a discussion of the true gnostic's need for encyclopedic learning in approaching the Scriptures.

25 Of its four books, three are given over to the linguistic and liberal arts necessary to the interpreter of Scripture. The fourth book is devoted to persuasion, rhetoric, and style. He quotes (4.12) Cicero's dictum that the eloquent man must teach, delight, and persuade. (*Orator* 21.) See also E. K. Rand's *Founders of the Middle Ages* (Cambridge, Mass., 1928), 49–64, 102–134.

26 R. P. McKeon's "Rhetoric in the Middle Ages," *Speculum* 17. 1–32. This highly compressed study supplants C. S. Baldwin's work.

27 *The Battle of the Seven Arts* (Berkeley, 1914), 19–20. Paetow's preface to this remarkable poem is as basic for these matters as his *Arts Course at Medieval Universities* (Urbana-Champaign, 1910). Henri D'Andeli's French poem about the battle of the arts at Paris in the twelfth century describes the war between the logicians and the humanists—that is, between the Schoolmen and the grammarians and rhetoricians. It is the same quarrel which occurred in fifth-century Athens, seventeenth-century France, and twentieth-century America.

28 President Hutchins complains that the only place in America where one can get a humanistic training in the arts of speech is a law school, *Education for Freedom* (Baton Rouge, 1943). It is true that in the past century the ab-

stract cadres of German scholasticism have completely disoriented American school and college organization away from humanistic ends, bringing our education into line with industrial technology. All industrialist organization of society is necessarily technological and abstract. New England and the northern states embraced abstractions readily. The southern tradition, however, is resistant with legalistic humanism.

29 Paetow, *op. cit.* (see note 27), 12: "Now the lowest ebb in the study of ancient classical literature occurred in the century which preceded Petrarch. So low it was that he and his contemporaries believed that the dry and barren period on which they had fallen must have extended back for centuries to the last days of classic Latin literature."

30 Erasmus refers to Colet, his inspirer, as "the vindicator and assertor of the old theology" against "this modern school of theologians who spend all their time in mere quibbling." J. J. Mangan, *Life of Desiderius Erasmus* (New York, two vols., 1927), 1. 109, 114–115.

31 *Education of a Christian Prince* (New York, 1934), 99. See also the Italian treatises published by W. H. Woodward in *Vittorino da Feltre and Other Humanist Educators* (Cambridge, 1921).

32 Cf. Ruth Kelso's *Doctrine of the English Gentleman in the Sixteenth Century* (Urbana, 1929). This work gives a complete picture of the primarily political aims of humanistic education which so strongly influenced English education and also southern education in America. Thomas Jefferson is the virtuoso of the Italian Renaissance in eighteenth-century dress. He is Ciceronian in all respects.

33 *The Secret Diary of William Byrd of Westover,* 1709–12 (Richmond, 1941), ed. L. B. Wright and Marion Tinling.

34 *Ibid.,* p. v.

35 Perry Miller's *The New England Mind* (New York, 1939) is the book which fully reveals the scholastic and dialectical bias of Calvinist theology as pursued in England, France, and New England.

36 Perhaps even more important as showing the basis of the economic as well as the cultural cleavage between North and South is the well-known work of Werner Sombart in the history of capitalism. He derives both industrial technology and the capitalist spirit from the great scholastic effort of abstraction during the twelfth to the sixteenth centuries.

A Bibliographical Note

BOOKS

The Mechanical Bride: Folklore of Industrial Man (New York: The Vanguard Press, Inc., 1951).

(As editor) *Selected Poetry of Tennyson* (New York: Rinehart & Co., Inc., 1954).

Explorations in Communication (with E. S. Carpenter) (Boston: The Beacon Press, 1960).

The Gutenberg Galaxy: The Making of Typographic Man (Toronto: The University of Toronto Press, 1962).

Understanding Media: The Extensions of Man (New York: McGraw-Hill, Inc., 1964).

Voices of Literature, an anthology of verse in 3 volumes, Marshall McLuhan and Richard J. Schoeck, eds. (New York: Holt, Rinehart & Winston, 1964).

Ibid., Vol. 2, 1965. (The third volume is forthcoming.)

Verbi-Voco-Visual Explorations, a reprint of *Explorations No. 8* (New York: Something Else Press, 1967).

The Medium Is the Massage, with Quentin Fiore (New York: Bantam, 1967).

War and Peace in the Global Village, with Quentin Fiore (New York: McGraw-Hill, 1968). Also a Bantam paperback.

Through the Vanishing Point: Space in Poetry and Painting, with Harley Parker (New York: Harper & Row, 1968).

ARTICLES

"G. K. Chesterton: A Practical Mystic," *Dalhousie Review,* Vol. 15 (1936).

"The Cambridge English School," *Fleur de Lis* (student magazine), St. Louis University (1937).

"Aesthetic Patterns in Keats' Odes," *University of Toronto Quarterly*, Vol. 12 (Jan. 1943).

"Herbert's Virtue," *The Explicator*, Vol. 1, No. 2 (Oct. 1943).

"Edgar Poe's Tradition," *Sewanee Review*, Vol. 52, No. 1 (Jan. 1944).

"Eliot's Hippopotamus," *The Explicator*, Vol. 2, No. 7 (May 1944).

"Kipling and Forster," *Sewanee Review*, Vol. 52, No. 3 (July 1944).

"Poetic vs. Rhetorical Exegesis," *Sewanee Review*, Vol. 52, No. 2 (April 1944).

"The Analogical Mirrors," in *Gerard Manley Hopkins, Kenyon Review*, eds. (New York: New Directions, 1946).

"An Ancient Quarrel in Modern America," *The Classical Journal*, Vol. 41, No. 4 (Jan. 1946).

"Inside Blake and Hollywood," *Sewanee Review*, Vol. 55, No. 4 (Oct. 1947).

Introduction to *Paradox of Chesterton* by Hugh Kenner (New York: Sheed and Ward, 1947).

"The Southern Quality," *Sewanee Review*, Vol. 55, No. 1 (July 1947).

"Henry IV, a Mirror for Magistrates," *University of Toronto Quarterly*, Vol. 17 (Jan. 1948).

"On Herbert's Virtue," in *Readings for Liberal Education*, L. G. Locke, W. M. Gibson, and G. Arms, eds. (New York: Rinehart, 1948). *Op. cit.*, 1943.

"Mr. Eliot's Historical Decorum," *Renascence*, Vol. 2, No. 1 (Autumn 1949).

"Pound's Critical Prose," in *Examination of Ezra Pound: A Collection of Essays*, Peter Russell, ed. (New York: New Directions, 1950).

"T. S. Eliot," *Renascence*, Vol. 3, No. 1 (Autumn 1950).

"American Novel Through 50 Years: John Dos Passos," *America*, Vol. 85, No. 3 (June 1951).

"John Dos Passos: Technique vs. Sensibility," in *Fifty Years of the American Novel: A Christian Appraisal*, Charles Gardiner, ed. (New York: Charles Scribner's Sons, 1951).

"Joyce, Aquinas, and the Poetical Process," *Renascence*, Vol. 4, No. 1 (Winter 1951).

"Poetry and Opinion: Examination of Ezra Pound and Letters of Pound," *ibid.*, Vol. 3, No. 2 (Spring 1951).

"Tennyson and Picturesque Poetry," *Essays in Criticism*, Vol. 1, No. 3 (July 1951).

"The Aesthetic Moment in Landscape Poetry," in *English Institute Essays* 1951, Alan Downe, ed. (New York: Columbia University Press, 1952).

"James Joyce: Trivial and Quadrivial," *Thought*, Vol. 28, No. 108 (Spring 1953).

"The Poetry of George Herbert and Symbolist Communication," *Thought* (Autumn 1953).

"Wyndham Lewis: His Theory of Art and Communication," *Shenandoah*, Vol. 4, Nos. 2–3 (Autumn 1953).

"Catholic Humanism and Modern Letters," in *Christian Humanism in Letters: The McAuley Lectures, Series 2, 1954* (West Hartford, Conn.: St. Joseph College, 1954).

"Joyce, Mallarmé, and the Press," *Sewanee Review*, Vol. 62, No. 1 (Winter 1954).

"Poetry and Society," *Poetry*, Vol. 84, No. 2 (May 1954).

"The Poetry of T. S. Eliot," *Renascence*, Vol. 3, No. 3 (Spring 1955).

"Eliot's Poetry and Plays," *Renascence*, Vol. 10, No. 2 (Winter 1958).

"Joyce or No Joyce," review of *Joyce among the Jesuits*, in *Renascence*, Vol. 12, No. 1 (Autumn 1959).

"The Letters of William Butler Yeats," *Renascence*, Vol. 11, No. 3 (Spring 1959).

"On Poetry and Poets," *Renascence*, Vol. 11, No. 2 (Winter 1959).

"The Books at the Wake," *Renascence*, Vol. 13, No. 4 (Summer 1961).

"James Joyce," *Renascence*, Vol. 13, No. 4 (Summer 1961).

"Joyce, Aquinas, and the Poetic Process," in *Joyce's Portrait: Criticisms and Techniques*, Thomas E. Connolly, ed. (New York: Appleton-Century-Crofts, 1962).

"John Dos Passos: Technique vs. Sensibility," in *Modern American Fiction: Essays in Criticism*, A. Walton Litz, ed. (New York: Oxford University Press, 1964). *Op. cit.*, 1951.

"Notes on Burroughs," a review of *Naked Lunch* and *Nova Express*, by William Burroughs, in *Nation*, Vol. 199 (Dec. 28, 1964).

"Art as Anti-Environment," *Art News Annual*, Vol. 31 (Feb. 1965).

"The Relation of Environment to Anti-Environment," University of Windsor *Review*, Vol. 11, No. 1 (Autumn 1966).

"The Relation of Environment to Anti-Environment," in *The Human Dialogue*, Floyd Matson and Ashley Montagu, eds. (New York: The Macmillan Company, 1967).

From 1953 to 1958 Professor McLuhan and E. S. Carpenter wrote and edited *Explorations* Magazine, Vols. 1 to 9. Currently he edits *Patterns of Literary Criticism* with R. J. Schoeck and E. Sirluck (University of Chicago Press). He is also editor of *The McLuhan Dew-Line Newsletter*, published by The Human Development Corporation, 200 Madison Avenue, New York, N.Y.

FORTHCOMING BOOKS

Counterblast (Harcourt, Brace [U.S.] and McClelland Stewart [Canada]).
Culture Is Our Business (McGraw-Hill).
From Cliché to Archetype, with Wilfred Watson (Viking).
The Place of Nashe in the Learning of His Time (Ph.D. thesis, McGraw-Hill).

About the author

(Herbert) Marshall McLuhan was born in Edmonton, Alberta (Canada), and received both a B.A. and M.A. from the University of Manitoba. He also received a B.A. and M.A. from Cambridge University, where he received a Ph.D. in 1943 for his dissertation *The Place of Thomas Nashe in the Learning of His Time,* which the McGraw-Hill Book Company will publish in 1970. Professor McLuhan began his teaching at the University of Wisconsin in 1936. After years at St. Louis University he spent two years at Assumption College and proceeded to the University of Toronto, where he is Professor of English and also the Director of the Centre for Culture and Technology.

Among his other writings Professor McLuhan is the author of: *The Mechanical Bride, The Gutenberg Galaxy,* and *Understanding Media*—which has been called "the most influential book by the most debated man of the decade." In 1970, McGraw-Hill plans to publish a revised and expanded edition of this seminal work in "the extensions of man."

About the editor

Eugene McNamara is Professor of English and Head of the Department of English at the University of Windsor, Ontario, Canada. He is also the editor of the *University of Windsor Review.*